Mediaeval Academy Reprints for Teaching

W.A. PANTIN

The English Church in the Fourteenth Century

BR 750 ,P3

Published by University of Toronto Press
Toronto   Buffalo   London
in association with the Mediaeval Academy of America

© Mediaeval Academy of America 1980
Printed in USA
ISBN 0-8020-6411-6

First published by the Syndics of Cambridge University Press in 1955
Reprinted by arrangement with Cambridge University Press

Great Britian - church history

To

SIR MAURICE POWICKE

WITH
AFFECTION AND GRATITUDE

CONTENTS

CONTENTS

PART III RELIGIOUS LITERATURE

PREFACE

This book represents the Birkbeck Lectures given in the University of Cambridge in the spring and summer of 1948. I have printed the lectures more or less as they were delivered, except that I have made certain additions and expansions. I must in the first place express my thanks to the Master and Fellows of Trinity College, Cambridge, who did me the honour of inviting me to deliver the Birkbeck Lectures. Next I wish to thank the friends who have helped me at various stages in the making of this book: Dr Daniel Callus, O.P., Professor V. H. Galbraith, Dr J. R. L. Highfield, Professor Aubrey Gwynn, S.J., Miss Beryl Smalley, and Fr Leonard Boyle, O.P., who have read the book in whole or in part in manuscript and have given me valuable advice and criticism; Mr A. B. Emden, who has helped me over the biographies of Oxford graduates; and Dr R. W. Hunt and Professor David Knowles, O.S.B., who have read the proofs. I must also thank the Master and Fellows of Corpus Christi College, Cambridge, and the Warden and Fellows of New College, Oxford, for permission to print extracts from their manuscripts. I am much indebted to the Syndics of the Cambridge University Press for undertaking to publish this book and to the staff of the Press for their skill and patience. Finally, I must also thank all those who have made my work easy in various libraries and archives in which I have worked over many years; and to conclude in the words of the martyrology—*et alibi aliorum plurimorum....*

W. A. P.

ORIEL COLLEGE, OXFORD
26 July 1954

LIST OF ABBREVIATIONS

Allen, *Writings*	H. E. Allen, *Writings ascribed to Richard Rolle, Hermit of Hampole, and materials for his biography* (Modern Language Association of America, 1927).
C and YS	*Canterbury and York Society.*
CPL	*Calendar of Papal Registers: Letters*, vols. I–III.
CPP	*Calendar of Papal Registers: Petitions*, vol. I.
DNB	*Dictionary of National Biography.*
EETS	*Early English Text Society (ES: Extra Series).*
EHR	*English Historical Review.*
Grandisson, *Reg.*	*Register of John Grandisson, Bishop of Exeter 1327–69*, ed. F. C. Hingeston-Randolph (Exeter, 1894–9).
Gwynn, *English Austin Friars*	A. Gwynn, *The English Austin Friars in the time of Wyclif* (Oxford, 1940).
Knowles, *Religious Orders I*	M. D. Knowles, *The Religious Orders in England* (Cambridge, 1948), vol. I.
Migne, *Pat. Lat.*	Migne, *Patrologia Latina.*
OHS	*Oxford Historical Society.*
Pantin, *Chapters*	*Documents illustrating the activities of the General and Provincial Chapters of the English Black Monks, 1215–1540*, ed. W. A. Pantin (3 vols., Camden Series, Third Series, XLV, XLVII, LIV, 1931–7).
Perroy, *Schisme*	E. Perroy, *L'Angleterre et le grand schisme de l'occident* (Paris, 1933).

PMLA	*Publications of the Modern Language Association of America.*
Raynaldus, *Annales*	Baronius, *Annales ecclesiastici*, continued by O. Raynaldus (Lucca, 1747 *seq.*).
RHE	*Revue d'Histoire Ecclésiastique.*
Rot. Parl.	*Rotuli Parliamentorum*, ed. Record Commission (London, 1832).
RS	*Rolls Series.*
RTAM	*Recherches de Théologie Ancienne et Médiévale.*
Rymer	T. Rymer, *Foedera, Conventiones*, etc.; the Record Edition (London, 1816–19) is cited down to 1377; after 1377, the original edition (London, 1704–35) is cited in the form 'Rymer (O)'.
SS	*Surtees Society.*
Tout, *Chapters*	T. F. Tout, *Chapters in the Administrative History of Medieval England* (6 vols., Manchester, 1920–32).
TR Hist. Soc.	*Transactions of the Royal Historical Society.*
Wells, *Manual*	J. E. Wells, *A Manual of the Writings in Middle English 1050–1400* (New Haven, London and Oxford, 1916); and Supplements (in progress).
Wilkins	D. Wilkins, *Concilia Magnae Britanniae et Hiberniae* (4 vols., London, 1737).
Wulf, De	M. De Wulf, *Histoire de la Philosophie Médiévale* (3 vols., 6th edition, Louvain and Paris, 1934–47).

CHAPTER I

INTRODUCTION: THE LEGACY OF THE THIRTEENTH CENTURY

In this book it is proposed to deal with three aspects of the Church in England during the fourteenth century. First, I want to consider the social and political aspect of the Church, particularly in such matters as the composition of the episcopate, the exercise of patronage in the Church, the influence of the Crown and papal provisions, and, in general, to try to explain the relation of the Church to the contemporary society in which it was embedded. Secondly, I want to consider the intellectual activities and controversies that exercised the Church in this century, and to see where these were carried on and what were the main topics of controversy, and to review some selected personalities, particularly some of the less familiar ones. The fourteenth century is above all things an age of continual controversy, of which the familiar Wycliffite controversy is but the culmination. Thirdly, I want to examine fourteenth-century religious literature, such as the manuals of instruction for parish priests, the religious and moral didactic works, and the relations of these writings with the mystical writings of the period. We are only slowly beginning to appreciate and understand this aspect of the age, and historians, I am afraid, have been much slower at this than students of literature. With all the faults and scandals of the times, and they were many, it was at the same time a profoundly religious period. It was the golden age of the English Mystics, when Englishmen made the greatest contribution they have ever made to the mystical and ascetical literature of Christendom. It was also the age of the devout layman, when it was becoming possible, more easily than before, for serious-minded laymen to have a deeper and more intelligent participation in the life of the Church; one has only to think of such diverse examples as Henry Duke of Lancaster and Margery Kempe.

The study of the fourteenth century, as of the later Middle Ages generally, has suffered much in the past from a habit of reading history backwards, of trying to trace signs and causes of the great changes to come, and of thinking of the period as the 'eve of the Renaissance' or the 'eve of the Reformation'. I think that the proper and really fruitful method is to tackle the problem from the other end, and to ask ourselves, how does the fourteenth century grow out of the thirteenth century? In what respects is it a logical continuation or a mishandling of opportunity? A climax or an anticlimax? These are the questions which the reader should bear in mind at every step of our inquiry. This method of approach is all the more feasible, because of the fine work that has already been done on the twelfth and thirteenth centuries.

It will be useful then to begin by recapitulating, very briefly, some of the outstanding features of the thirteenth century which we may expect to find carried over into the fourteenth century. In the first place, the thirteenth century was an age of centralization and reform in the Church, in which the lead had been taken by Innocent III and the Lateran Council of 1215. The effect of this reform had been, among other things, to raise the standard of the bishops, in England at least, and to give scope to men like Langton, Grosseteste and Pecham. How far this promising beginning was carried on in the fourteenth century remains to be seen. Side by side with this, was the growing centralization of the Church under the Papacy, so that the pope's *plenitudo potestatis* made itself felt every day in legislation, in judicial appeals and in finance. The centralization of the Church was not then a morbid growth of the declining Middle Ages, but a characteristic of its most vital period. Some of the most active reformers were also the most active centralizers; a man like Grosseteste, however much he protested against particular abuses, held the most Ultramontane views, writing of the bishops as the mere delegates and assistants of the pope. Thus the centralization which we shall see at work in the fourteenth century, in such matters as papal provisions, is very much a legacy from the previous century.

Besides the centralization of the existing machinery of the Church, the thirteenth century also saw the creation of new organs in the Church, such as the universities and the friars. The universities produced a new class of men, the *scholares*, the men of the schools, to be fitted in and made use of in the Church; it remains to be seen how far the fourteenth century exploited this opportunity. The universities were also the cockpits of scholastic debates which go on into the next century and help to make the fourteenth century the age of controversy. The friars on the one hand revolutionized the technique of pastoral work, particularly by the revival of preaching, and on the other hand made their noble but extremely difficult experiment in apostolic poverty. Both sides of the friars' activities, their pastorate and their poverty, were to provide material for some of the most violent of the fourteenth-century controversies.

Finally, the thirteenth century was an age of administrative centralization and development in the English state. Centralization in the Church, through the growth of the Roman Curia, and in the State, through the growth of the Curia Regis, were closely analogous. That was perhaps why Crown and Papacy cut across one another, and also why they understood one another and in practice came to terms more easily than one might expect. Here were two great centralized bureaucracies face to face: deep calling unto deep. It is important to realize that 'nationalism' and the 'national state' were not things invented at the Renaissance or in the days of Philip the Fair; on the contrary, ever since the eleventh century men had in fact been familiar with the problem of a universal Church working in the framework of a number of highly organized and jealous national states. Indeed, by the fourteenth century, most of the problems of the relationship of Church and State had become so familiar that they had been worked out into a series of dignified checkmates and compromises. It was an over-readiness to compromise rather than intransigence that was the besetting fault of the late medieval Church. It is this readiness to compromise which gives an air of unreality to the extreme theorists on either side, whether regalists like Wyclif or papalists like Adam Easton. Nevertheless the theorists were clearly valued, up to a point, by those whom they served; it would be a mistake to dismiss them as 'remote and ineffectual dons'.

In its geographical scope this book deals with that part of the Church which was situated in the kingdom of England: that is to say, with the provinces of Canterbury and York, which between them contained seventeen English dioceses and four Welsh ones. I shall in general be more concerned with the English than the Welsh dioceses, and I shall not be concerned with the Church in Scotland or Ireland at all. The provinces of Canterbury and York did not technically form a single unit of ecclesiastical government; in spite of the efforts of William the Conqueror and Lanfranc, the Archbishops of Canterbury did not succeed in exercising a direct control over the province of York, and strictly speaking the province of Canterbury had no closer ties with the province of York than with the province, say, of Bordeaux or Cologne. But in practice, of course, the fact that these two provinces had now for centuries existed within the political framework of a well-organized national state gave them innumerable ties of common conditions and problems, common race and speech, and so forth. To give one tiny illustration of this: parish priests throughout England, in explaining the various categories of excommunication to their flocks, would need to explain how a man might incur excommunication by infringing the clauses of Magna Carta and the Charter of the Forest. At a higher level, too, the *de facto* existence of England as an ecclesiastical unit had long been recognized by the sending of papal legates. This English ecclesiastical unit was called by the convenient name of the English Church (*ecclesia Anglicana*). Such a name did not of course imply

4

any of that claim to ecclesiastical autonomy which was afterwards made in the sixteenth century. Nothing could be more clear than that the fourteenth-century English Church was very consciously part of the universal Church, in ecclesiastical government and in its intellectual and spiritual life. And this was achieved without any diminution of national characteristics—for this was the age of Rolle, Chaucer and Langland. This combination of genuine Englishry with being part of an international Church and culture is one of the most interesting features of medieval England.

Finally, it must be emphasized that the purpose of this book is to deal only with certain selected topics of fourteenth-century English church history; it does not aim at providing an exhaustive survey of the period. Two examples of deliberately adopted limitation may be mentioned. In the first place, while I have a good deal to say about certain individual monks and friars, I have not attempted to give an account of the life and organization of the religious orders as such. Secondly, in dealing with the intellectual life of the period, I have been concerned mainly to present some of the less familiar sides of the subject. I have, it is true, included the well-known figure of FitzRalph, but I have not attempted to give a systematic account of the life and teachings of Occam, for instance, or of Wyclif, or of the great English mystics.

PART I

CHURCH AND STATE

CHAPTER II

THE SOCIAL STRUCTURE OF THE ENGLISH CHURCH

IN order to get a view of the social structure of the Church, and its relation to contemporary society, it will be necessary to examine the different kinds of offices and benefices, and to inquire how men were appointed to them, and what sort of men these were.

THE BISHOPS[1]

The method of appointment of bishops in England, since King John's charter of 1214, had in theory been that of free and canonical election by the cathedral chapters; but, in fact, by the fourteenth century the appointments were being made more and more by royal and papal intervention, as we shall see when we come to consider papal provisions. I shall only remark here that while papal provision became the general method formally, the king generally got the bishops he wanted, at any rate after the reign of Edward II, and that the provision of aliens to English bishoprics was virtually unknown in this period. The only exceptions would seem to be the provision of Rigaud de Asserio (Assier) to the see of Winchester in 1320, and Lewis Beaumont (at the king's request) to Durham in 1317.

The various types of bishops may be roughly classified according to their previous careers and qualifications, as civil servants, scholars, religious, diocesan administrators, papal officials and aristocrats. It must always be remembered, however, that the same man may belong to more than one category.

[1] For lists of bishops see *Handbook of British Chronology*, ed. F. M. Powicke (Royal Historical Society, 1939), 132–94, and W. Stubbs, *Registrum Sacrum Anglicanum*, 2nd ed. (Oxford, 1897). For careers of bishops, see *DNB*; K. Edwards, 'The political importance of the English bishops during the reign of Edward II', in *EHR*, LIX (1944), 311–45; Waldo E. L. Smith, *Episcopal appointments and patronage in the reign of Edward II* (Chicago, 1938).

Before analysing the fourteenth-century bishops, it will be useful to glance briefly at the composition of those of the thirteenth century.[1] Of the seventy-eight bishops who ruled between 1215 and 1272, eight were religious. Forty-two may be classed as administrators and magnates, of whom twenty-two were officials of the normal type, employed in the household, exchequer, or law departments of the Curia Regis, and fourteen seem to have been *magistri*. In all, forty of the bishops seem to have been *magistri* or university graduates, and of these, thirty were men whose academic experience had been a factor in their promotion and careers. Thirty-seven had had some experience as diocesan administrators or members of cathedral chapters. One bishop was a papal legate, Pandulf, who held the see of Norwich. Again, one might take a cross-section of the seventeen English bishoprics at intervals throughout the century. In 1225 there were one religious, five *magistri*, twelve administrators and magnates, and two from the diocesan or capitular clergy. In 1250 there were one religious, eight *magistri*, nine administrators and magnates, and six from the diocesan or capitular clergy. In 1275 there were four religious, eight *magistri*, ten administrators or magnates, three from the diocesan or capitular clergy. One notable feature is the small part played by the religious. There had been a time, in the later eleventh century, when the monks and the royal clerks had divided the bishoprics among them. Now the monks had dwindled, while the coming of the friars, which had so much influence on the Church in other respects, did not affect the episcopate in the thirteenth century, apart from Kilwardby and Pecham at Canterbury. The two most important groups, which overlap, are clearly the administrators, who comprise between one-half and two-thirds of the bishops, and the *magistri*, who rise from about one-quarter to one-half. The scholar bishops include important men like Stephen Langton and Alexander Stavensby in

[1] For the bishops between 1215 and 1272, see M. Gibbs and J. Lang, *Bishops and Reform 1215-1272* (Oxford, 1934).

1225, Grosseteste, Walter Cantilupe, St Richard Wych, and Roger Weseham in 1250, Kilwardby and Stephen Berksted in 1275. What happened in the fourteenth century was that the administrators or civil servants continued to be prominent; and while the number of graduate bishops increased, the professional scholars gradually ceased to hold key positions in the episcopate. We can now turn to analyse the fourteenth-century bishops.

I. CIVIL SERVANTS. Here we have a striking example of fourteenth-century conditions as the outcome of thirteenth-century developments. The steady growth of the civil service throughout the two centuries, as described by Tout, meant that there was an army of civil servants, ever growing in numbers and dignity, to be provided with benefices, from bishoprics downwards, and the civil servants form perhaps the most important of all the groups among the bishops. If you want to find out about bishops of the tenth or eleventh or twelfth century, you will naturally consult the monastic chronicles, or Migne's *Patrologia Latina*, or *The Lives of the Saints*; if you want to find out about the fourteenth-century bishops, you will do well to start by looking at the index to Tout's *Chapters in the Administrative History of Medieval England*. If we take the seventeen English bishoprics, it may be roughly reckoned that in 1300 there were two civil servants holding bishoprics; in 1325, twelve; in 1350, eight; in 1375, ten; in 1400, seven; that is to say, the proportion of civil servant bishops rises sharply at the beginning of the century, and is at its height in the second and third quarters of the century. The term 'civil servant bishops' may be taken to include both those who held office in the service of the Crown before becoming bishops and those who held certain high offices while bishops.

The different departments of the civil service contributed to the episcopate in varying degrees. Wardrobe officials were conspicuous at first, in the reign of Edward II, as can be seen from the careers of Walter Reynolds (promoted to Worcester and Canterbury),

William Melton (promoted to York), and Roger Northburgh (promoted to Lichfield); but in the reign of Edward III the wardrobe officials decline in importance in the episcopate.[1] The office of Treasurer of the Exchequer was generally held by a bishop throughout the century, and the same is true of the chancellorship, though there were the well-known experiments with lay chancellors in the 1340's and 1370's. The Keepers of the Privy Seal become increasingly prominent in the Church about the middle of the century; in 1350, six out of the seventeen English bishops had held this office, and Tout has pointed out that between 1345 and 1355 every Keeper received either an archbishopric or an important see.[2] Men employed as diplomatic envoys were particularly prominent among the bishops, including both those trained as envoys before becoming bishops, and those employed as envoys while bishops. Diplomatic missions on behalf of the king to the Roman Curia and elsewhere gave churchmen an opportunity for indulging their various hobbies in a way that is very revealing. Thus careerists like Adam Orleton, William Airmyn and John Stratford used their presence at the Roman Curia on the king's business to angle for bishoprics for themselves.[3] On the other hand, Richard de Bury tells us in his *Philobiblon* that he used his opportunities as ambassador, as well as his position as Chancellor and Treasurer, to collect books, preferring to take gifts and douceurs in that form: 'we loved codices more than florins, and preferred slender pamphlets to pampered palfreys.'[4] Bishop John Sheppey, an enthusiastic preacher and connoisseur of sermons, seems to have used his embassy to Spain in 1345 to collect Gascon sermons,[5] and it was while acting as the king's representative at the Roman Curia in 1350 that Richard FitzRalph delivered his first broadside against the friars.[6]

[1] Tout, *Chapters*, III, 217–19, for the period 1345–60.　　　　[2] *Ibid.* 219.
[3] Tout, *Chapters*, II, 307–8, III, 16; K. Edwards in *EHR*, LIX (1944), 312, 333, 342–3; Waldo E. L. Smith, *op. cit.* 27–8, 39–40, 43–4. The case against Airmyn is doubtful.
[4] *The Philobiblon of Richard de Bury*, ed. E. C. Thomas (London, 1888), 68–9, 199.
[5] New College, Oxford, MS. 92, fo. 5 ff.　　　　[6] See below, pp. 152, 155.

Not all the leading servants of the Crown got the bishoprics they wanted; some had to wait several turns, and some found themselves permanently rejected. Thus Robert Baldock on three successive occasions, 1321–5, failed to get a bishopric, in spite of the king's support;[1] and William Kilsby, the 'stormy petrel of curiality', after contesting for the see of York against Zouche from 1340 to 1342, gave up the struggle and took to a military career instead.[2] Pope John XXII took a particularly strong line in refusing to provide royal nominees on half a dozen occasions between 1317 and 1325, on account of which the Westminster chronicler praises the pope for his determination to 'restore the enslaved English Church somewhat to its former dignity'.[3] It should be noted, however, that when the pope turned down a royal nominee, he generally tried to satisfy him on a later occasion.[4] It was said that in 1345, when the cardinals objected to a royal nominee (Thomas Hatfield), as 'levis et laicus', Clement VI, a pope notorious for his liberality, declared that if the king of England asked for an ass to be made bishop, he would grant his request.[5] But later popes, Innocent VI and Urban V, showed a growing reluctance to promote royal servants automatically; Robert Stretton, a clerk of the Black Prince, and a candidate for the see of Lichfield, was three times examined on his 'literature', and three times 'ploughed', twice by the archbishop and once by the pope, though he was at length consecrated in 1360; and there were similar difficulties over the consecration of John Buckingham, Keeper of the Privy Seal, to the see of Lincoln,[6] c. 1362–3.

If eminent royal servants were sometimes branded as 'illiterate', it should be remembered that the category of civil servant bishops

---

[1] Tout, *Chapters*, II, 310. [2] Tout, *Chapters*, III, 116ff., 161–3.
[3] *Flores Historiarum*, ed. H. R. Luard (*RS* 1890), III, 175–6.
[4] Waldo E. L. Smith, *op. cit.* 48.
[5] *Chronicon Angliae 1328–88*, ed. E. M. Thompson (*RS* 1874), 20; cf. Tout, *Chapters*, III, 220.
[6] Tout, *Chapters*, III, 254–5.

did to a considerable extent come to overlap with the category of graduate bishops. At the beginning of the century, there was indeed a striking contrast between the scholar bishops like Winchelsey, and the mere administrators, especially those promoted from the wardrobe, like Reynolds or Walter Langton, men with no academic background. But from about 1316, there emerged a new type of civil servant bishop, with an academic training, often a distinguished one; good examples of this type were Archbishop John Stratford and his brother Robert Stratford, Chancellor of Oxford University, Chancellor of the kingdom, and Bishop of Chichester. Such men were specially useful as diplomatic envoys. Half the graduate bishops in the reign of Edward II were also civil servants.[1] And even Bradwardine, the *Doctor Profundus*, was for a time a clerk of the household of Edward III.[2]

2. SCHOLARS. One of the chief aims of ecclesiastical reform in the thirteenth century had been the raising up of a new type of bishop, and particularly the encouragement of scholar bishops, men who had made their name in the schools, like Grosseteste and Pecham. Was this early promise continued in the fourteenth century? It is first of all necessary to make a distinction between two classes of 'scholars'. On the one hand there are the university graduates in general, men who had passed through the schools; and these are fairly constant and numerous among the fourteenth-century bishops, including, as we have just seen, the graduate civil servants. In the reign of Edward II, out of forty-five bishops, about twenty-nine are known to have been graduates;[3] and the same proportion, roughly two-thirds, seems to be true of the century as a whole. The majority were graduates of Oxford, but some were from Cambridge and Paris. To this extent then the

[1] K. Edwards in *EHR*, LIX (1944), 312; K. Edwards, 'Bishops and learning in the reign of Edward II', in *Church Quarterly Review*, CXXXVIII (1944), 60.
[2] Tout, *Chapters*, IV, 114.
[3] K. Edwards in *Church Quarterly Review*, CXXXVIII (1944), 58 ff.

universities had left their mark on the majority of the bishops, and the lamentations of the chroniclers and sermon-writers about the illiteracy of the bishops seem to be exaggerated. On the other hand, within this wider class just mentioned, there is the smaller number of men with distinguished academic careers, owing their position in the Church primarily to their academic distinction, and it is the role of these 'scholars', in the stricter sense, in the episcopate, that I want to consider here.

Among the seventeen English bishoprics, in 1300, we find such scholars occupying some of the key positions: Winchelsey at Canterbury, Simon of Ghent at Salisbury, John Dalderby at Lincoln. In 1325 there were Roger Mortival at Salisbury and Thomas Cobham at Worcester. In 1350 there were John Grandisson at Exeter, Ralph Shrewsbury at Wells, and one who was perhaps the greatest scholar of the day, Richard FitzRalph, far away at Armagh. In 1375 there were William Rede at Chichester and Thomas Brunton at Rochester. In 1400 there were no such outstanding scholars to be found among the bishops. This does not mean that the type of scholar bishop was to disappear, for a little later we find scholars such as Philip Repingdon, Robert Hallam, and Richard Fleming. But on the whole, the general process is clear: the scholars were gradually edged out of the greater sees like Canterbury, and confined to lesser or distant sees like Rochester or Chichester or Armagh; that was as high as a scholar could hope to get. This was a tragedy, a great opportunity missed, for the opening years of the fourteenth century had promised to carry on the tradition of scholar bishops like Langton, Grosseteste and Pecham, as envisaged by the thirteenth-century reformers. Thus, in particular, there was a very interesting group of scholars at Oxford in the last quarter of the thirteenth century, consisting of four successive Chancellors of the University between 1288 and 1293, namely Robert Winchelsey, John of Monmouth, Simon of Ghent and Roger Mortival, all of whom became bishops in the last years of the thirteenth or the first years of the fourteenth century.[1] The greatest among these, probably the master and inspirer of the rest, was Winchelsey. Two of this group, Ghent and Mortival, succeeded one another at Salisbury, and Ghent in particular made some efforts to pack the Salisbury chapter with scholars. It is in the early fourteenth century, too, that we find most traces of theological lectures being delivered at the cathedrals.[2]

The change of policy tending to diminish the importance of the scholars in the episcopate may perhaps have come about the second decade of the century. On the one hand, the masterful personality of Pope John XXII (1316–34), as Tout reminds us, left a deep mark on English ecclesiastical history.[3] Himself a canonist, he seems for a time at least to have favoured canonists rather than theologians and was responsible for providing six lawyer bishops to English sees between 1317 and 1325.[4] We must not, however, exaggerate John's preference for lawyers, for a contemporary document assures us that after a time he transferred his favour from lawyers to theologians.[5] This document is a letter from an Englishman at the Roman Curia, Master Stephen de Kettelbergh, to Master John Lutterel, Chancellor of Oxford University (c. 1317–22), urging him to come out to the Curia; it throws so much light on the scholars' prospects of ecclesiastical preferment that it is worth quoting at length:[6]

Concerning the state of this Court, I signify to you by these presents that the great and special affection which hitherto our Lord the Pope had felt towards jurists, for the sake of civil learning, he has now wholly and perfectly transferred to theologians and especially to masters of the sacred page; so that any master, expert in theology in name and deed,

[1] Snappe's Formulary, ed. H. E. Salter (OHS, LXXX, 1923), 323f.
[2] See below, pp. 111 ff.
[3] T. F. Tout, The place of Edward II in English history (2nd ed. Manchester, 1936), 207; Church Quarterly Review, CXXXVIII (1944), 60.
[4] Bishops Orleton, Newport, Assier, Burghersh, John Stratford, Ross.
[5] In any case it must be remembered that canonists as well as theologians might be 'scholars', like Brunton, or a man might be both, like William of Pagula.
[6] Snappe's Formulary, 304. Lutterel did not in fact get a bishopric.

who comes here to the Apostolic See, does not leave the Court. In the first place the lord pope freely provides them with great dignities and prebends, and according to the various conditions of the persons, transfers some to the pinnacle of episcopal dignity and others to archiepiscopal sees, granting to each, as is becoming, that which their merits demand.

Moreover the lord king of Sicily [Robert the Wise], who among all the clerks in the world that I have ever seen, both in oppositions and responsions really shows himself well and elegantly a man of great learning and as it were most perfect in every art, and very much excelling in moralities, honours immensely men of your faculty, endears and extolls them with great rewards. Wherefore, if it please your immense discretion to consent to the foolishness of my head, I counsel you, for your honour and no little profit, and I believe it is a healthy counsel, that you should make a journey here to the Curia after Christmas as the envoy of some great king or earl or bishop, making a stay only for one quarter of a year, unless subsequently there is given to you a greater hope and richer confidence of making here a longer stay. I know for certain that when you have come here, and have made a couple of disputations here among the theologians of this court, in some good matter of theology well planned and thought out by you beforehand, then in a short time, you will have carried off more profit and honour, than ever you have had from all your acts in the schools. Since therefore you have (blessed be the most High!) plenty of vigour and youth and bodily power for work, and together with these there shines out in your person the fulness of all wisdom, subtlety of opposing, and a great gift for disputing well and solemnly, do not give yourself over to ease and quiet, but, for the good and profit of yourself and all your friends, as I have said, undertake a little labour for the present; and write back and let me know what you think about this, by the next messenger.

About the same time, in the second decade of the century, the Crown was increasing the appointment of civil servants to bishoprics, including, admittedly, the new type of graduate civil servants. A significant episode took place in 1313. On the death of Winchelsey, the monks of Canterbury tried to elect another scholar, Thomas Cobham, the 'good clerk', the 'Flower of

Kent'; he was one of the group who had been at Oxford *c.* 1288–93 with Winchelsey and Ghent. But Cobham was turned down, and the primatial see given instead to Walter Reynolds, a royal clerk, who was said to have won the king's favour by his skill in private theatricals.[1] Whoever was responsible, and whatever the motives, the main trend towards the exclusion of great theologians from high places is clear. In the middle of the century there was one striking exception, a very notable experiment, in the appointment of the great theologian Bradwardine to Canterbury in 1349, but unfortunately he died within a few weeks, so that one will never know what he might have done in that position. But when we see a typical scholar bishop later in the century, Bishop Brunton of Rochester, standing out as a famous preacher, a courageous critic of political and social ills, and a champion of ecclesiastical liberties, we cannot help wondering what such a man might have done at Canterbury; could he have played the part of another Pecham or Winchelsey?

3. RELIGIOUS. In the past, religious had played a great part in the episcopate; not only were there the great monk bishops of the tenth and eleventh centuries, but there had also been, more recently, in the later thirteenth century, the interesting experiment in friar bishops, such as the Dominican Kilwardby and the Franciscan Pecham at Canterbury, while in 1265 the pope had offered the see of York to the great Franciscan theologian and mystic, St Bonaventure. Here again is a promising development of the thirteenth century which was not continued. In actual numbers, the religious among the fourteenth-century English bishops were not negligible; during the reign of Edward II, for instance, they comprised nine out of forty-five bishops, seven being Benedictines, one an Augustinian canon, and one a Domi-

---

[1] 'Monk of Malmesbury' in *Chronicles of...Edward I and Edward II*, ed. W. Stubbs (*RS* 1883), II, 197: 'In ludis theatralibus principatum tenuit, et per hoc regis favorem optinuit.' But see also Tout, *Place of Edward II*, 71 n.

nican. But with one exception (Simon Langham at Canterbury) the fourteenth-century religious bishops did not occupy prominent positions, and they fall into certain rather specialized types.

First, they occupied mostly minor sees which had monastic cathedral chapters. Thus in the course of the century there were five monk bishops at Rochester, four at Ely, and one at Norwich. The reason for this was that the monastic chapters, great and small, continued gallantly to make attempts at electing monk bishops; in most cases they were unsuccessful, but sometimes they were allowed to have their way, in cases where it could not make much difference, and where the sees were not required for 'Very Important People'. The suitability of a monk candidate, however, even for a minor see might sometimes be challenged; and here we must remember that a monk would have to face not only the competition of royal protégés, but a certain amount of academic prejudice from those bishops who had been trained in the schools. Thus in 1302 the monks of Ely elected their prior, Robert Orford, as Bishop of Ely. The Archbishop of Canterbury, Robert Winchelsey (himself a distinguished theologian), examined Orford and quashed the election on account of his 'insufficient literature'. The elect therefore appealed to Rome, appeared before the pope and explained to him how the archbishop had examined him:

'Holy Father, My Lord of Canterbury put three questions [argumenta] to me. To the first I gave such an answer, and to the second, such an answer; but to the third, because I found it very difficult and as it were insoluble, I answered not theologically but logically, so as to avoid a conclusion.' At which the Lord Pope and the Cardinals burst out into laughter, and the Lord Pope said: 'Truly my son, you answered well; We do not find you an empty vessel, as Our Brother of Canterbury described you, but rather We approve of you as a vessel full of all goodness and knowledge.' And he confirmed the election, and had him consecrated there and then.[1]

[1] H. Wharton, *Anglia Sacra* (London, 1691), I, 640.

That at any rate is the Ely chronicler's account. This is not only a very amusing story, but also a very significant one, because answering 'logically' instead of 'theologically' does seem to have been a recognized weakness of Englishmen in the early fourteenth century. Just about thirty years after Orford's examination, about 1333–4, John Lutterel, ex-Chancellor of Oxford, was at the papal Curia when the controversy over the views of John XXII about the Beatific Vision was at its height; he writes to expound his views on the subject to a friend at the Curia, and among other things he remarks:

But you will object against me, what people here frequently object against us Englishmen, you will say: 'Now, you are answering according to logic; *tolle, tolle*—away with that, answer according to theology.' But is logic then superfluous among theologians? Indeed, there is no more dangerous beast than a presumptuous theologian without logic. To try to treat a question without logic, is like building a wall without cement. When I was a young man, I heard a great man say that a theologian without good logic was like an ass with horns.[1]

The sending of monks to graduate at the universities, which became an established custom by the fourteenth century, may have lessened the academic objection to monk bishops, for no one could accuse men like Adam Easton or Thomas of Brunton of 'insufficient literature'; all the same, the number of monk bishops did not noticeably increase.

Secondly, there was, as Tout has pointed out, a 'curious recrudescence of monastic tenure of great offices of state' in this period,[2] though needless to say these monastic administrators were in a very different position from a Lanfranc or a Suger. Thus John Sheppey, Benedictine, Bishop of Rochester, was Treasurer of the Exchequer, 1356–60; Simon Langham, another Benedictine, Abbot of Westminster and later Archbishop of Canterbury, was

[1] Cambridge University Library, MS. Ii. III, 10, fo. 94v; and see below, p. 263.
[2] Tout, *Chapters*, III, 205.

Treasurer of the Exchequer, 1360–3 and Chancellor, 1363–7; and John Gilbert, Dominican, Bishop of Hereford, was Treasurer of the Exchequer, 1389–91. In Langham, then, we have the last monk to hold the see of Canterbury or indeed any other major see, but this was clearly a reward for administrative ability and not because he was a monk.

Finally, there was a curious group of religious among the 'courtier bishops' of Richard II's making[1] consisting of two of the king's Dominican confessors, Rushook and Burghill;[2] Robert Waldby, an Austin friar, said to have been the king's physician (promoted to Chichester and York); Tideman, a Cistercian, also the king's physician (promoted to Llandaff and Worcester); and Thomas Merke, monk of Westminster (promoted to Carlisle).

4. OFFICIALS OF THE ROMAN CURIA. The most outstanding bishop of this class was Rigaud de Asserio (Assier), canon of Orleans and papal tax-collector, provided to the see of Winchester in 1320; he is the only example of a foreign papal official so appointed, and his provision perhaps represents the high-water mark of papal pressure on English church patronage, under the strongest pope and the weakest king of the century. There are, however, several examples of Englishmen who were officials at the Roman Curia being promoted to bishoprics, such as John Ross, Auditor of the Sacred Palace and clerk to two cardinals (promoted to Carlisle); William Bateman, another papal auditor (promoted to Norwich); Thomas Fastolf, also a papal auditor (promoted to St David's);[3] and Simon of Sudbury, also a papal auditor (promoted to London and Canterbury).

---

[1] A. Steel, *Richard II* (Cambridge, 1941), 220.

[2] Other Dominican bishops in the later fourteenth century were Thomas de Lisle (Ely), John Gilbert (Hereford), and William Bottesham (Rochester).

[3] Thomas Fastolf was a canonist of some distinction, being the author of the earliest known collection of Decisions of the Roman Court of the Rota (I owe this information to Mr Derek Hall). He is also possibly to be identified with the English canonist who wrote the *Memoriale presbiterorum* at Avignon in 1344, cf. below, p. 205.

5. DIOCESAN ADMINISTRATORS AND CATHEDRAL CLERGY. A good many bishops had previously held archdeaconries, deaneries and canonries, such offices being in fact by this time very generally treated as sinecures. John Stratford, later Archbishop of Canterbury, had among other things been Official to Bishop Dalderby of Lincoln. On the whole, the men who became bishops had usually combined diocesan or cathedral offices with a distinguished academic or civil service career, and I think it would be difficult to find an example of a man reaching a bishopric solely or mainly on the strength of administrative and pastoral work done in his diocese. Thus what is now a common avenue to the episcopate seems to be curiously lacking in this period.

6. ARISTOCRATS. Last but not least there was the high aristocratic element among the bishops, which became noticeable in the second half of the fourteenth century. This seems to have been a new development, though it was not unprecedented. The twelfth-century English bishops had included men of very high rank, some of them of royal kin, such as Henry of Blois, Geoffrey Plantagenet of York, and Hugh Puiset. In the intervening period of the thirteenth and early fourteenth centuries we find, it is true, bishops from the baronial families, such as the Cantilupes, the Becks, Burghersh, and Cobham, and in the reign of Edward II about one-fifth of the bishops were drawn from baronial families;[1] but there is a marked absence of bishops from the great comital families in that period. We do not find Warennes, Clares and Bigods among the English bishops, and it is significant that while Bogo of Clare at the end of the thirteenth century received many benefices, he did not get a bishopric.[2] The only exception to this rule, in the early fourteenth century, was Lewis Beaumont,

[1] *EHR*, LIX (1944), 312.
[2] For Bogo of Clare, see A. H. Thompson, 'Pluralism in the Medieval Church', in *Associated Architectural Societies' Reports*, XXXIII (1915-17), 53-7; *Archaeologia*, LXX (1920), 1-56.

Bishop of Durham, related to the kings of England, France and Sicily. On the whole, there was no question in England of a noble monopoly of bishoprics and other high church offices, such as we find in parts of the Continent.

From about 1350 onwards, and throughout the fifteenth century, the situation changed, and a new type of bishop appeared, drawn from the higher aristocracy. Examples of this are William Courtenay, son of the Earl of Devon (at Hereford, London and Canterbury); Thomas Arundel, brother of the Earl of Arundel (at Ely, York and Canterbury); Henry Beaufort, son of John of Gaunt (at Lincoln and Winchester); Edmund Stafford, related to the Earls of Stafford (at Exeter); and in the north, Alexander Neville and Richard Scrope at York. This was continued during the fifteenth century, and between about 1350 and 1480 there were about twenty bishops of this type. It should be noted that these aristocratic bishops occupied key positions, such as Canterbury, York, London, and Lincoln, very different from the reward of a scholar or a religious. The aristocrats had this advantage over the civil servants or the scholars, that they started their episcopates early, and held office longer; thus Courtenay became a bishop at about twenty-five years of age, Arundel at twenty-one, Beaufort at about twenty-three. It may be noted too that with such men translations became more frequent, as though it had become a point of prestige, as well as profit, to occupy the highest place available at any given time.

This infiltration of the aristocracy accompanied a certain decline in the preponderance of the civil servants among the bishops in the later fourteenth century. Thus whereas in the reign of Edward III bishoprics had been given as administrative salaries or rewards, in the reign of Richard II we find them given as political rewards or retainers. As a result the bishops like others suffered from the growing vindictiveness of politics in the period. Under Richard II, there was a new and deplorable feature, whereby both the king and the baronial opposition, with the aid of the Papacy, used episcopal translations to reward supporters and punish opponents. Already, earlier in the century, Edward II had tried to get the pope to remove opposition bishops, such as Orleton and Burghersh, but without success,[1] and the pope had protested against the victimization of Walter Langton and the Scottish bishops.[2] It was a period when the Papacy could take a creditably strong and independent line, for which it received due praise, as we have seen, from an English chronicler. Now, in the reign of Richard II, after the outbreak of the Great Schism, the popes were in a weaker position and more complaisant, and the provision of royal nominees had become more of a habit. Consequently bishops were translated as reward or punishment, on political grounds.[3] Thus in 1388 as a result of the triumph of the magnates in the Merciless Parliament, royalist bishops were banished or demoted; Alexander Neville was translated from York to St Andrews (which was a kind of ecclesiastical Botany Bay, being in the hands of the adherents of the anti-pope), Rushook went from Chichester to Kilmore in Ireland, Fordham from Durham to the smaller and poorer see of Ely; while a baronial supporter like Arundel was promoted from Ely to York. In 1397, with Richard's 'second tyranny', the tables were turned, and this time royal protégés were promoted, Tideman, the king's physician being moved up from Llandaff to Worcester, Waldby from Dublin to Chichester, Medford from Chichester to Salisbury, while on the other hand Arundel was banished from Canterbury to St Andrews, and the veteran John Buckingham, whose promotion had been pressed on the pope by Edward III with so much difficulty, was now, after more than thirty years at Lincoln, removed to Lichfield to make way for the youthful Henry Beaufort. After the revolution of 1399, Arundel was brought

[1] Rymer, II, 464, 504f., 515, 536, 537, 549, 553, 601, 629.
[2] Ibid. 41, 44, 53, 59, 64, 65, 138, 147, 154.
[3] Steel, Richard II, 164, 218, 220, 235; Tout, Chapters, III, 436; Perroy, Schisme, 303–4, 340, 344, 347; A. H. Thompson, The English clergy and their organization in the later Middle Ages (Oxford, 1947), 13–14.

back in triumph to Canterbury, and his supplanter, Roger Walden, was moved down to London; while Thomas Merke was removed from Carlisle and translated to a see *in partibus infidelium*. These political ups and downs inevitably coloured men's attitude towards their ecclesiastical superiors. Thus when Archbishop Arundel in 1411 attempted a visitation of the University of Oxford, one of his leading opponents, John Rote, Dean of Oriel, is reported as saying: 'The archbishop had better take care; he tried to visit the University once before [i.e. in 1397], and at once was banished from the realm.' 'Sir John,' replied a colleague, taking the part of the archbishop, 'why do not you remember what happened to those [i.e. Richard II and his party] who insulted the archbishop, and how gloriously he himself returned?'[1] This impinging of purely secular politics upon the Church in the fourteenth century was on the whole a new thing. The great churchmen who had become involved in political struggles in the past, such as St Anselm, St Thomas, Langton, Pecham, even to a certain extent Stratford, had acted as churchmen, because ecclesiastical claims and privileges had seemed to be at stake.

The growth of the aristocratic element among the bishops seems to coincide with that new phase of feudalism which, rightly or wrongly, has come to be called 'bastard feudalism'. Does this mean that the power of the Crown over church patronage was weakening, and that the magnates were helping themselves? If so, there is a contrast with earlier practice, for the baronial oppositions of the thirteenth and early fourteenth century do not seem to have been able to affect the nomination of bishops to any appreciable extent.

This survey of the fourteenth-century English bishops may perhaps be summed up very roughly as follows: at the beginning of the century, it is the scholar bishops, of whom Winchelsey may be taken as the type, who are most notable, though the civil servants are already in evidence. In the mid century the civil

[1] *Snappe's Formulary*, 200-1.

servants, of whom Wykeham may be taken as the type, predominate. At the end of the century, the aristocratic bishops, of whom Arundel may be taken as the type, are prominent.

With the other classes of ecclesiastical benefices, it is only possible to deal summarily here, partly because we still lack sufficiently full and trustworthy data to make it possible to generalize.

THE GREATER BENEFICES IN CATHEDRAL AND COLLEGIATE CHURCHES[1]

The cathedral chapters comprised in the first place a group of dignitaries, usually four in number (dean, precentor, treasurer, chancellor); secondly, the body of canons, each with his own prebend or share of the church's property; thirdly the archdeacons of the diocese. The collegiate churches consisted of a body of canons, presided over by a dean or provost.

As regards methods of appointment, in the cathedral chapters, the deans were elected by the chapters, while the other dignitaries, canons and archdeacons were normally appointed by the bishop; hence the importance of the bishop's patronage. In the collegiate churches, the methods of appointment varied, though here too the bishops had much patronage.

Some of these cathedral and collegiate benefices, particularly the dignities and archdeaconries, were very lucrative, and by the fourteenth century had in fact largely come to be treated as sinecures whose duties could be performed in absence by deputies; and in the cathedral chapters, the canons were divided into a small group of residentiary canons, who were bound to residence and received extra emoluments, and a much larger group of non-resident canons. Dignities, archdeaconries and prebends, being both lucrative sinecures and held in plurality, were therefore the

[1] For the cathedral and collegiate churches see K. Edwards, *The English secular cathedrals in the Middle Ages* (Manchester, 1949); A. H. Thompson, *The English clergy*, chapter III; and below, p. 59, 99.

class of benefice most sought after for royal officials and papal provisors, as we shall see.

Some of the most important and wealthy cathedrals in England had chapters consisting of monks instead of secular canons, as at Canterbury, Winchester and Durham, and therefore provided no prebends available for papal provision, royal nomination, or episcopal collation. This fact made the competition for prebends in the secular cathedrals, such as York, Lincoln or Salisbury, all the more keen. It also put the bishops whose cathedrals were served by monastic chapters at a serious disadvantage, in having no prebends and dignities to dispose of to their followers; it was perhaps partly for this reason that we find such bishops founding collegiate churches in their dioceses, such as Wingham, founded in 1286 by Archbishop Pecham (Canterbury), and Lanchester (1283) and Chester-le-Street (1286) founded by Bishop Beck (Durham), not to mention the well-known and unsuccessful attempt of earlier Archbishops of Canterbury to create secular collegiate churches at Hackington and Lambeth.

THE PARISH CLERGY[1]

It is even more difficult to generalize about the parish clergy than about the capitular clergy. A good deal of work needs to be done by way of analysing the parish clergy and attempting to work out their social background and family connexions, their intellectual standards, their relations with their patrons, the methods by which they obtained preferment. One thing can, however, be safely said: the parish clergy were not at all a homogeneous class. They were heterogeneous and stratified; they consisted in fact of several different classes. In the first place there were those who held parochial benefices but were non-residents or pluralists. A careful analysis of the returns of pluralists in 1366[2] would tell us a good

[1] A. H. Thompson, *The English clergy*, chapter IV.
[2] Now published in *Registrum Simonis de Langham*, ed. A. C. Wood (*C and YS*, 1947–8), 1–109; and *Registrum Simonis de Sudbiria*, ed. R. C. Fowler and C. Jenkins (*C and YS*, 1930), II, xxxvi–xliv, 148–82.

deal about these men, though of course not all non-residents were necessarily pluralists; a study of the dispensations for non-residence in the bishops' registers would also help. Here again we must remember that the non-residents and pluralists were not all of one type. They ranged from what canon law called 'sublime and literate persons', and important and wealthy officials like William of Wykeham or Hugo Pellegrini, down to quite humble people who subsisted on a couple of minute benefices.[1] Thus the great dividing line[2] in the Church between the important and wealthy, the administrators in Church and State on the one hand, and the rank and file of the clergy on the other, cuts right across this sub-section of non-residents and pluralists.

Secondly, there were the beneficed clergy who resided in their parishes, whether from inclination or necessity. Chaucer in his 'poor parson' has given us a famous picture of this type at its best, and it is only fair to regard him as at least as characteristic as the Friar or the Pardoner. An example from real life can probably be seen in William of Pagula,[3] a distinguished canonist and theologian, who nevertheless seems to have ended his life as a working parish priest and local penitentiary. This was perhaps unusual for a distinguished academic person; Wyclif, for instance, who held three parish churches in succession from 1361 to 1384, habitually resided at Oxford until the last two and a half years of his life.[4]

Thirdly, there was a very large clerical proletariate of priests working for a salary, 'parish priests' or 'chaplains' (*capellani curati*), who acted as assistants to or deputies for the beneficed parish priests, whether resident or non-resident.[5] Some of these chaplains were necessary for serving outlying chapels in the larger parishes. These unbeneficed clergy were very numerous, and in some districts they outnumbered the beneficed clergy by nearly two to one. As we shall see, John Mirk, when writing his hand-

---

[1] Cf. below, p. 36.
[2] Cf. below, p. 98.
[3] Cf. below, p. 195.

[4] A. H. Thompson, *The English clergy*, 103.
[5] *Ibid.* 122–3.

book for parish priests, presupposes that his reader will be a 'hired man', working for an employer, whether as assistant to a priest or chaplain to a lord.[1] Socially and economically, this class must have been poles apart from the 'sublime and literate persons', though the case of Langland shows us that a more or less submerged cleric might be the intellectual equal of anybody. The unbeneficed clergy were the ecclesiastical equivalent of the landless labourers, and like the latter, they became restive during the years after the Black Death and demanded higher pay. John Ball no doubt belonged to this class.

In their intellectual formation and pastoral training the parish clergy were also heterogeneous. We must not expect to find that they have been through a uniform and systematic training like the modern seminary system. This is perhaps the most important of all differences between the clergy of medieval and modern times. The training of the secular clergy in this period was, to modern eyes, very haphazard. Some of the parish clergy were able to get to a university for a few years, and some of these (though not all) were able to stay there long enough to take a degree.[2] But those who did well at the university were likely for that very reason to be drawn away from parochial work to academic or administrative work. Even for those who did get there, the university did not perform the function of a seminary; its studies were organized on a different basis. Those parish clergy who did not get to a university must have got their training from attendance either at cathedral schools (where these were functioning),[3] or at the schools of the friars, or at the grammar schools, or from experience in helping senior priests, or from the manuals that were put out for the instruction of the clergy. There were, as we shall see, plenty of writers ready to teach the parish priest (in English verse if necessary) what he should do, what he should teach, and how he should live.[4]

[1] Cf. below, p. 215.
[2] The list of medieval members of Oxford University, which Mr A. B. Emden is preparing, will throw valuable light on this aspect of the clergy.
[3] Cf. below, pp. 110ff.   [4] Cf. below, pp. 195ff.

CHAPTER III

PATRONAGE AND THE
USE OF BENEFICES

PATRONAGE or appointment to offices and benefices in the Church was exercised by a variety of persons: by the Crown, by lay magnates, by bishops and abbots, and by the country gentry. The Crown exercised a vast amount of ecclesiastical patronage which was made up in various ways:

In the first place, there were the appointments made by the Crown in its own right, *pleno iure*, such as the advowson of Crown livings, the appointment to masterships of certain hospitals, and to the 'Royal Free Chapels'.[1] These last consisted of about a dozen collegiate churches, composed of deans and canons, such as St Martin-le-Grand, Wimborne, Bridgnorth, Wolverhampton, and Tamworth (which last reverted to the Crown in the course of the fourteenth century); to these were added two important new foundations, St Stephen's Westminster (1348) and St George's Windsor (1349), the creation and lavish endowment of which shows how much the king valued such ecclesiastical 'pocket boroughs'. In some of these chapels the king only appointed the dean, in others he also appointed the canons.

Not all the Crown livings were filled by the king himself, for by ancient custom the Chancellor had the right to nominate to those benefices in the king's gift which were valued at twenty marks a year (£13. 6s. 8d.) or less; these were to be given to clerks of the Chancery, the Exchequer, and the Judicial Benches. We may even find the king asking the Chancellor to present particular persons to benefices nominally in his own gift.[2]

---

[1] A. H. Thompson, *The English clergy*, 81 ff.; *Archaeological Journal*, LXXXIV (1926), 26–9.
[2] H. C. Maxwell-Lyte, *Historical notes on the use of the Great Seal of England* (London, 1926), 220ff.

Secondly, the king enjoyed a variety of accidental patronage, 'windfalls', which were even more valuable than the patronage *pleno iure*. In the first place, as a result of his exercise of the feudal right of wardship over the heirs of tenants-in-chief, the king, during the period of wardship, disposed of his wards' patronage, such as the advowson of churches. Secondly, and above all, there was the 'regalian right', by which, during the vacancy of a bishopric, the king not only took over the bishop's lands and revenues, but also exercised the bishop's patronage, that is to say, the king presented to those offices and benefices which the bishop would have filled if he were there. This right was stretched to the utmost, and was of the greatest importance, because the bishops had so many important and valuable offices in their gift, such as archdeaconries and canonries. These were just what the king wanted for his servants, and it was precisely here that the Crown most often came into conflict with the Papacy, which also specialized in these dignities for purposes of provision.[1]

Another windfall came during the Hundred Years War, when the king had the custody of the alien priories and therefore of their advowsons. Again, the Crown was not above borrowing a little patronage from the Papacy itself: thus in 1363 we find the pope authorizing the appointment of five persons nominated by the king to a deanery and four prebends, about to be void by the consecration of John Buckingham, bishop-elect of Lincoln[2]— benefices which would normally have been claimed for papal provision.

From all these sources, high and low, the king derived a formidable amount of patronage. It has been estimated, from the evidence of the Patent Rolls, that during the thirty-five years of the reign of Edward I, the Crown presented about 600 persons to about 1000 benefices, disposing, that is to say, on an average of rather less than 30 benefices a year; and probably only about one in twelve of these presentations was made *pleno iure*, the rest being

---

[1] See below, p. 80.   [2] *CPL*, IV, 87.

windfalls.[1] During the rest of the fourteenth century, the volume of patronage seems to have risen even higher: an examination of certain years, taken at intervals, in the Patent Rolls, shows an average annual presentation to about 15 prebends and dignities and about 45 lesser benefices, while during the Hundred Years War the custody of alien priories for a time brought in between 30 and 60 additional presentations annually.

The magnates also had a good many benefices and offices in their gift. Such patronage had a definite social value, as a way of building up a body of ecclesiastical retainers and rewarding servants. This is illustrated in the fifteenth-century treatise on the royal household known as the *Liber Niger Domus Regis Edwardi IV*, which among other things gives a series of model budgets for the households of various degrees of nobility and gentry, from dukes to squires. The expenses and resources of each household are analysed, and among the resources there are given lists of posts, secular and ecclesiastical, which are likely to be in the gift of the nobleman concerned. Thus concerning the establishments of dukes and marquesses we are told:

These lords reward their knights, chaplains, esquires, yeomen and other of their servants, after their deserts. Some of his chaplains with officialships, deaneries, prebends, free chapels, parsonages, pensions or such other; and for the secular men, stewardships, receivers, constables (*etc.*). And this causeth lords to rule at need.

And concerning an earl's establishment:

This lord may give deaneries, prebends, free chapels, corrodies, or else he is founder of some canons, monks or friars singers [?]; thus he may raise up a chapel by help of yeomen and household children, which after, if they may not serve in the chapel, shall serve in the household, or else be preferred by the lord.[2]

---

[1] R. A. R. Hartridge, 'Edward I's exercise of the right of presentation to benefices as shown by the patent rolls', in *Cambridge Historical Journal*, II, 171 ff.

[2] 'Liber Niger Domus Regis Edwardi IV', in *A collection of ordinances and regulations for the government of the Royal Household* (published by Society of Antiquaries, London, 1790), 27, 28.

Bishops and abbots naturally had even more benefices to give away, and this too was an important social asset. Some heads of religious houses had a waiting list of 'pensionary clerks', men waiting to receive suitable benefices, who took an oath of fidelity and were employed by the monastery in various capacities such as legal counsel; the system is perhaps comparable to the secular indentures of retainer. A late thirteenth-century formula from Durham Cathedral priory for the engagement of a pensionary clerk runs as follows:

Know that we have granted and confirmed by this present charter to our beloved and faithful clerk N. by way of charity a rent of ten marks to be received yearly out of our chamber at such terms, until it shall please us to provide him more richly with an ecclesiastical benefice. The said N. has sworn to us on the Gospels that he will keep fealty to us in all things, and that he will faithfully see to the forwarding of our business, both beyond the seas and at home, and that he will not reveal our counsel to our harm, nor will he seek any art or device, whereby we may in anything be the losers.[1]

These pensioned counsellors sometimes included very important people; thus a Durham list of c. 1265–72[2] includes the high-born pluralist Bogo of Clare (at a fee of £66. 13s. 4d.), Robert Burnel the future Chancellor, and two archdeacons (who only cost £4 the pair); and a list of nineteen pensioned counsellors at Christ Church, Canterbury, 1291–2, includes two royal justices, three royal clerks, Gilbert of St Liffard (the saintly Bishop of Chichester), and Thomas of Cobham (the future Bishop of Worcester); there are also pensions paid to resident proctors and a cardinal at the Court of Rome. A generation later Christ Church was retaining the chronicler Adam Murimuth as a pensioned proctor at the Court of Rome.[3]

When the colleges came to be founded at the universities, they too had to have patronage to dispense to their alumni or friends,

---

[1] Durham annals and documents of the thirteenth century, ed. F. Barlow (SS, CLV, 1945), 86.
[2] Ibid. 87.
[3] R. A. L. Smith, Canterbury Cathedral Priory (Cambridge, 1943), 75, 79.

hence the acquisition of college livings. Throughout the ecclesiastical world, the great men and corporations were surrounded by a host of little men, constantly looking up to them for support and promotion: *ecce sicut oculi servorum in manibus dominorum suorum....*

An important factor was what may be called indirect patronage. A bishop or an abbot might often be pressed by the king or a magnate to give a living to one of the latter's protégés, so that while a clerk seemed to owe his promotion to one patron, in reality he owed it to some great man in the background. In this way the king, for instance, enjoyed much more patronage in fact than he appeared to do on paper. Some idea of the volume of this indirect patronage can be got from the fact that Edward II, when Prince of Wales, during a single year (1304–5), sent sixty-four letters to abbots and priors asking for benefices or pensions for his clerks, and another thirty letters asking for corrodies or pensions, while he sent eight letters to bishops asking for prebends or benefices.[1] It would be interesting to know how many of these applications were successful. In one case at least Edward, Prince of Wales, was scandalously successful. In 1305, with the help of the Chancellor, he forced the Prior of Worcester, after much resistance, to present Ingelard of Warley, Keeper of the Prince's Wardrobe, a man not yet in holy orders, to a benefice already occupied; the incumbent had to make room for the Prince's nominee.[2] This was no doubt a particularly bad case, but the repetition of this kind of pressure, capable of being pushed to such lengths, must have contributed to that hostility towards the Crown and its servants which was intermittent throughout the fourteenth century.

Sometimes a patron was able to elude pressure. Thus (to take an example from a later period) when the Duchess of Gloucester

[1] *Letters of Edward Prince of Wales 1304–5*, ed. H. Johnstone, Roxburghe Club, 1931, *passim*.
[2] J. M. Wilson, *The Worcester Liber Albus* (London, 1920), 49–52.

in 1476 asked the Prior of Durham for the vicarage of Bossall for her clerk, Nicholas Headlam, the Prior had his excuses ready: 'for I have a little overseen myself in my simpleness for lack of remembrance'; in fact, he had already presented someone else![1]

Which of the various types of patrons exercised the greatest influence in the Church? I think undoubtedly the Crown, both directly and indirectly. This is illustrated by the way in which the royal servants never lacked for benefices, great and small, as can be seen from the careers described in Tout's *Chapters*.

Underlying all this patronage and method of distribution was a regular system of the use and exploitation of ecclesiastical benefices. One element in this system was a certain utilitarian conception of the ecclesiastical benefice.[2] Every position in the Church, whether that of bishop, archdeacon, canon or parish priest, has two aspects. It can either be regarded as an office, a mass of duties and functions to be performed, such as administration of the sacraments, preaching, visitation, and so forth. Or it can be regarded as a benefice, as a mass of rights and emoluments to be received, tithes, fees, rents, and so forth, to be reckoned in pounds, shillings and pence. In theory, of course, the benefice is given for the sake of the performance of the duties: *beneficium datur propter officium*; and conscientious churchmen in every age and place would try to keep this in view. But it was easy to pay more attention to the benefice than to the duties, and to regard a church as a 'fat benefice' (*beneficium pingue, beneficium uberius*) worth, say, £50 a year; and the corollary to this was to argue thus: if a benefice is worth £50 a year, and you can get a priest to do the work for £5 a year, why not do so, and divert the surplus £45 to the higher purposes of Church and State? This in fact was what often happened throughout the Church from top to bottom. Thus a bishopric or archdeaconry would be held by

---

[1] *Historiae Dunelmensis Scriptores Tres*, ed. J. Raine (*SS*, IX, 1839), ccclviii.
[2] Cf. G. Barraclough, *Papal provisions* (Oxford, 1935), 71 ff.

a royal or papal official, and the bishop's or archdeacon's work would be done by a substitute. In the cathedral chapter, many a canon would be non-resident, and his place in the choir would be taken by a vicar-choral. In many parishes, the tithes would go to a non-resident rector, who might be anything from the Keeper of the Privy Seal to a university student, or to a monastery or a college, and the work would be done by a substitute, a vicar or chaplain. So we find a widespread system of sinecurism, absenteeism, and pluralism, with the work done by substitutes. If we wanted to imagine a modern equivalent to this system, we should have to suppose a cabinet minister, for instance, instead of drawing a salary, holding the headship of three or four colleges at Oxford and Cambridge, the professorships, let us say, of Roman Law, Forestry, Gynaecology and Classical Archaeology at various other universities, Directorships of Education in several counties, and the headmasterships of two or three of the more expensive public schools, drawing the revenues of all these offices, and performing the duties by deputy. Such a picture will give us some idea of how an important official in the medieval Church or State was provided for.

It is possible to give some concrete examples of how this system worked in the fourteenth century. For instance, a return of pluralists in the diocese of London in 1366 shows that there were 169 pluralists, great and small, holding benefices to a total value of £7,500. More than a third of the total value of these benefices was held by nine pluralists alone, and of these, there were three outstanding pluralists: William of Wykeham, Keeper of the Privy Seal, who held the Archdeaconry of Lincoln and ten prebends to the annual value of £873 (perhaps £30,000 of modern money); David of Wollore, another civil servant of long standing in the Chancery, who held seven prebends, one parish church and one hospital, to the value of £270; Hugo Pellegrini, a papal envoy, who held the treasurership of Lichfield, two prebends and one parish church, to the value of £293. It is worth noticing that most of these offices were without cure of souls. About one-fifth of the pluralists were civil servants, holding about £3,000 worth of benefices, that is to say, nearly half of the total value.[1] A similar return of pluralists in the diocese of Lincoln in 1366 shows 136 pluralists, of whom 37 were royal officials, two papal officials, and five men in the service of bishops; 44 of the pluralists can be identified as university graduates or students.[2]

It would be a mistake to imagine that the typical 'pluralist' was a man of enormous wealth drawn from numerous benefices, like William of Wykeham or David of Wollore. A clearer picture of the medieval pluralist can be got from a further examination of the returns of English pluralists made in 1366, just quoted.[3] Thus in Salisbury diocese there were 56 pluralists holding 132 benefices, in Lichfield diocese 38 pluralists holding 95 benefices, and in Norwich diocese 20 pluralists holding 41 benefices. Each pluralist thus on an average held two or three benefices, which brought in to each individual an average aggregate income ranging from about £26 (in Salisbury) to about £30 (in Norwich), the equivalent perhaps of about £1,000 or £1,200 a year in modern money, or roughly the salary of a senior university lecturer. About one-third of the pluralists had incomes of over £30. Only two men in the diocese of Salisbury had over £100, and only one man in each of the other two dioceses. The typical pluralist would hold one prebend in a cathedral or collegiate church together with one parish church with cure of souls. Such benefices were 'compatible', and needed no papal dispensation, which was only required for the holding of two benefices with cure of souls. In fact there seem to have been only two pluralists in the three

[1] *Registrum Simonis de Sudbiria*, ed. R. C. Fowler and C. Jenkins (*C and YS*, 1938), II, xxxvii–xliii.

[2] A. H. Thompson, in 'Pluralism in the Medieval Church', in *Associated Architectural Societies' Reports*, XXXIII (1915–16), 35–73, XXXIV (1917), 1–26, XXXV (1918–20), 87–108, 199–242, XXXVI (1921), 1–41, gives an annotated list of the Lincoln pluralists, preceded by a very valuable essay on pluralism.

[3] *Registrum Simonis de Langham*, ed. A. C. Wood (*C and YS*, 1947–8), I, 1–109; for Salisbury diocese, see pp. 16–29; for Lichfield, see pp. 84–98; for Norwich, see pp. 5–10.

dioceses who needed such a dispensation. Some of the 'pluralists' were quite small men, combining the office of vicar-choral with a small parish or chapelry in the neighbourhood, and so bringing in a small income of perhaps £8 or £10. In other words, while 'pluralism' could mean a princely income, it could also mean an attempt to make ends meet by combining two or more exiguous benefices. The rule which forbade the holding of two cures of souls simultaneously without a papal dispensation was no doubt intended to make it possible for a man to reside on his cure, but the man who held two 'compatible' benefices, one with cure of souls and one without, did not necessarily reside in either. Judged by modern standards, the curious and unsatisfactory feature was not so much the pluralism—the accumulation of prebends might have no worse effect than a thin attendance in choir in some distant collegiate church like Abergwili or Penkridge—as the lack of insistence on the performance of the cure of souls in person.

We may approach the subject from a different angle, and take the history of a particular benefice, such as the valuable Rectory of Houghton-le-Spring, in the diocese of Durham, assessed at £86. 13s. 4d. in 1291.[1] Of its ten incumbents between 1294 and 1400, four were civil servants, three were in the service of the bishop, one was a papal auditor (an Englishman), and another a Frenchman from the diocese of Le Mans; one of the civil servants, Richard Clifford, ultimately became Bishop of Worcester and London.[2] Yet in 1343 Bishop Richard de Bury, when petitioning to the pope to have this church of Houghton-le-Spring turned into a collegiate church, stated that in the past the church had been conferred by bishops at the request of the kings and queens of England on 'courtiers, insufficient and light persons, who turn the income to lascivious and profane uses'.[3] The bishop may have been thinking of the notorious royal clerk, John Mansel, who held

[1] *Taxatio Ecclesiastica...Nicholai IV* (London, 1802), 314; later reduced to £50, ibid. 329.

[2] *Fasti Dunelmenses*, ed. D. S. Boutflower (SS, cxxxix, 1926), 172.

[3] *CPP*, i, 25.

the benefice c. 1260, but on the whole his words seem to be a libel upon a succession of responsible royal and ecclesiastical administrators, and show with how much caution we must treat contemporary *plaidoyers* of this sort.

In theory, canon law forbade or severely restricted pluralism and non-residence, as in the constitution *De multa* of the Lateran Council of 1215 and the constitution *Execrabilis* of John XXII (1317). But even canon law had explicitly to make exceptions for 'sublime and lettered persons', the great officials of church and state, and it hardly affected those benefices, such as ordinary prebends, which had no cure of souls.[1] Moreover, among the recognized reasons for non-residence was study at a university, and the more zealous bishops were as promoters of learning, the more lavish they were in granting incumbents leave of absence for the purpose of university study; indeed the frequency of such dispensation is a good index of a scholar bishop's zeal.[2] Thus even the most respectable motives conspired to support the system of exploitation.

This system of exploiting or diverting ecclesiastical benefices for the higher purposes of Church and State was taken for granted and found defenders among various shades of opinion, clerical and lay, strict and lax, during the thirteenth and fourteenth centuries. Thus, for instance, Bishop Walter Cantilupe, though himself a reformer, in 1237 expressed his sympathy with the influential clerks who protested against anti-pluralist legislation:

> It would be exceedingly hard for such men to be despoiled of their benefices and thrust into ignominious poverty. Indeed some young men, ferocious and strenuous, would face the greatest dangers, sooner than let themselves be deprived of their benefices, and reduced to a single benefice. I myself, before I was called to my present dignity, determined in my mind, that if I had to lose one benefice under such a decree, I would give them all up.[3]

---

[1] *Associated Architectural Societies' Reports*, XXXIII, 42–50, 61–73.

[2] Bishop Simon of Ghent gave leave of absence to 308 scholars in seventeen and a half years; Walter Reynolds as Bishop of Worcester to 156 in five years, *Church Quarterly Review*, CXXXVIII (1944), 79.

[3] Matthew Paris, *Chronica Majora (RS)*, III, 418.

39

The bland assumption that the Church's benefices exist for the benefit of influential people and their relatives is well illustrated in a memorandum drawn up in 1274 for the royal and baronial proctors sent to the Council of Lyons. There is a protest against the effects of papal provisions: 'Item concerning the straitened plight of noble and well lettered clerks, whose kinsfolk have to be supported by them, or else they are exposed to dangers and unlawful gain (*questui*).' It is argued that pluralism is necessary because of primogeniture, for (it is explained for the benefit of foreigners) in this country 'only one succeeds, and the inheritance is not divided among many; it is therefore important that the rest [that is, the younger sons], who become clerks, should be admitted to the said dignities, personages, offices and benefices, by canonical election or presentation or collation; through them help is given to the poor'.[1]

In the return of pluralists made in 1366, Master Roger Otery, *clericus commensalis* of the Bishop of Hereford, makes the following apologia. After explaining that he has been busily employed for many years in the correction and reform of the morals of subjects of bishops according to the custom of the Church in England and Wales, he goes on to say:

And it is laid down in the sacred canons that a good and industrious and literate person can govern two or even ten churches better than another can govern one; and both he who resides and he who does not reside are understood to serve the altar, so long as they live a good life and expend well the income they derive. And I say also that by the custom of the English Church it was and is the used and approved custom, from time out of mind, and tolerated by the Roman Church, that the bishops and other patrons of the said realm of England can provide their well-deserving clerks with benefices, especially sinecures, up to any number, without any contradiction or offence to the Holy See.[2]

[1] H. Cole, *Documents illustrative of English history in the thirteenth and fourteenth centuries* (London, 1844), 358–60.
[2] A. H. Thompson, *The English clergy*, 246.

The point of view of the Papacy is expressed in a letter from Honorius III to Archbishop Gray of York in 1220:

Since those who faithfully serve the Apostolic See, as the head of the universal Church, are held to give useful service as it were to all the members, it is right that they should be honoured with suitable benefices; lest otherwise, if they had to serve at their own cost and were defrauded of special revenues, they might be slower to serve. Whence it is the practice that clerks who reside at the Apostolic See (not without many labours and expenses), have received for the time being ecclesiastical benefices in England and other parts of the world; and these not infrequently have striven in their time to serve those from whom they have received their benefices so efficaciously, that it has been as much to the advantage of those who gave the benefices as of those who received them.[1]

The same idea is echoed in a document of c. 1352, which speaks of the benefices of the cardinals, who 'being employed about Us [the pope] in the service of the Universal Church, procure the advantage of their benefices, no less than if they personally resided in them'.[2]

We must be careful not to exaggerate the scandals or the unreasonableness of this system. The paid substitutes who did the work of the absentees may have been efficient up to a point; and the funds were on the whole diverted to genuinely useful purposes, to support the administration of Church and State, and not to be dissipated in riotous living, in spite of what Richard de Bury stated. By the middle of the fourteenth century, at any rate, the type of ecclesiastical drone like Bogo of Clare, living at ease on the fruits of his many benefices, seems to have disappeared, and, as we have seen, the outstanding pluralists in the 1366 returns were busy men in official positions.

One must remember too the difficulties facing a medieval pope or king. Medieval men hated taxation, and would not recognize

---

[1] *Register of William Gray* (SS, LVI, 1872), 137–8.
[2] Durham Cathedral Muniments, Register N, fo. 29 ff.; cf. below, p. 73.

the necessity of supporting the central government in Church and State; the king should live of his own, and so should the pope. Hence the king and the pope were reduced to this indirect use of ecclesiastical endowments to support their administration; there seemed no other way out. The more sensible and honest plan of a direct income tax levied on the whole Church to support the papal Curia, for instance, though repeatedly suggested—at the end of the twelfth century, in 1225, and again at the Council of Vienne in 1311—came to nothing.[1]

This system of exploitation was simply an early example of something we are all too familiar with, something that might be called the priority mentality: the doctrine that the convenience of an official organization must always outweigh the claims of the private individual. It is the same principle throughout the ages, whether it is applied to the reservation of prebends or the reservation of sleeping berths.

Again, we must not exaggerate the extent of the system. Not all fourteenth-century churchmen were absentee officials; there were bishops like Simon of Ghent, Cobham, and Brunton, and in the cathedral chapters, for instance, there was a substantial core of resident canons, larger than has been realized, keeping up the life of the cathedral. It is dangerous too to judge by appearances and by imperfect data. Thus if we had only certain official records, such as the papal registers, to go upon, we might dismiss men like Richard de Bury, Grandisson, FitzRalph, Adam Easton and Wyclif as place-hunters, absentees, nepotists, chronic litigants and so forth; we happen to know, from other sources, that these men were very different.

If official records may be misleading, so may be chroniclers; some of their best stories are sometimes rendered dubious by historical research. Thus the Durham chronicler, Robert Gray-

---

[1] For the scheme put forward by the Emperor Henry VI and again in 1225 by Honorius III, see F. M. Powicke, *Stephen Langton* (Oxford, 1928), 83, 158; for the proposal of 1311 (put forward by the canonist Iohannes Andreae), see J. Haller, *Papsttum und Kirchenreform* (Berlin, 1903), 54.

stanes, has given us a well-known picture of the aristocratic Lewis de Beaumont, Bishop of Durham, as illiterate (*laicus*), unable to understand Latin, and stumbling over the Latin words of the liturgy, such as *metropolitice* and *in aenigmate*, and exclaiming in French, in the middle of the service, 'By St Louis, he was no gentleman who wrote that word!' Yet in fact Lewis de Beaumont must have been a graduate, for he is consistently described as *magister* in records. Similarly Bishop Henry Burghersh was censured by another chronicler for his youth and lack of learning, yet Bishop Cobham tells us that he had studied for more than fifteen years at various universities and was skilled in letters.[1]

When all allowances are made, this system by which one set of men did the work and another set of men received the rewards was unreal and unfair, and a tragic falling short of the promise of the thirteenth-century reform. Men like William of Wykeham and Thomas Arundel were worthy enough men in their own way and cannot be called scandalous; but neither were they the type of zealous and learned bishop envisaged by Innocent III. The Keeper of the Wardrobe or the *Auditor litterarum contradictarum* in the Court of Rome was no doubt an able and deserving man and very necessary to Church or State, but that was no guarantee that he was the best man to make Archdeacon of Middlesex or Dean of York. To take a particular instance: Adam Easton, the Benedictine monk, theologian and cardinal, was one of the most creditable products of his order and of his age, but there was some absurdity in a system which loaded him with benefices and made him Archdeacon of Shetland and Precentor of Lisbon.[2]

But it is not enough to criticize; we must try to understand. All this system is really part of the perennial problem of the entanglement of the Church in the world, in the ambient society. *Nemo militans Deo implicat se negotiis saecularibus*, says the Apostle, but the difficulty is to know how to apply this, except by going

---

[1] *Church Quarterly Review*, CXXXVIII (1944), 62–5; cf. *Hist. Dunelm. Scriptores Tres*, 118.
[2] Cf. below, p. 63.

into the desert. Entanglement takes different forms in different periods. Thus in the age of the investiture contest there were characteristically gross abuses, such as open simony, or the career of Odo of Bayeux. Since then, manners had improved, and the Church had emerged technically free, except for lay patronage of parish churches; but now, in the later Middle Ages, there was a more subtle control and exploitation of the Church by lay society. During the Middle Ages, the lay power was always generous to the Church, but always kept a tight hand on it; what it gave with one hand, it held on to with the other. The 'Caesarian prelates' whom Wyclif denounced were not spiritual men arrogantly seizing secular power—that bogey of the anticlerical—but for the greater part they were secular administrators, for the convenience of the government disguised as spiritual men. In other words, the Church was the exploited, not the exploiter, a point which so many contemporary and later critics seem to miss. Grosseteste was one of the few men who saw clearly and disinterestedly the dangers of the situation, and desired to separate the clergy from all secular activities.[1] And yet this entanglement and exploitation was part of the price paid for a noble conception of Christian society, in which Church and State were interwoven and identified, a conception which had great merits.

In this connexion there is an interesting contrast to be made between conditions in England and France. Guillaume le Maire, Bishop of Angers, in a memorandum to the Council of Vienne, complains of the effects of papal provisions, and tells us that promising clerks, finding their promotion in the Church thus blocked, in desperation take to matrimony and a secular career, and take service in secular courts and the councils of princes; and these disappointed men become the most bitter enemies and persecutors of the Church.[2] One supposes that he was thinking

[1] F. M. Powicke, *Henry III and the Lord Edward* (Oxford, 1947), I, 287–8.
[2] C. Port, *Mélanges historiques* (*Collection de documents inédits sur l'histoire de France*, Paris, 1877), II, 481–2.

of the counsellors, lawyers and knights, in the service of King Philip the Fair of France, men like Pierre Flotte and Guillaume de Nogaret, who took a leading part in that king's struggle against the Papacy. There does seem to have been a real gulf and hostility, in France, between the leading servants of the king and the Church, at least in the time of Philip the Fair. But in England that gulf, on the whole, did not and could not exist because the king's servants were for the most part themselves churchmen; if Nogaret or Flotte had been an Englishman, he would have had half a dozen prebends and a bishopric at the end. Thus in England anticlericalism comes from the commons and the magnates, but not from the Crown and the royal servants. It is true that in 1341 and in 1371 attempts were made to get rid of clerical ministers and substitute laymen, and this at first sight looks like a dangerous experiment, which if successful might have produced a division between Crown and Church on the French model. But these attacks must not be exaggerated; in both cases it was more of a personal attack on a few highly placed clerical ministers than a general purge of clerical officials.

English royal servants were very conscious and proud of their position as mediators and 'hinges' between the kingdom and the Church and conscious of their power for good or ill; this is well brought out in a manifesto on behalf of the king's clerks in 1279, to which Sir Maurice Powicke has drawn attention:[1]

He [the Pope], saving his reverence, does not realize the merits of the clerks of the Lord King, that is, how useful and necessary they are in the business of the court and government of the kingdom, and how the court of the kingdom of England has always been governed principally and for the greater part by clerks, spaciously endowed with ecclesiastical benefices and honours; by whose assistance the interests not only of the kingdom of England, but also of the Church are consulted with healthful circumspection, and the indemnity of both is looked after. For they as lawful sons of the Church, nourish and preserve peace,

[1] Cole, *Documents*, 369; cf. Powicke, *Henry III*, II, 716.

unity and the devotion of the kingdom towards the Church, and as good mediators, hinder and extinguish anything to the contrary; which the laity would be not at all likely to do these days, as was shown clearly during the recent disturbance of the kingdom, when the laity were the hinge upon which everything turned [*dum revolveretur axis sub cardine laicali*].

The document goes on to warn the pope of the dangers of alienating these powerful clerks.

CHAPTER IV

PAPAL PROVISIONS

So far we have been considering the exercise of patronage by local, English authorities, of which the Crown was the most important. Competing with this local patronage, however, was another system of patronage: papal provision.[1] This subject has often been treated merely as one of the 'abuses' of the late medieval Church, along with simony or incontinent clerics. But in fact papal provision was simply part of the growing centralization of the Church which had been going on during the twelfth and thirteenth centuries; it was centralization applied to patronage, just as appeals to Rome, the use of judges delegate, and so forth, represented centralization applied to the judicial system. The system of papal provision meant that men were promoted to offices and benefices by the central authority, the pope, instead of by local methods of appointment. It was a system which could of course be used or abused, but it was not in itself an abuse; indeed it was capable of being used as an instrument of reform.

It is necessary here to pass over the earlier history and the theoretical basis of papal provision. It need only be said that the pope's right to dispose of all benefices was based on and indeed was part of the *plenitudo potestatis* which he wielded. Two thirteenth-century writers may be quoted on this point. Robert Grosseteste, opposed as he was to any misuse of provision, was very clear about the pope's right: 'I know and I truly know,' he wrote in 1238, 'that the Lord Pope and the Holy Roman Church

---

[1] For papal provisions in general, see G. Barraclough, *Papal Provisions* (Oxford, 1935); F. M. Powicke, *Henry III and the Lord Edward* (Oxford, 1947), I, 274 ff.; F. W. Maitland, *Roman Canon Law in the Church of England* (Cambridge, 1898), 66 ff.; G. Mollat, *La Collation des bénéfices ecclésiastiques sous les Papes d'Avignon 1305-78* (Paris, 1921; it is the introduction to vol. VIII of the *Lettres communes de Jean XXII*); A. Deeley, 'Papal provision and rights of royal patronage in the early fourteenth century', in *EHR*, XLIII (1928), 497–527.

have this power, that they can freely dispose [*ordinari*] of all ecclesiastical benefices.'[1] And Pope Clement IV began an important decretal on this subject, *Licet ecclesiarum* (1265), by saying: 'Although the full disposal of churches, parsonages, dignities and other ecclesiastical benefices is known to belong to the Roman Pontiff, so that he can not only confer these by right when they are vacant, but can also grant a right to those that shall fall vacant....'[2]

What we are concerned with here is to consider how the system of papal provision worked, and what were its effects. First we must consider the procedure, the successive stages that led up to papal provision.[3] Here it is important to remember that the initiative normally lay with the petitioner, not with the pope, at any rate with benefices other than bishoprics. This is in contrast to the local methods of appointment, where the initiative lay, at least formally, with the electors, collators or patrons of a benefice, though of course many candidates would have no hesitation about bringing themselves to the notice of patrons, as the formularies and letter books show.

Papal provisions might be exercised by virtue of either a special reservation or a general reservation. By a special reservation, the pope reserved to himself the right to appoint to a particular benefice. By a general reservation, he reserved to himself the right to appoint to a whole class of benefices or to all the benefices in a particular area. By canon law, for instance, all the benefices vacated by those who died at the papal Curia or who were promoted to higher offices by the pope were automatically reserved to the pope. And in 1265 the pope had reserved to himself all the benefices about to become vacant in England. Papal provision might take the form of immediate appointment to a benefice already vacant, and this was commonly the case with important

---

[1] *Roberti Grosseteste Epistolae*, ed. H. R. Luard (*RS*, 1861), 145.
[2] *Corpus Iuris Canonici*: Sext. lib. III, tit. iv, c. 2.
[3] For procedure, see Mollat, *La collation*, esp. 39–62.

offices like bishoprics. But it might also take the form of a promise of a benefice when it should fall vacant in the future; this was called an 'expectative grace', and was the method commonly used in providing to lesser benefices.

The procedure for obtaining a papal provision was as follows:

(i) The first stage was for the petitioner to get his petition for a benefice presented to the pope, backed if possible by some influential person, a cardinal or a bishop or the king or a lay magnate. Failing such backing, he must do the best he could; and it is clear that some desperate petitioners literally bombarded the pope. 'Whereas certain persons,' writes Pope Clement VI in 1343, 'as We have frequently learned from experience, casting from them their regard for decent manners and the reverence due to Ourselves, have presumptuously dared, and still do dare, when We are in Consistory, and at other times when We are out riding, to cast before Us, and sometimes upon Us, their petitions, in which they even wrap up stones, to Our perturbation....' The pope therefore forbids this 'unbridled audacity' under severe penalties.[1]

The *Calendar of Papal Petitions* throws some light on the promoters or supporters of petitions for provisions. Thus between 1342 and 1366 King Edward III asks for 49 prebends and dignities and 20 lesser benefices (of which 41 are for his own clerks); Edward the Black Prince asks for 67 prebends and dignities and 38 lesser benefices (of which 42 are for his clerks); Henry Duke of Lancaster asks for 66 prebends and dignities and 32 lesser benefices (of which no less than 80 are for his clerks); and another active promoter of provisions was Thomas Beauchamp, Earl of Warwick.[2] Ricard de Bury, Bishop of Durham, is said on one visit to the Curia to have obtained over three hundred graces for his clerks.[3] It is curious to find the king being outdone by Prince Edward and Henry of Lancaster, but we must remember that the

[1] *CPP*, I, vii.   [2] *CPP*, I, *passim*.
[3] *Hist. Dunelm. Scriptores Tres (SS*, IX, 1839), 127.

king exercised a vast amount of patronage in his own right, as we have seen, and no doubt he wisely concentrated on pressing for more important things such as the provision of suitable bishops. On the whole, during the period 1342–66 the number of petitions supported by ecclesiastical patrons decreases, while the number supported by the Crown, members of the royal family and royal officials increases, as does also the number of independent petitioners.

Analogous to the backing of petitioners by magnates, lay and ecclesiastical, was the practice in universities of sending to the pope periodically rolls of graduates and scholars asking for benefices; they range from chancellors, ex-chancellors and senior doctors, who ask for dignities or prebends, down to under-graduates.[1] It is not clear when these university rolls began, whether under John XXII or later. The practice may perhaps be implied in the numerous provisions to Fellows of Merton and other graduates in July, 1317,[2] and there is other evidence from Oxford that the university was asking for provisions about the years 1335 and 1337.[3] Four Oxford rolls for 1343, 1362, 1363 and 1366 are entered in the papal registers.[4] Cambridge is even more fortunate in possessing the original drafts of three rolls for 1370, c. 1389–90, and 1399, containing 75, 265 and 109 petitions respectively.[5] In this as in other ways we can see the universities acting as a kind of corporate magnate or patron. It is clear from these collective petitions that papal provision offered an opportunity for promotion that was invaluable to university men, especially to those who had no claim on a private patron. Then, as in later times, it may be said that the pursuit of learning, to borrow Dean Gaisford's words, 'frequently leads to positions of considerable emolument'.

---

[1] E. F. Jacob, 'Petitions for benefices from English Universities during the Great Schism', in TR Hist. Soc. (IV), XXVII, 41 ff.   [2] CPL, II, 137, 157–64 (July, 1317).
[3] Oxford Formularies, ed. H. E. Salter, W. A. Pantin and H. G. Richardson (OHS, Second Series, IV, 1939), I, 85–92.
[4] CPP, I, 60–2, 390–2, 402–4, 514–17.   [5] Jacob, art. cit., 47 ff.

(ii) If the petitioner was successful in the first stage, he was submitted to an examination (from which university graduates were exempt); the candidates were put into four classes—*bene, competenter, debiliter, male*. Any attempt to employ a substitute disguised as the candidate was punished with excommunication. Contemporary descriptions of medieval examinations must be rare, and I doubt if one exists of the examination of a petitioner for provision. But some idea of the proceedings may perhaps be got from surviving descriptions of the examination of bishops-elect.[1]

(iii) If the petitioner passed the examination, the next step was for a bull of provision to be granted, and this was sent to local executors to be put into effect.

(iv) But there was one last hurdle to be cleared; there was the possibility of an appeal against the provision, by a rival claimant, for instance, or by the normal patrons.

It is important to remember that not all those who petitioned succeeded in getting a provision in actual fact. A very large proportion of petitioners, perhaps as much as half, fell by the way and failed to get possession of their benefice in the end; or even if successful, they might suffer long delays. Consequently the number of effective provisions was much less than appears on paper. There was a certain amount of devolution or delegation of the right of papal provision. Thus bishops might be empowered by the pope to make provisions; in 1344 the Archbishop of York, for instance, was empowered to make provisions in each of the churches of York, Ripon, Beverley, Southwell and Howden.[2] Similar rights were granted to fourteen English bishops between 1343 and 1354.[3] On occasions the pope granted the same right to the king, as in 1378, when Urban VI granted to Richard II the right to fill the first two vacant canonries in every cathedral and collegiate church in England, Wales and Ireland.[4] In some cases

---

[1] See above, p. 19.   [2] *CPP*, I, 46.
[3] E.g. *CPP*, I, 48, 63, 85; the Abbot of Glastonbury asks for a provision to a benefice in the gift of his own monastery in 1355, *ibid.* I, 282.
[4] Wilkins, III, 130; Rymer (O), VII, 215; cf. also above, p. 31.

such grants must have meant that the bishops were simply being authorized to exercise their own patronage, but presumably the advantage was that appointments so made were immune from litigation or challenge from provisors.

How did papal provisions work out in practice, and what were their effects? In answer to this question we are usually given a lurid picture of English benefices filled with aliens, with disastrous results. This picture has a long tradition behind it and goes back to the complaints of contemporary writers and to the protests, petitions and statutes that were made throughout the fourteenth century. Thus the petition of the lords and commons in the Parliament of Carlisle (1307) states:

Whereas Holy Church in all the estates of prelacy in this realm has been founded by the king and by his ancestors and by the said earls and barons and their ancestors, in order to teach them and the people the faith of God and in order to make prayers and alms and hospitality in the places where the churches are founded, for the souls of the founders and of their heirs...and of such prelates the king and his ancestors have always had the greater part of the counsel that was needed for the safety of the realm; now comes the pope...and by his provisions and in other ways gives the said dignities, prebends and churches to aliens...and then elections will fail, the prayers, alms and hospitality in the aforesaid places will be withdrawn, the king and other lay patrons will lose their presentations in time of vacancies, the said counsel will perish, goods will be taken out of the realm, from which all manner of evils will openly follow.[1]

Again the king in a letter to the pope in 1343 describes the effect of provisions:

Thus Christian worship is diminished, the cure of souls neglected, hospitality withdrawn, the churches' rights perish, church buildings fall down, the people's devotion weakens; the clerks of this realm, men of great learning and honest conversation, who might advantageously

---

[1] *Rot. Parl.* I, 219. This and other protests are conveniently printed together in Haller, *Papsttum und Kirchenreform*, 544–9.

undertake the cure and rule of souls there, and would be useful in our public councils, are deserting study, because the hope of suitable promotion is taken away. The rights of our Crown are perishing, the treasure of our realm is exported to foreigners, not to say our enemies perhaps in the subtle conjecture that our realm will be rendered the weaker in adversity.[1]

Similar grievances were set out in the Parliament of Stamford (1309) and in the preamble to the Statute of Provisors (1351).[2] Certain themes run throughout these complaints: neglect of divine service, hospitality, alms, etc.; the frustration of the founders' intentions and the destruction of patrons' rights; the exportation of treasure to enemies; the lack of councillors and betrayal of the kingdom's secrets; the lack of advancement for scholars and therefore the decay of learning.

Historians have sometimes taken these complaints at their face value. What we really need, however, are facts and statistics, to test the effects of papal provisions. In any given chapter or diocese in England, how many men got their benefices by way of provision? And what proportion of these provisors were foreigners? What sort of people were these provisors? What difference did they make to the number of non-residents and pluralists? What contribution did they make to the life of the Church and of the State? Considering the wealth of materials available, in bishops' registers and elsewhere, it is extraordinary how little has been done so far systematically to answer these questions. There is need for much work to be done here, diocese by diocese, chapter by chapter.

In the meantime, let us try to examine how the various classes of benefices were affected by papal provisions. Here, at the outset, one extremely important distinction is to be made, namely the distinction between papal provision and the occupation of English benefices by aliens. In other words a papal provisor was

---

[1] Rymer, II, 1233.
[2] *Chronicles of the reigns of Edward I and II*, ed. W. Stubbs (RS), I, 161 ff.; *Statutes of the Realm*, I, 316; Rot. Parl. II, 232.

not necessarily an alien, and indeed aliens were greatly out-numbered by English provisors. Another general point to be borne in mind is that although the pope had the theoretical right to dispose of all benefices, as a general rule he did not intentionally interfere with the rights of lay patrons; provisions were made as far as possible at the expense of ecclesiastical patrons or electors.

1. THE BISHOPS. In the course of the fourteenth century papal provision became the normal method of appointment to a bishopric. In the thirteenth century papal provisions to bishoprics had still been exceptional; there were, for instance, only six direct provisions to bishoprics between 1216 and 1272.[1] But papal provision, or at least papal intervention, had been helped on not only by the formulation of papal claims, but also by disputed elections which were referred to Rome, and by the growing practice of translation from one bishopric to another, a process which always needed papal authorization. From 1272 to 1300 only one in forty of episcopal appointments was by way of translation; during the fourteenth century the proportion was one in four, and during the fifteenth century, one in three. In other words, it became more and more normal for a man to move on to a more important or richer see whenever the opportunity occurred.[2] This meant that favoured persons had a much greater chance of reaching the top of the tree in time, and it also meant that they needed papal approval in order to do so.

It was the reign of Edward II that was the turning point in the development of the provision of bishops.[3] Of the twenty-eight episcopal appointments in this reign, fifteen represented elections by chapters, of which ten (all before 1318) were undisputed and five disputed but confirmed. The other thirteen appointments were papal provisions; in six cases these were in accordance with

[1] Gibbs and Lang, *Bishops and Reform*, 81.
[2] Cf. A. H. Thompson, *The English clergy*, 13.
[3] For the appointment of bishops in the reign of Edward II, see Waldo E. L. Smith, *Episcopal appointments*, chapter II.

the king's wishes; in a seventh case the candidate, Thomas Cobham, Bishop of Worcester, was supported by Thomas of Lancaster; and in the six other cases the provision was more or less against the king's wishes. Among those provided in accordance with the king's wishes were Bishops Reynolds, Beaumont, and Burghersh; among those provided against his wishes were Rigaud d'Assier, John Stratford, and Orleton. The papal provisions against the king's wishes all came after 1316, that is to say, under Pope John XXII. In these cases, the pope often provided a royal servant, but not the particular one that the king had asked for, and where the pope turned down the king's nominee, he sometimes tried to satisfy him later on. For instance, Burghersh, disappointed of Winchester in 1319, was provided to Lincoln in 1320. The climax came in 1323-5, when the pope made four provisions in succession against the king's will.

The prevalence of provisions was still only partial during the period 1327-42, that is to say, during the early years of Edward III, under Popes John XXII and Benedict XII; out of twenty-three bishops, ten were elected and thirteen were provided. It was not until after 1342, in the time of Pope Clement VI, that papal provision to bishoprics became normal. Bishop Trilleck of Hereford (1344) seems to have been the last English bishop who was not provided to his see. From then on the general rule seems to have been provision by the pope, more or less at the king's nomination. The form of election by the chapter was still gone through, even though it was regularly superseded by a provision. It was not at first obvious that free election was a thing of the past; as late as 1362 the king thought it necessary to overawe the chapter of Lincoln by armed force, when he wanted his nominee John Buckingham elected.[1] The pope too might sometimes reject the

---

[1] The king objected to the canons of Lincoln holding a hasty election in order to prevent the non-resident canons engaged in the royal service from taking part, and he sent the sheriff and a body of knights to prevent this, Rymer, III, 676. It looks as though the king relied on his protégés in a chapter in order to get his way in an election, which supplies an additional motive for the Crown's loading its servants with prebends.

king's candidate, as we have seen. But if the king's success was not always a foregone conclusion, he generally got the bishops he wanted by papal provision. In 1344 Pope Clement VI wrote claiming that to abolish papal provisions to bishoprics would be against the interests both of the English Crown and the English Church; by no other means was the king so likely to get his ablest counsellors promoted, and capitular elections were likely to be carried out under the pressure of lay interference (*per impressionem militarem*).[1] To this period (1345) belongs the story that Clement VI said that if the king of England asked him to make an ass a bishop, he would do so.[2] The pope's readiness to oblige the king must have increased after the outbreak of the Great Schism; the climax came with the provisions and translations of the reign of Richard II, when bishops were moved up or down for political reasons by the king and his opponents in turn.[3]

While the appointment of bishops by papal provision gradually became the normal procedure, it is extremely important to notice that the appointment of aliens to English bishoprics was almost unknown in the fourteenth century; the only examples are the appointment of Rigaud d'Assier, a papal collector, to Winchester (1320–23), and of Lewis de Beaumont (a royal nominee) to Durham in 1318. There had been a small group of alien bishops in the time of Henry III, like Boniface of Savoy (the queen's uncle) and Aymer of Lusignan (the king's half-brother), but these owed their position to royal rather than papal influence.[4] There is also a rather unexpected group of Italian bishops at Worcester, Salisbury and Hereford in the time of Henry VII and Henry VIII, which probably means that the Crown found this a convenient way to reward useful diplomats.[5] Alien bishops are thus extremely

---

[1] MS. Cotton Cleopatra E II, fo. 47v. I owe this and the reference in the previous footnote to Mr J. R. L. Highfield.
[2] See above, p. 13.   [3] See above, p. 24.
[4] On the alien bishops under Henry III, see Powicke, *Henry III*, I, 264.
[5] A. H. Thompson, *The English clergy*, 26–7.

rare. It cannot be said therefore that papal provision had the effect of filling English sees with aliens. That was only to be expected; no English king, except Edward II at his weakest, faced by John XXII at his strongest, was going to have aliens intruded against his will among his tenants-in-chief and counsellors. Thus on the whole, after the time of Edward II, papal provision had the effect of giving the king the bishops he wanted, and he had little reason to complain about the way the system worked.

It may be asked whether abbots as well as bishops came to be appointed by papal provision in England during the fourteenth century. The answer seems to be that papal provision of English abbots was not unknown, but that it seems to have been rare, and liable to cause some stir or opposition, especially as the greater monasteries were generally under the king's patronage. Those monasteries most likely to be affected by provision seem to have been the great houses which were exempt from the local bishop's jurisdiction and immediately subject to the Holy See, since their abbots were bound to go to the papal Curia to have their elections confirmed by the pope, and the pope sometimes took this opportunity to make a provision.[1] In 1327, for instance, Richard of Wallingford was elected Abbot of St Albans; on his going to the Curia, the pope quashed his election on the grounds of some technical irregularities in procedure, and reappointed him by provision.[2] At St Augustine's, Canterbury, in 1346, William of Kenington was elected Abbot, but the pope, instead of confirming him, provided to the abbey John Devenish, a monk of Winchester, who had been elected to the see of Winchester but set aside to make way for a royal nominee, William Edington. The king protested to the pope against Devenish's provision to St Augustine's, and withheld the temporalities from him. Devenish died in 1348 at the Curia, while attempts were being made to get his

[1] On papal provisions to English monasteries, see A. H. Street, in *Speculum*, xxvin (1953), 473–5.
[2] T. Walsingham, *Gesta abbatum mon. S. Albani*, ed. H. T. Riley (*RS* 1867), ii, 186–91; *CPL*, ii, 269.

provision changed into an election.[1] Perhaps the most famous case of a monastic provision was at Bury St Edmunds in 1379. John Tymworth was elected abbot, but the pope provided instead Edmund Bromfield, a monk of Bury who was at that time proctor of the English Black Monks at the Roman Curia. This aroused the greatest opposition from Tymworth's supporters and still more from the Crown. Bromfield had himself installed at Bury in October 1379, but was almost at once arrested by the king's officers and imprisoned for three years; it was not until 1384 that the pope agreed to Tymworth's election.[2] At Westminster in 1387 the pope at first wished to quash the election of William of Colchester and provide him instead, but was persuaded to confirm the election.[3] In most of these cases there seems to have been more concern about the form of appointment, election or provision, than about the person appointed; and papal provision, in the rare cases where it operated, does not seem to have made much difference to the type of abbot appointed; there was no question of intruding aliens so far as one can see. Nor does the king seem to have imposed royal nominees. Since commendatory abbots were at this time unknown in England, abbeys were not much used as a means of endowing either papal or royal officials.

2. THE PARISH CHURCHES. At the other end of the hierarchical scale was the great mass of parochial benefices, the rectories and vicarages. How were these affected? Here the number of aliens and the practical effect of papal provisions on the cure of souls seem to have been much exaggerated. In the first place, a large proportion of these benefices were in lay patronage, and therefore not touched by papal provision. Secondly, of the benefices which were in the gift of ecclesiastical patrons, bishops and abbots, the richer ones might well be in demand for provisors, but these

---

[1] Twysden, *Hist. Anglicanae Scriptores Decem* (London, 1652), col. 2082 ff.
[2] *Memorials of St Edmunds*, ed. T. Arnold (*RS*, 1896), III, xxii ff., 113–37.
[3] Higden, *Polychronicon*, ed. J. R. Lumby (*RS*, 1886), IX, 89, 98, 102, 103.

benefices would probably in any case be given to a non-resident pluralist, such as a civil servant, so that it was merely a question whether the non-resident incumbent would be a royal nominee or a papal provisor, and in fact a papal provisor might himself be a royal servant. We have already seen how the rich living of Houghton-le-Spring, in the diocese of Durham, was held by a succession of royal and ecclesiastical administrators. The number of aliens holding parochial benefices in England seems to have been small; among nearly 3,000 incumbents in the diocese of Durham, listed in the *Fasti Dunelmenses*,[1] there are only about forty aliens, roughly about 1·4 per cent. A very simple test is available. As one goes about the country, one will often find in old churches a list of the medieval and modern incumbents, compiled by local antiquaries from the bishops' registers; it is comparatively rarely that one finds a foreign name among these, at any rate after the thirteenth century. The idea therefore that many thousands of English parishioners were groaning under the extortions and negligence of alien incumbents, though it was an idea clearly present in the minds of medieval petitioners, seems to represent an exaggeration. In fact, except in the case of a few 'golden rectories', which would be sufficient to create a sense of grievance, the number of provisors, and still more of alien provisors, would be comparatively small. Even under the lavish Clement VI the average number of provisions to parochial benefices per annum was 42 to Englishmen and 1·8 to aliens.

3. THE CATHEDRAL CHAPTERS. As Maitland pointed out,[2] the 'staple commodity' of papal provision consisted of the dignities and prebends in the cathedral chapters and collegiate churches; that is to say, the offices of dean, precentor, chancellor, treasurer, the archdeaconries and the ordinary prebends or canonries. These benefices were very considerably affected by papal provisions,

---

[1] Ed. D. S. Boutflower (*SS*, cxxxix, 1926), *passim*.
[2] Maitland, *Roman Canon Law*, 67n.

and in some chapters the proportion of alien provisors was high. This was to be expected, for, as has already been pointed out, these capitular benefices were of a type that made them much sought after by non-residents employed in the service of both Church and State. Ordinary canonries were not deemed by canonists to involve the cure of souls, and by the fourteenth century the majority of the canons were not even supposed to be resident; the duty of residence in the cathedral was undertaken by a small minority of residentiary canons, generally about a third or a quarter of the whole chapter.[1] Even the dignitaries, such as deans, precentors, etc., and the archdeacons, while they had important duties to perform and were technically bound to reside, in fact also often treated their offices as sinecures and performed their duties by deputy. The chapters most heavily affected by the provision of aliens were York, Lincoln and Salisbury, probably because they contained the most lucrative benefices, whereas London, Wells, Hereford and Exeter were hardly affected by alien provisions at all. Thus at York, for instance, in the time of Archbishop Greenfield (1306–15), out of 34 collations to canonries, 12 were papal provisions (of which 7 were to aliens) and 12 were nominations by the Crown, leaving little more than a quarter as normal appointments by the archbishop.[2] At York, too, about this time, we find that three out of the five archdeacons were cardinals. It is possible to get a very rough idea of the proportion of aliens among the dignitaries and archdeacons of these three chapters of York, Lincoln and Salisbury during the fourteenth century.[3] At York, the proportion of aliens among the deans was one in three (4 out of 13); among the treasurers one in three (6 out of 17); among the archdeacons

---

[1] K. Edwards, *The English secular cathedrals*, 83.

[2] *Abp. Greenfield's Register*, ed. A. H. Thompson (*SS*, CXLV, 1931), I, appendix I, 289–98, cf. xiv–xx.

[3] These figures are based on the lists in J. Le Neve, *Fasti Ecclesiae Anglicanae*, ed. T. D. Hardy (Oxford, 1854); imperfect as these are, they probably give a rough indication of the true proportions.

nearly one in three (18 out of 62); as many as 9 out of 12 of the archdeacons of the West Riding were aliens. At Lincoln, the proportion of aliens among the deans was one in six (2 out of 13); among the precentors one-half (4 out of 8); among the archdeacons one in eight (11 out of 84). At Salisbury, the proportion of aliens among the deans was unusually high, three-quarters (6 out of 8); among the precentors one in four (3 out of 12); among the treasurers one in three (3 out of 9); among the archdeacons one in seven (7 out of 49). Some of the lesser chapters were also heavily drawn on; seven out of sixteen canons of Southwell were alien provisors in 1306. On the other hand, we only find a single alien among the dignitaries and archdeacons at Exeter, and three among those of Hereford, during the whole century. I have been dealing here with the effect of provisions in its most extreme form, namely the presence of aliens in the chapters, which is easily detected. To estimate the number of English provisors in the various chapters would require more research into the personnel of the chapters, a thing which is badly needed.

It was precisely over these cathedral dignities and prebends that the Crown and the Papacy were most likely to come in conflict; they were normally in the gift of the bishops and therefore seemed fair game for papal provision, particularly as they were often vacated by men promoted by the pope to bishoprics, and they provided just what the pope wanted for cardinals and other papal officials. But on the other hand, being in the gift of the bishops, they were constantly being claimed by the king during the vacancy of bishoprics; it was in fact the king's regalian right, his claim to exercise episcopal patronage during vacancies, that brought him into conflict with the pope.[1]

Much of all this consideration of the number and distribution of provisors must be tentative, because at present we have to rely on imperfect data. But this much seems clear, that papal provisors

[1] Cf. A. Deeley in *EHR*, XLIII (1928), 497–527, especially 508–27.

and especially alien provisors did not exist in vast numbers. They were not an invading 'army of provisors', as contemporaries seemed to think, but rather a small group of highly privileged 'Very Important Persons' such as cardinals, a general staff rather than an army, enjoying a comparatively small number of extremely lucrative benefices. It was, I think, the value and not the number of the provisors' benefices that caused resentment.

The effect of papal provisions can be examined from another angle. What different classes of persons benefited from provisions? First, there is a fundamental distinction to be made between English provisors and alien provisors. As has been pointed out, it is quite wrong to imagine that all or even a majority of papal provisors were aliens; in fact, the great majority were Englishmen. Thus in the pontificate of Pope John XXII (1316–34), the average numbers of recorded provisions per annum were as follows: for prebends and dignities in cathedrals and chapters, 27 English provisors to 9 aliens (a proportion of three to one); for lesser benefices, 19 English provisors to 3 aliens (a proportion of six to one). In the pontificate of Clement VI (1342–52), the annual average for prebends and dignities was 52 Englishmen to 10 aliens (a proportion of five to one); for lesser benefices, 42 Englishmen to 1·8 aliens (a proportion of over twenty to one). Clement VI was famous for his lavishness, but this seems to have operated more in favour of English than of alien provisors. These figures represent what may be called 'paper' provisions, that is, provisions which are recorded as granted in the papal registers, and these provisions did not necessarily all take effect; but since Englishmen had at least as good a chance as aliens of getting possession of their benefices, this consideration does not materially weaken the proportions given above.[1] This large majority of

---

[1] Some allowance must also be made for the imperfect recording of provisions in the papal registers, and for the imperfect calendaring of the registers; but the proportions given above probably still hold good.

English over alien provisors and the extent to which natives used the system seem very important facts which are little realized in the popular estimate of papal provisions.

The men who benefited from papal provisions can also be classified according to their status or occupations. In the first place there were the officials of the papal Curia, from cardinals downwards. Many of these of course were aliens, such as Cardinal Raymond de Got (d. 1310), a brother of Clement V, who was at various times Dean of York, Lincoln and London, and Precentor of Lichfield;[1] or Annibaldus de Ceccano, Cardinal Bishop of Tusculum (d. 1350), who was Archdeacon of Nottingham and Buckingham, Precentor of Lichfield, and Treasurer of York.[2] But there were also native Englishmen at the Curia who benefited by papal provision. There was, for instance, the English Cardinal Adam Easton, a monk of Norwich, and a very distinguished scholar and writer, as we shall see later; in the last years of his life, between 1389 and 1395, after his recovery from disgrace and imprisonment under Urban VI, he received a number of provisions, and was made Archdeacon of Shetland, Provost of Beverley, Rector of Wearmouth, Prebendary of Aylesbury in the cathedral chapter of Lincoln, Precentor of Lisbon Cathedral, and Prior of the Priory of St Agnes at Ferrara in Italy.[3] Three of these benefices were estimated to bring in 600 marks a year, which was more than the income of most Oxford colleges. Adam's benefices were well scattered, from Shetland to Lisbon; they have a pleasing suggestion of far-flung empire and 'dominion over palm and pine'. A less exalted English curialist, Master Thomas Walkington, Auditor of Causes in the Apostolic Palace, and a protégé of Adam Easton's, was stated in 1391 to hold the archdeaconry of Cleveland, prebends in Exeter, St Martin-le-Grand and Beverley, and the church of Houghton-le-Spring (Durham), to the total value of 460 marks, together with the expectation of prebends in York,

---

[1] Abp. Greenfield's Register, I, 7n.   [2] CPL, II, 379, 384; III, 95, 314.
[3] CPL, IV, 335, 343, 385, 468, 536.

Lincoln, Salisbury, Beverley, Howden, Auckland and Ripon; he had a few years earlier been Dean of Exeter.[1]

Another class of persons who benefited by provisions were royal officials. A good example is Roger Northburgh, Keeper of the Wardrobe, Keeper of the Privy Seal, Treasurer of the Exchequer, and Bishop of Lichfield 1322–59; in 1317, when he already held prebends in St David's, York, Lincoln, London and Beverley, and four parish churches (ranging from Cumberland to Cornwall), he was provided at the king's request to a prebend in Wells.[2] On a single day in 1329 the queen's chancellor and eight more of her clerks or chaplains received prebends in various churches.[3]

Another class who benefited were the university graduates. We have already seen how the universities made a habit of sending up the names of deserving graduates to the pope, and how a friend of the Oxford Chancellor, John Lutterel, wrote urging him to come out to the Curia to show his academic prowess and gain promotion.[4] Professor Jacob has discussed the promotion of graduates in the late fourteenth century.[5] The university was prepared to write in the strongest terms to recommend a graduate to the pope for provision. Here is a good example:

In the garden of the Church Militant, among other fruit-bearing trees, God's providence with perpetual constancy has rooted the Tree of Knowledge; the sweetness of whose fruit the faithful in the Church taste every day, when with aroused devotion they are healthfully instructed by catholic doctors in the observance of the Divine Law. But lest, for lack of watering, such a health-giving tree should at any time wither away with dried up branches; from the seat of Your Holiness a certain fountain of affluent grace is known to spring, by God's institution, so that from it a river, coming out as it were from the paradise of pleasure, may everywhere fertilize the Church's garden of delights with unfailing fruitfulness. Since therefore our beloved in Christ A. de B., divinely propagated from the fruitful stock of the

[1] *CPL*, IV, 343, 344, 420. [2] *CPL*, II, 143.
[3] *CPL*, II, 292f. [4] See above, p. 16.
[5] *Tr. Hist. Soc.* (IV), xxvii, 41ff.

Sacred Page, an egregious doctor, an excellent preacher, serene both in the purity of his conscience and the honesty of his morals, has not as much of the richness of the earth as the vigour of such branches demands; therefore prostrate at the feet of Your Beatitude, we humbly implore the clemency of Your Holiness, that having regard to the merits of the said colleague, a river of grace may flow out from the apostolic plenitude, to the relief of his indigence; mercifully deign to make provision for him, if You please, in the church of York, so that while he is watered by the dew of Your munificent liberality, he may more abundantly bear fruit for others unto salvation.[1]

On another occasion the university writes to the pope, recommending a Master who is the son of an earl, 'wonderfully decorated by profound solidity of doctrine, integrity of fame and life, and decency of stature', and asking that he may hold a benefice with cure of souls, although he is under the canonical age.[2]

A fortunate scholar might support himself for years at the schools by papal provisions. Thus Hugh of Wymundewold, whose brother Richard was an advocate in the Roman Curia, first appeared in the papal registers in 1344 as 'literate in civil law', with the promise of a couple of benefices, and continued for nearly twenty years, studying and collecting benefices. By 1362 he had the precentorship of York, three prebends and a church; when he asked for five more years' leave of absence for study, he was told 'It is time to leave off studies and reside on one of your benefices'.[3]

We have therefore two rival systems of patronage facing each other: a native system, in which royal patronage predominates; and a central system, consisting of papal provision. What was the attitude of various sections of opinion in England towards this contest?

The most violent and vocal opposition to papal policy came from the laity, especially from the magnates and the commons, expressing themselves in a series of protests and petitions in parliament

---

[1] *Oxford Formularies*, II, 266.   [2] *Ibid.* 267.
[3] *CPP*, I, 44, 108, 386.

throughout the fourteenth century.[1] It is true that the laity suffered little directly from papal provisions, which were normally at the expense of ecclesiastical patrons, but laymen might see the promotion of their relatives and protégés blocked by provisions, and above all, they felt a strong antipathy to aliens. Parliamentary protests were much concerned with aliens and their benefices, especially during the periods c. 1326–47 and c. 1372–86.[2] One of the most interesting things about the anti-papal and anti-clerical feeling among the laity of this period is that it took the form of parliamentary pressure, capable of influencing the king, sometimes rather against his will.

The position of the king was less simple. In general, he naturally desired to maintain the Crown's rights to the full, and on more than one occasion he reminded the pope that he was bound to do this by his coronation oath;[3] the pope, it was implied, could hardly press the king to give way and so imperil his soul by perjury! Richard II pointed out to Boniface IX (c. 1393) that the king's regalian right to dispose of the patronage of vacant bishoprics, which was then being threatened, had been respected during the worst days of the Avignonese papacy; it was not right that the king should be worse off under the leadership of the 'true Moses' (i.e. the Roman, Urbanist line of popes) than under the oppression of Pharaoh among the fleshpots of Egypt (i.e. the Avignon popes).[4] Half a century earlier (1342), Edward III had written to the officials of the Roman Curia, politely and patiently explaining his royal rights.[5] Though no doubt learned in the imperial laws and other general matters, they might not understand English customs and laws and the royal prerogatives, so he explained that in England causes about advowsons belonged exclusively to the lay courts, that advowsons could be bought and sold like real property, that the king exercised the regalian right over the property

---

[1] See especially the protests printed in Haller, *Papsttum und Kirchenreform*, 544–9.
[2] *Rot. Parl.* II, 9–173, 312–72; III, 18–222, *passim*.   [3] Rymer, II, 130, 1243.
[4] E. Perroy, *The diplomatic correspondence of Richard II*, Camden Third Series, XLVIII (1933), 134–9.   [5] Rymer, II, 1208.

and patronage of vacant bishoprics, and so forth—all of which suggests that perhaps the Avignon days were not quite so rosy as Richard II liked to think.

On the other hand, while the king maintained his claims, he was more realistic, less bald-headed in his opposition than the lay magnates and the commons; he knew that he could get more by diplomacy than by blustering. He frequently made use of papal provision for rewarding his servants with benefices, from bishoprics downwards.[1] He paid retaining fees to selected cardinals,[2] protected them, their agents and their English benefices,[3] granted them exemption from taxes and licences to export their wool.[4] In return, when he wanted something done at the Curia, he used to write round to the cardinals as well as to the pope. When Edward II was pressing for the canonization of Thomas of Cantilupe in 1307, he wrote to twenty-five cardinals;[5] in the same year, when protesting against certain attacks on his royal rights, he wrote on one occasion to eleven cardinals, and on another to six cardinals.[6] In 1320 when asking for Roger North-burgh to be made a cardinal, he wrote to twenty-one cardinals.[7] Similarly Edward III in 1329 wrote to twenty-four cardinals, papal relatives and officials, to urge the promotion of Robert Wyvill to the see of Bath and Wells.[8] The royal policy of trying to influence the pope through the cardinals throws an interesting light on the constitutional character of the Roman Curia at this time.[9] This mutual relationship between the English king and the cardinals makes one understand why, after the election of Urban VI in 1378, one of Cardinal Aigrefeuille's first thoughts was to ask what the English king would think of their choice; and on being told

[1] See for instance *CPP*, I, Index, *s.v.* Edward III; and Rymer, II, *passim*.
[2] E.g. Rymer, II, 69 (1309), 348 (1317), 854 (1333).
[3] E.g. Rymer, II, 1002, 1090; III, 105, 154; IV, 56, 86, 89, 90, 128, 134.
[4] E.g. Rymer, II, 423, 595, 1037, 1089, 1133, 1218, 1223; III, 29.
[5] Rymer, II, 21. [6] *Ibid.* 24, 29.
[7] *Ibid.* 433. [8] *Ibid.* 766.
[9] Cf. G. Mollat, 'Contribution à l'histoire du Sacré Collège de Clément V à Eugène IV', in *RHE*, XLVI (1951), 22ff., 566ff.

by his English friend Adam Easton that the reaction would be favourable, he exclaimed, 'It was in a good hour that we elected Urban, and the Holy Ghost was working for us'.[1]

It seems clear that the policy of the king, if left to himself, would have been neither to be wholly intransigent, like the lay magnates and commons, nor to give in to papal claims *in toto*; what suited him best was to maintain his own claims to the full in principle, while being ready to make individual exceptions whenever it suited his purpose. This explains why the Crown and the Papacy on the whole were able to work together in practice, while being unwilling to concede general principles or to bind themselves for the future.

The king must often have been subjected to both papal pressure and parliamentary pressure. In his dealings with the pope, he showed an interesting tendency to put the responsibility on the magnates; he could do nothing in these matters, he said, without consulting them, and they, by reason of their fealty, would allow nothing that would diminish the rights of the Crown.[2] Later on in the century, in 1343, it was the commons as well as the magnates whom the king quoted as objecting;[3] and in 1344, when he restored the temporalities of the see of Norwich to a papal provisor, William Bateman, the king said that he did this *non sine periculoso murmure communitatis*.[4] We need not take this too seriously, perhaps, for the king may have been using the tactics of Spenlow and Jorkins. Nevertheless, the fact that the king should make these explanations at all is an interesting index of the growth of parliamentary power, and I think that the anti-papal measures which culminated in the Statute of Provisors represent in some way a royal surrender to parliamentary pressure, for it seems likely that the king, left to himself, would have preferred to take a more diplomatic, less intransigent line.

[1] L. Macfarlane, 'An English account of the election of Urban VI, 1378', in *Bulletin of the Institute of Hist. Research*, XXVI (1953), 77, 84.
[2] Rymer, II, 20, 53, 105, 111, 130.   [3] *Ibid.* 1232.
[4] Raynaldus, *Annales*, VI, 366ff.; *CPL*, III, 9; E. Deprèz, *Les préliminaires de la guerre de cent ans* (Paris, 1902), no. 957.

The attitude of the English clergy, especially the bishops, abbots and other ecclesiastical patrons, was also complex. Officially and in principle, the clergy were bound to support the claims of canon law and papal authority, as Grosseteste had done, and to agree with the papal protests against lay 'encroachments' and 'novelties'. On at least one occasion, in 1390, the prelates in parliament made a formal protest against anti-papal legislation, 'in so far as such statutes are known to tend to the restriction of the Apostolic power or the subversion, enervation or derogation of ecclesiastical liberty'.[1] In 1343 the prelates had tried to retire from parliament when anti-papal protests were made.[2] Moreover the king was careful, on several occasions, to exculpate the bishops and point out the correctness of their attitude. Thus in 1343 he wrote to tell the pope that the Archbishop of Canterbury is *libertatis ecclesiasticae zelator praecipuus* and not responsible for the recent anti-papal agitation; similarly he wrote on behalf of the Bishop of Chichester in 1344, and of the Bishop of Worcester in 1345, pointing out their devotion to the Holy See, contrary to the suggestions of their enemies.[3]

In practice, however, the feelings of churchmen must have been mixed. It was chiefly at the expense of bishops and abbots that papal provisions operated. Many of the bishops had been royal servants, and may have sympathized with government policy in this matter, just as they sympathized with government demands for clerical subsidies.[4] Many of them must have owed their promotion to both royal and papal patronage. We must not think of papal provisors and royal protégés as two separate and opposing armies, for they were often the same people. The king was constantly pushing his clerks for papal provisions, and a man might owe half his benefices to the king, and half to the pope. The mixture of respect for papal authority and dismay at the

[1] *Rot. Parl.* III, 264.
[2] Adam Murimuth, *Continuatio chronicarum*, ed. E. M. Thompson (*RS*, 1889), 138.
[3] Rymer, II, 1232, 1242; III, 27.
[4] M. V. Clarke, *Medieval representation and consent* (London, 1936), 27 ff.

effects of papal policy is well expressed in a letter of Bishop
Grandisson of Exeter, who himself owed some of his preferments
to papal provision, and had been a chaplain to John XXII and
a pupil of Benedict XII when at the University of Paris. In
November 1342, after a meeting of the Convocation of Canterbury in London, Grandisson writes to Clement VI, then in the
first year of his pontificate:[1]

When I see on all sides the disturbances of kings and kingdoms, from
which the Church Militant and its Ruler cannot hope to be free, I must
confess I am not a little anguished within and weighed down with
weariness without. For suffering together with the Head, I hope also
likewise to be consoled with it. For I am weak with those that are
weak, and on fire with those that are scandalized; and there is added to
the grief of my wounds, whenever I hear my fellow-servants mur-
muring against the master of the household of God. Lately, indeed, on
the Ides of October I was present in the Council of the province of
Canterbury held in London, where among other things, if I may say so
by your leave, no small wonder arose at the burdensome and hitherto
unknown multitude of apostolic provisions. For it was said that from
now onwards prelates, both greater and lesser, indiscriminately, without distinction of estate or person, will never be able to provide for the
well deserving or necessary servants of their churches or of themselves.
What has perhaps added to the astonishment at these novelties is the
fact there is no doubt that many better and more worthy men have
stayed at home, doing their own duty, or in the service of others,—
more than all those other ambitious men who have flown to the Roman
Curia. Nor was there lacking displeasure as well as wonder among my
brethren, in as much as from now onwards they will scarcely be able to
find useful and skilled cooperators in the pastoral office, since all hope
of reward is taken away. Moreover this was the chief and almost the

[1] Grandisson, *Reg.* I, III. In 1327 Bishop Mortival of Salisbury wrote to Pope
John XXII a similar letter, complaining of the great number of provisions made to the
chapter of Salisbury and of his own consequent difficulty in promoting his own *familiares
clerici.* He gave a list of thirty-six persons provided to prebends and dignities in the
chapter of Salisbury. Of these, one Englishman and seven aliens had been provided under
Pope John's predecessors; ten Englishmen and ten aliens under Pope John (i.e. since 1316);
and five Englishmen and three aliens were still 'expecting' their prebends; Salisbury
Diocesan Registry, Reg. Mortival, II, fo. 215 (234).

only thing that many found commendable in Benedict XII of good memory, namely that he did not burden any churches or prelates. Let your holy discretion therefore see and judge concerning these matters, having had experience of like cases. And if by chance, while you are bent on unaccustomed and arduous business at the beginning of your rule, you find yourself overcome by the surreptitious action or importunity of claimants or petitioners, pray think in your heart of your fellow servants and brethren in Christ, among whom you have been made the first-born. And moreover forgive me, the least of your servants, if, as truth is my witness, out of a pure heart I speak directly to my Lord, since charity alone urges me.

The comments and criticisms of the chroniclers are specially interesting, as representing a kind of free-lance ecclesiastical opinion. These writers have something of the traditional anti-alien feeling of men like Matthew Paris, and they were particularly outspoken critics in the days before the Lollard menace tended to close the ranks of the clergy. Thus Adam of Murimuth (c. 1274–1347), a chronicler who was also an active ecclesiastical lawyer, makes the provisions or elections to bishoprics one of the chief themes of his chronicle. He complains of the various forms of papal exactions that have gone on since the time of Clement V down to the time of writing in 1345; the cardinals and the *curiales*, he says, hold the better benefices of the kingdom, which it would be difficult to number; it seems likely that the riches which go from England to the papacy and aliens exceed the annual income of the king, and that out of this money the king's enemies are for a large part supported:

Whence among the *curiales* of the Apostolic See it has become a proverb that the English are good asses, ready to carry all the intolerable burdens that are put upon them. Against which no remedy can be ordered by the prelates and bishops, because, since they are almost all promoted by the Apostolic See, they do not dare to utter a word that might offend that See. The king also and the nobles, if they ordain or establish any remedy against the aforesaid inconveniences, yet they themselves shamelessly procure the contrary by the letters and prayers

71

that they pour out on behalf of their unworthy servants, as has been said above, and they grow slack in every good purpose, as they did formerly at the time of the Council of Lyons held under Innocent IV.[1]

The Continuator of the *Flores Historiarum* at first praises John XXII for saving the English Church, by his reservations, from the appointment of unworthy and illiterate royal nominees —though this comment is probably inspired more by anti-royalist bias than by zeal for the papacy. He also praises John XXII for attacking pluralism in the Decretal *Execrabilis*. But a few pages on, speaking about the taxation of the Church, he complains that the pope and the king make a deal (*mercatio*) over the Church, as though over an ox or an ass.[2]

Another chronicler, the so-called 'monk of Malmesbury', is much given to moralizing. He comments on Clement V's policy in general, and the preferment of Walter Reynolds over Thomas Cobham to the see of Canterbury in particular, and he makes a well-known outburst: 'Why does the pope presume to make greater exactions from the clergy, than the emperor himself from the laity?...Lord Jesu, either take the pope away, or diminish the power that he presumes over the people; because he who abuses his power, deserves to lose his privilege.'[3]

There is another and rather more fanciful type of record of public opinion, which resembles both the comments of the chroniclers and the protests of the magnates and commons. This consists of certain more or less fictitious letters that were produced from time to time. Thus the chronicler Walter of Hemingburgh gives us the text of a mysterious document, which he says appeared suddenly 'as if sent down from heaven', in the Parliament of Carlisle (1307), when papal exactions were being discussed. This purports to be a letter from 'Peter son of Cassiodorus, a catholic knight', to the 'noble English Church, enslaved among

---

[1] Adam Murimuth, *Continuatio Chronicarum*, 173-6.
[2] *Flores Historiarum*, ed. H. R. Luard (*RS*, 1890), III, 175-6, 177-8, 182.
[3] *Chronicles of...Edward I and Edward II* (*RS*), II, 198.

the clay and the bricks'. With a wealth of scriptural allusions, it denounces papal exactions, mercenary shepherds, nepotism, tenths and first-fruits. Let the knighthood of England beware: the kingdom is being weakened in the face of its French enemies. Let the king and the magnates, who have endowed the English Church, resist these extortions.[1]

Later in the century a Durham formulary gives what purports to be an exchange of letters between the pope and the king.[2] The pope's letter begins: 'Ventrem suum dolet alma mater ecclesia'; he complains that King Edward has seized the benefices of the cardinals and other non-residents, and after pointing to the fate of Ozias and Eliodorus as examples of the divine punishment of lay encroachments, he warns the king that he must restore the benefices within four months, under pain of excommunication. The king's reply begins: 'Caput suum dolet ecclesia nobilis Anglicana'; it consists of a long complaint put into the mouth of the 'noble English Church', addressed to the magnates of the kingdom. Aliens and hirelings have come, and have fleeced and milked the English Church. Pope Clement has not lived up to his name; evil counsellors have turned him against the 'most glorious King of England and France'. The pope is reminded of the evil fate of Boniface VIII. More money is sent from England to Avignon than from any other island province. The evil effects of provisions are described in the familiar terms, and the letter ends with an appeal to the English nobility, since Church and State are so closely connected, to intervene and protect the English Church from the exactions of the Curia,[3] so that Englishmen shall no longer be called the 'asses of the Curia'. A copy of this appeal has been stuck up on the door of Westminster Hall, that they may see and judge, who judge the world. We can

---

[1] Walter de Hemingburgh, *Chronicon*, ed. H. C. Hamilton (London, 1849), II, 254ff.
[2] Durham Cathedral Muniments, Register N, fo. 29vff.
[3] Cf. the letter to the English nobility, probably spurious, ascribed to Grosseteste (*Roberti Grosseteste epistolae*, ed. H. R. Luard, RS, 1861, 442). Grosseteste would have been the last person to invoke lay intervention.

hardly take these two documents as representing genuine products of the papal and English chanceries, but the alleged papal letter does in fact embody certain phrases taken verbatim from a genuine papal letter, dated 15 October 1352, protesting about the seizure of the cardinals' benefices,[1] so that it was probably about this time that these two letters were fabricated. They seem to be partly in the nature of a pamphlet or manifesto, partly an exercise in epistolary rhetoric—hence their presence in a formulary. The appeal to the laity, both here and in the 1307 letter, is significant for the future. But however much exasperation is shown, it seems to be the exasperation of those who still fundamentally believe in papal authority; it resembles the impatience of Langland rather than the radical denial of Wyclif.

Probably the one class that had most to gain and least to lose from papal provisions were the university graduates. It is significant that they petitioned for relief from the Statute of Provisors, and ultimately gained some exemption from it.[2]

It was not of course only on the English side that views and protests were expressed. The Papacy from time to time put forward its claims and grievances. Thus quite early in the century, in 1308 and 1309, the pope made elaborate protests against lay encroachments; against the imprisonment of English and Scottish bishops; against the action of royal officials in obstructing the execution of papal provisions and the payment of annates, in impeding the exercise of ecclesiastical jurisdiction and refusing to capture excommunicates, and in having clerks tried and punished by lay courts; against the extortions and abuse of custody rights practised by the lay patrons of monasteries and churches.[3] These papal protests have a good deal in common with the *gravamina*

[1] Raynaldus, *Annales*, VI, 562–3; *CPL*, III, 51, 468.

[2] *Collectanea* III (*OHS*, XXXII, 1896), 136, 151, 153; Wilkins, III, 275; Rymer (O), VIII, 339; *Rot. Parl.* III, 301; IV, 81. In 1373 the Pope blamed the English universities for the large number of provisions, see below, p. 90. It is amusing to find the Commons in 1415 attributing the decay of learning to the stoppage of provisions, whereas earlier it had been attributed to the prevalence of provisions.

[3] Rymer, II, 41, 97.

against the oppressions of the lay power, brought forward by the clergy of various nations in the Council of Vienne (1311),[1] and with the *gravamina* brought forward by the English clergy from time to time.[2] While churchmen might have varied feelings about the operation of papal provisions, they would all agree in opposing lay attacks upon the jurisdiction and liberties of the Church.

The mass of claims and counter-claims put forward by clergy and laity taken all together constitute an interesting body of legal and political theory which deserves careful study.

[1] Denifle and Ehrle, *Archiv für Literatur- und Kirchengeschichte*, iv, 361 ff.
[2] *Registrum Roberti de Winchelsey*, ed. R. Graham (*C and YS*, 1942), 1013–31.

CHAPTER V

ANGLO-PAPAL RELATIONS

THE relations between England and the Papacy during the fourteenth century can be divided roughly into three periods: the first from about 1300 to about 1342; the second from about 1342 to about 1360; and the third from about 1360 to the end of the century.

THE FIRST PERIOD (1300–1342)

This period covered the last years of Edward I, the reign of Edward II, and the early years of Edward III, and among the popes, the early Avignon popes, Clement V (1305–16), John XXII (1316–34) and Benedict XII (1334–42).[1] It was on the whole a period of fairly smooth relations. In the last years of Edward I's reign, the great struggle with Boniface VIII was over, and the king was able to get from the compliant Clement V much of what he wanted, such as the suspension of Archbishop Winchelsey and a share in papal taxation. Such things benefited the king but not his subjects, and we can begin to see a divergence of interest and opinion between the two. The resentment of the laity against such things as provisions and papal taxation expressed itself at the Parliament of Carlisle in 1307, in the statute forbidding the export of money, but this was partly nullified by the king's action.

Under Edward II and in the early years of Edward III, the Papacy was established at Avignon. The effects of this upon Anglo-papal relations were not so bad before the outbreak of the Hundred Years War. The English king had possessions and interests in south-west France; Clement V was himself an English subject by birth, and in 1308 he could claim that he had never provided anyone to an English benefice who was not a subject of

[1] For the popes of the Avignon period, see G. Mollat, *Les Papes d'Avignon* (new ed., Paris, 1949).

the English king in either England or France.[1] Clement V was succeeded by two masterful popes, John XXII and Benedict XII, bent on the centralization of the Church. John XXII seems to have taken a paternal interest in Edward II, sending him letters of advice about prudent housekeeping, the appointment of good judges, the avoidance of youthful and imprudent friends and of extravagance in clothes, feasting and presents, and the importance of good relations with Thomas of Lancaster—together with reminders that Peter's pence and tenths were in arrears and hints that the political troubles of the kingdom may be a judgment for the injuries done to the rights of the Church.[2] In the face of these two strong popes, both Edward II and the youthful Edward III were in a comparatively weak position and conciliatory.

One of the most interesting and moving documents in the history of Anglo-papal relations is the letter sent by the young King Edward III to Pope John XXII in 1330. The king, then aged eighteen, was still under the control of his mother Isabella and her paramour Mortimer, though he was about to throw off their yoke; he might have to set his seal to letters which were far from representing his personal views, and he therefore sent to the pope, at the pope's own suggestion, in great secrecy, a private sign by which the pope could tell which letters represented the king's true wishes. It is like a letter for help smuggled out of prison.

Most Holy Father, because it will behove us many times to send letters to Your Holiness, not only for Our own needs, but also for the advancement of the people of Our household and for others, and on this matter We are informed by My Lord William de Montague that You will be pleased to have from Us some private countersign [*prive entresigne*], by which You can tell which petitions we have tenderly at heart, and which not; We affectionately beseech Your Holiness that the petitions which We shall send You in future by Our letters in Latin or French, sealed under Our Privy Seal or under Our Signet, on which

[1] Rymer, II, 42. [2] CPL, II, 414, 430, 433, 434, 439.

shall be written these words in Our hand 'Pater Sancte'—that these You will please to have specially recommended and You will understand for a certainty that We have them at heart; for Our intention is not to press You over these matters by this sign, but to use it at least where we can and as we ought to; and know, Most Holy Father, that this matter is not known to anyone except to My Lord William aforesaid and to Master Richard de Bury Our secretary, of whom We are certain that they will keep it secret in every event. This document was written by the hand of the said Master Richard, for by reason of diverse occupations that We had at the time of despatch of these letters, We could not devote Ourselves to so much writing.[1]

At the foot of the letter is written, in careful, deliberate, rather disjointed characters, in the young king's own hand, the password: 'Pater Sancte'. It is probably the earliest surviving autograph of an English king. The main part of the letter, as it states, is written by the hand of Richard de Bury, the king's tutor and secretary, the famous book-collector and future Bishop of Durham, and one of the most interesting men of his age. The man who took the letter to Avignon, William Montague, was shortly to carry out the *coup d'état* which was to overthrow Isabella and Mortimer. Notice that the king, even in this weak and humiliating position, never for a moment forgets to be a 'good lord', a good patron; what he has at heart is to advance his dependents, to see that the right men get the right benefices. It must have been a real pleasure to the king's secretary to pen a letter like this. The system of patronage, which is apt to seem so much jobbery and snobbery to modern eyes, is here seen in its better and more generous side—the lord's duty to look after his dependents. Nothing could illustrate better than this letter the strength of patronage and the importance which the king attached to papal co-operation in exercising that patronage. The anti-papal protests of the lay magnates and commons must have

---

[1] Tout, *Chapters*, III, 27–30; *EHR*, XXVI (1911), 331; the letter is reproduced in facsimile in C. Johnson and H. Jenkinson, *English Courthand* (Oxford, 1915), II, plate xxii. I have to thank Professor V. H. Galbraith for drawing my attention to this.

seemed rather irrelevant and tiresome to those at the centre of government.

The king who wrote this letter was a boy of eighteen; the pope who received it was an old man of eighty-four. Medieval kings were hereditary, and generally succeeded young and died comparatively young; popes were elective, and sometimes began to rule about the age that modern professional men have to retire. Hence there must normally have been a large age-gap between the two, occasionally, as here, amounting to nearly three generations. This is a point always to be remembered in considering Anglo-papal relations. It helps to explain the paternal attitude of John XXII towards Edward II and Edward III. It may also help to explain the exasperation which broke out from time to time between the Crown and the Papacy. For the time being things ran smoothly. The young king continued to correspond with the pope, in 1330 and 1331; he consulted him, for instance, on the advisability of going over to reform Ireland. The pope replied with good advice; he also reminded him that he would find much in his (the pope's) letters to his father which would be useful to him in the government of the realm, and he exhorted him to treat his mother with honour (in spite of the recent *coup d'état*), in order to preserve her good fame. He combined all this with the inevitable exhortations to maintain the liberties of the Church.[1]

On the whole this was the hey-day of papal provisions, and the period when provision was becoming the normal method of appointing bishops. The advantages, however, were not all one-sided; the pope was generous in giving to the king a large share in the papal tenths levied, amounting to about £230,000 between 1301 and 1324—a convenient arrangement by which the pope incurred the odium and the king got the money.[2]

---

[1] *CPL*, II, 498, 500; Raynaldus, *Annales*, v, 520.

[2] W. E. Lunt, *Financial relations of the Papacy with England to 1327* (Medieval Academy of America, 1939), chapter VII. It was this kind of thing, the taxation of the Church for the benefit of the king, with the pope's backing, that Grosseteste had opposed in the previous century; Powicke, *Henry III*, I, 299–300, 368–9.

Underneath this comparatively smooth relationship there was, however, an undercurrent of difficulties. There was, for instance, a succession of *causes célèbres* between the Crown and the Papacy over appointments to benefices. In theory the extension of papal provision need not have come into conflict with the king's rights, because normally provisions were at the expense of ecclesiastical electors or patrons. But one cause of conflict was the extension of the king's rights, especially the very wide interpretation put upon his regalian right to dispose of the patronage of a vacant bishopric, so that the king might be exercising such patronage years after the bishopric had been filled. This meant that cathedral dignities and canonries were specially likely to be in dispute, as we have seen, both because they were so often claimed under the king's regalian right, and because they formed the favourite subject of papal provisions.[1] Another cause of conflict was the fact that the Papacy did not recognize the claim of the king's courts to have jurisdiction over advowsons; this meant that the disputes over provisions and the like were really an extension of the age-old conflict of jurisdiction between the royal and ecclesiastical courts.

A dispute between the Crown and the Papacy over a benefice might go on for half a century. In 1297 the pope had deprived John Colonna of the treasurership of York. Both pope and king claimed the appointment of his successor, and there followed a succession of papal claimants on the one hand (Theobald of Bar, Cardinal Francis Gaetani and Cardinal Peter of Mortemart) and royal nominees on the other hand (Walter Bedewynd, Robert Baldock and William de la Mare). At one point, in 1307, the case came before the king's Council; later on, in 1331, Edward III seems to have given way and allowed the case to be settled in the Court of Rome, as a personal favour to Cardinal Peter. Finally, *c.* 1349–51, the king revived his claim, and a compromise was reached by which the king's nominee, John Winwick, was also

[1] See above, p. 31.

provided by the pope.[1] A shorter dispute was over the prebend of Aylesbury in Lincoln Cathedral chapter, c. 1321-4, between Cardinal Gaillard de la Motte and Ralph Baldock, which also ended in a compromise; the king claimed to have recovered his presentation to the benefice, but left Gaillard a portion of its revenues during his life.[2] A provisor who was determined to make the most of his benefice might find himself in conflict with other bodies besides the Crown. Thus the Cardinal Gaillard de la Motte just mentioned was, among other things, Archdeacon of Oxford, and as such he attempted to challenge certain archidiaconal rights exercised by the University of Oxford. But the university was a more powerful adversary than the cardinal perhaps realized, and after prolonged litigation c. 1330-45, it was confirmed in its right of the correction of its clerks and the proving of their wills.[3]

THE SECOND PERIOD (1342-1360)

This was a period of crisis and struggle. It opened with the pontificate of Clement VI (1342-52);[4] a monk, a distinguished scholar, and sometime chancellor of the French king, he was thoroughly French in his sympathies. He had the habits and tastes of a *grand seigneur*—his magnificent additions to the papal palace at Avignon contrast with the austere style of his predecessor's work; he used to remark that no one should leave the presence of a prince dissatisfied, and he was particularly lavish in granting provisions. This was also the middle and most vigorous period of Edward III's reign. Above all, the Hundred Years War now complicated Anglo-papal relations both practically and psychologically. There

---

[1] Mollat, *La collation des bénéfices*, 104; *Select cases before the King's Council*, ed. I. S. Leadam and J. F. Baldwin (*Selden Soc.* xxxv, 1918), lviff., 18 ff.; *CPL*, III, 420. For the career and preferments of John Winwick, a good example of a successful, well-beneficed royal clerk, see Tout, *Chapters*, v, 36, 96; he contemplated founding a college of scholars.
[2] Mollat, *La collation des bénéfices*, 102; Rymer, II, 492-3, 568.
[3] *Oxford Formularies*, I, 86, 101-4; *Statuta Antiqua Univ. Oxon.* ed. S. Gibson (Oxford, 1931), lxxi; *Medieval archives of the University of Oxford*, ed. H. E. Salter (*OHS*, LXX, 1917), I, 114-16; *Munimenta Academica*, ed. H. Anstey (*RS*, 1868), I, 148.
[4] Mollat, *Les Papes d'Avignon*, 84-92.

was a divergence of policy between the Papacy and the king; the Papacy had a natural sympathy for France, while it genuinely desired to promote peace between the two countries, and it had long disapproved of King Edward's alliance with Lewis the Bavarian, the Papacy's enemy. As we have seen, the English king had relied much on the diplomatic use of the cardinals, but some of these were now more of a liability than an asset; in particular Cardinal Talleyrand de Perigord was regarded as one of England's bitterest enemies.[1] Both sides were hard pressed for money, the king because of the war, the Papacy because it was living in expensive exile, cut off from its Italian patrimony. There was a good deal of jingoism and anti-French feeling in England, which strengthened the laity's hostility to papal demands and papal policy. Particularly with the victories of Crécy and Poitiers, it seemed intolerable that the Papacy should be so pro-French, when Providence was so obviously on the side of the English.

> Ore est le Pape devenu Franceys,
> e Jesu devenu Engleys.
> Ore serra veou qe fra plus,
> ly Pape ou Jesus.

Knighton tells us that this verse was found written up in various places in France.[2] *Jesu devenu Engleys*: national pride could hardly go further, though the Wilton diptych, showing the angels wearing the badge of Richard II, comes close to it.

During this period the parliamentary protests that had been raised at Carlisle in 1307 and Stamford in 1309 were renewed, and now that there was more coolness between the king and the pope, the king was less able and less disposed to ignore popular protests than before. Anti-papal protests and action reach a climax between 1343 and 1347, and in fact continue throughout the pontificate of Clement VI. In the Parliament of 1343 the lay magnates and commons petitioned against the holding of benefices by aliens;

[1] *Rot. Parl.* II, 143-4. [2] Knighton, *Chronicon*, ed. J. R. Lumby (*RS*, 1889), II, 94.

the pope, they complained, had granted to two cardinals benefices worth 2,000 marks, and so year by year the land would be filled with aliens, and native clerks, sons of magnates and others, would find no benefices for their advancement; the commons could not and would not endure this.[1] On 18 May the lay magnates and commons sent a letter of protest against the provision of aliens to the pope; the king also wrote to the pope on 30 August and again on 10 September, drawing up a full-dress complaint against provisions and their evil effects and asking the pope for a remedy, and in the meanwhile he had issued writs to prevent the introduction and execution of bulls of provision.[2] In the parliament of 1344 there were more petitions against provisions; they asked that the ordinances made in the previous year should be affirmed by perpetual statute, and that benefices void by reason of provisions should be filled by the king or other patrons.[3] In 1346 the king seized the revenues of the aliens' benefices, to pay for the expenses of the war.[4] In the parliaments of 1346 and 1347 there were more petitions against provisors and aliens' benefices.[5] In the meanwhile the pope had replied in 1344 with a volley of protests against these 'novelties' attempted against the Church; he not only wrote to the king, but also to the queen and the queen-mother, to about seventeen earls and other magnates, and six bishops.[6] But in fact, while these protests and counter-protests were going on, the king and the pope continued to co-operate. The king was ready to receive parliamentary petitions and to make protests, but does not seem willing to do much more. In February 1345 he wrote a long and tactful letter of explanation to the pope, telling him that the rumours of anti-papal legislation were unfounded.[7] The king's favours to the cardinals and his requests for

[1] Rot. Parl. II, 141–5.
[2] Adam Murimuth, Continuatio Chronicarum, 138; Rymer, II, 1230, 1232, 1233; cf. above, p. 52.
[3] Rot. Parl. II, 153–4.
[4] Rymer, III, 68, 81; Adam Murimuth, Continuatio Chronicarum, 245.
[5] Rot. Parl. II, 162, 172.   [6] CPL, III, 5, 9, 12.   [7] Rymer, III, 31.

provisions continued; so did the pope's complaisance, and it was at this time that the papal provision of royal servants was at its height.[1]

The climax of parliamentary pressure came with the enactment of the Statutes of Provisors in 1351 and of Praemunire in 1353.[2] What were the purpose and effects of these celebrated statutes?

The Statute of Provisors was ostensibly aimed at protecting ecclesiastics against papal provisions. In the face of a papal provision, the ordinary ecclesiastical patrons or electors, a bishop or a cathedral chapter, for instance, might not dare to appoint to a vacant office or benefice; for instance, when the Bishop of Lichfield collated to the precentorship of that cathedral in 1339, the chapter said that they were willing to accept and admit the bishop's nominee, provided that the pope had not provided someone.[3] Hence, according to the Statute, if the patrons or electors dare not act, the king as 'patron paramount' of all such benefices steps in and fills the vacancy himself. Papal provisors must be kept out at all costs; if the ecclesiastics will not act, then the king will act for them. Moreover, the introduction of bulls of provision is forbidden under severe penalties (forfeiture and imprisonment). Thus in a very ingenious manner the king appeases popular clamour against provisions, poses as a defender of the rights and liberties of English churchmen against the Papacy, and at the same time increases the royal patronage; for by the Statute, it is not the ecclesiastical patron who gains, but the Crown. Moreover, the Statute was frequently suspended or evaded by the king, whenever he chose. The king knows from of old how to use papal provision to advant-

---

[1] See above, pp. 13, 56.

[2] For the text of these statutes and their reissues, see *Statutes of the Realm*, I, 316, 329; II, 69, 73, 84; E. C. Lodge and G. A. Thornton, *English constitutional documents 1307–1485* (Cambridge, 1935), 300, 303, 310, 311; F. Makower, *Constitutional history and constitution of the Church of England* (London, 1895), 476; cf. also Maitland, *Roman Canon Law*, 67–71; E. B. Graves, 'The legal significance of the Statute of Praemunire', in *Anniversary Essays ...by students of C. H. Haskins* (New York, 1929); W. T. Waugh, 'The great Statute of Praemunire 1393', in *EHR*, XXXVII (1922), 173–205.

[3] Bodleian, MS. Ashmole 794, fo. 64v–65 (5 April 1339); cf. also *ibid*. fo. 31–2 (chancellorship, March 1339).

age, to get bishoprics and so forth for his protégés. If the pope is complaisant, the king will let him provide the royal nominee; if the pope is difficult, the king will be able to invoke the Statute of Provisors, and step in to nominate to the benefice himself, as indeed he has so often done in the past. It is a case of 'Heads I win, tails you lose!'

The Statute of Praemunire is a rider to the Statute of Provisors. Bulls of provision were already excluded, but a bishop or other patron who ignored a papal provision might, on appeal, be cited to the Court of Rome by an aggrieved party, and so forced to comply with the pope's commands. Hence the Statute of Praemunire forbids cases cognizable in the king's courts being taken abroad (i.e. to the Roman Curia), and what it has specially in view are patronage cases. As Professor Graves has pointed out, this was not a novelty; for half a century the king had been prohibiting such appeals to Rome. Again, this was not intended to interfere with appeals to Rome in unquestionably spiritual matters, i.e. in cases not claimed by the lay courts. It is therefore a mistake to imagine that the Statute of Praemunire (or for that matter the Statute of Provisors) was a general or direct attack on papal authority or papal supremacy as such; it was not the first blast of the Reformation. Its only purpose was to prevent the pope from meddling with those cases (such as patronage) which the king had always claimed as temporal and not spiritual matters.

The theoretical basis of the Statutes of Provisors and Praemunire is most interesting. From one point of view they represent a most important survival of traditional feudal rights and the principle of the *Eigenkirche*, the proprietary church, ideas which were still very much alive in the fourteenth century. The ancestors of the king and other lords have founded and endowed churches, great and small, for certain specific purposes, for the spiritual welfare and charitable relief of the local inhabitants, and not for the benefit of aliens (nor, it might perhaps be added, for the benefit of the clerks of the Chancery and the Wardrobe). This point of view had been expressed not only by laymen in the Statute of Carlisle, for instance, but by Archbishop Romeyn of York in the late thirteenth century.[1] The founders' intentions and rights must be respected; the king and other lords still have certain rights over the churches their ancestors have founded. In particular, the king, whose ancestor (King John) had granted free elections of bishops to the churches, must safeguard those elections, or else reclaim the right of appointment for himself. Above all there is the general principle that the patronage or advowson of any church, great or small, is a piece of real property, and a matter for the king's courts alone to deal with. It is easy to exaggerate the modernity of Provisors and Praemunire; they are really more survivals of the primitive world of feudalism than the beginnings of the omnicompetent or totalitarian state.

From another point of view, the Statutes of Provisors and Praemunire represent one more battle in the long warfare—essentially a border warfare—between the royal courts and the church courts, which had been going on ever since the separation of the courts under William the Conqueror. Some conflicts had already been settled, such as benefit of clergy; but there was one everlasting bone of contention, namely suits about the advowson or patronage of benefices, which were claimed both by the king's courts and the church courts. By the thirteenth century, writs of prohibition were a well-established practice by which the king prevented an ecclesiastical judge from meddling with lay matters, and in spite of the protests of men like Grosseteste, this method was extremely successful, especially in keeping advowson suits in the king's courts.[2] But with the centralization of the Church's judicial system the battleground was bound to shift in time from prohibitions directed against local church courts (the bishop's or the archdeacon's) to prohibitions, or an equivalent device, directed against the central ecclesiastical court, that is the Roman Curia. Now the king's writ

[1] Cf. A. H. Thompson, *The English clergy*, 10n.
[2] G. B. Flahiff, 'The writ of prohibition to court Christian in the thirteenth century', in *Medieval Studies*, VI, 261.

does not run abroad, and he cannot stop the pope from trying these disputed cases about patronage; but he can stop provisors from introducing bulls into the country, by having the ports watched, and he can stop them taking their cases to Rome and citing Englishmen to Rome. So the tactics change, but the war of the king's courts *versus* the church courts is the same. In this respect Provisors and Praemunire represent an extension of the existing principle of the writs of prohibition.

The Statutes of Provisors and Praemunire have perhaps seemed more important to later observers than they did at the time. The chroniclers do not seem to have taken much notice of the 1351 and 1353 statutes (as distinct from the reissues of 1365, 1390, and 1393), and it seems doubtful even whether they were generally published; at any rate the Commons were asking in 1352 for the publication and execution of the statute of the previous year, and received a non-committal reply.[1] Perhaps the king preferred to keep them as a secret weapon or rod in pickle, to be used or not, as he wished. It seems clear that the pope's anger was much more provoked over the seizure of the revenues of the cardinals' benefices than over the Statute of Provisors. About 1352 Clement threatened the kingdom with excommunication and interdict; 'the patience of God and of the Church' was at an end. But in October he suspended the censures for four months, and in 1353 he died.[2] In 1360 the benefices were restored,[3] and there was by then peace with France.

THE THIRD PERIOD (1360–1399)

This period of Anglo-papal relations consisted of negotiations, serious attempts to reach an agreement, interspersed or accompanied by protests and conflicts.[4] On the English side it corresponds to the last years of Edward III, and the whole reign of Richard II. On the papal side, the years 1360–78 saw among other things costly

---

[1] *Rot. Parl.* II, 241.
[2] Mollat, *La collation des bénéfices*, 109; Raynaldus, *Annales*, VI, 562; *CPL*, III, 50, 51, 468, 610.
[3] Rymer, III, 544, 602.   For this period, see Perroy, *Schisme, passim*.

wars of reconquest in Italy, and from 1378, the return to Rome and the Great Schism. It was a difficult time both for the Crown and for the Papacy.

The popes' financial needs led them to make demands on England which would have been out of the question earlier, when England was actively at war with France. In 1365, the pope raised the question of the arrears of the tribute due from England by reason of King John's submission, but this was dropped in the face of the opposition it aroused.[1] In 1372 he made another demand, this time for a 'charitable subsidy'.[2] What was the English attitude? The Statutes of Provisors and Praemunire had already been renewed, this time by royal initiative, in 1365. In the 1370's anti-clericalism and anti-papalism were particularly strong; it was the period of the attack on William of Wykeham and the alliance of John of Gaunt and Wyclif, on the one hand, and, on the other hand, the complaints, more exhaustive and violent than ever, in the Good Parliament against the Roman Curia, the cardinals' benefices, and the 'brokers of benefices in the sinful city of Avignon'.[3] This seemed to be one of the few things on which Gaunt and his opponents would agree. The 'charitable subsidy' was forbidden by the king, but the government's reaction was not altogether intransigent; perhaps they saw it as an opportunity for getting a *quid pro quo*. At any rate a series of negotiations between the Crown and the Papacy began, which went on intermittently until the end of the century. In 1373 an embassy was sent to Avignon, and in 1374-5 a conference, which included Wyclif among the English representatives, was held at Bruges.[4] The outcome was that between 1373 and 1377 a serious attempt was made to arrive at an Anglo-papal concordat. In the embassy of 1373, the king put forward the following demands:[5]

(i) The pope should stop proceedings in the Roman Curia in those cases where the king's regalian right was concerned; this would refer to those benefices, particularly cathedral dignities and

[1] Perroy, *Schisme*, 28.　　[2] *Ibid.* 29.　　[3] *Rot. Parl.* II, 337ff.
[4] Perroy, *Schisme*, 32-3, 35-40.　　[5] *Ibid.* 32; cf. Raynaldus, *Annales*, VII, 258.

prebends, where, as we have seen, the pope and the king were both claiming the right of appointment.

(ii) During the war with France, on account of the dangers of travel, English subjects should not be cited personally to the Court of Rome.

(iii) All existing reservations of benefices, which had not yet been put into effect, should be quashed.

(iv) The pope should abstain in future from making any provisions or reservations.

(v) During the war with France, the payment of the charitable subsidy from the English clergy should be suspended.

The fourth point would have wiped out the whole system of papal provisions, while the fifth point, on the other hand, seems to admit that the subsidy might be paid at some future date. The pope naturally protested against these far-reaching demands, but he saw the need for compromise. A compromise was in fact slowly reached in a series of three sets of documents, which it is worth examining; namely, some promises made verbally by the pope in 1373; five bulls issued by the pope in 1375; and two ordinances issued by the king in 1377.

In 1373 the pope made the following promises, presumably to the embassy at Avignon:[1]

(i) With regard to reservations, the pope was not willing to restrict his rights, and could not decently revoke existing reservations; but he promised to moderate his use of them in the future, so as not to aggrieve the king and the kingdom.

(ii) As regards bishoprics, he would not give up his right of provision, but he would give time for an election to take place, would meet the king's wishes as far as possible, and would 'provide' the elect, if suitable. (This was in fact by now the normal procedure.)

(iii) As regards elective dignities, abbeys, etc., he would give them to those who would reside, and would enforce the duty of repairs to property.

[1] Rymer, III, 1072; Perroy, *Schisme*, 47.

(iv) The question that raised the most discussion [*magnas alter-cationes*] was that of the aliens' benefices; the pope said that in his time he had never given a benefice to any alien except cardinals, with one exception and that was a Roman who resided in England. But since complaints had been made that the cardinals took more revenue from England than from France, and that the money went to England's enemies, the pope promised to moderate provisions to aliens.

(v) The pope could not afford to do without taking first-fruits, owing to the cost of his wars, but he hoped to be able to do something to lighten the burden on the churches.

(vi) As regards the large number of expectative reservations and provisions, the pressure from the English universities and through the letters of magnates was to blame; the pope was quite prepared to be more sparing [*difficilem*], but without restricting his right.

It is clear that the pope was unwilling to give up any right in principle, but was prepared to moderate his practice; and while this was far from meeting the king's demands, it provided a basis for further discussion.

The next step was that on 1 September 1375, the pope issued five bulls:[1]

(i) The pope confirmed the king's nominees in their benefices, even if these benefices had been the subject of papal reservations or of litigation in the Curia.

(ii) He put a stop to nine lawsuits between certain named English clerks, royal nominees, on the one hand, and cardinals or other provisors on the other, and confirmed the royal nominees in their benefices.

(iii) He quashed certain reservations of benefices made by himself or his predecessor, if these had not yet taken effect, and confirmed the existing holders of benefices.

(iv) Those who were thus confirmed were exempt from paying first-fruits.

[1] Rymer, III, 1037; Perroy, *Schisme*, 39.

(v) Owing to the dangers of the war, for the next three years Englishmen cited to the Roman Curia were to be allowed to appear at Bruges or some neighbouring town instead.

In return for these concessions, the pope was allowed to raise a charitable subsidy of 60,000 florins.

Edward III, on his part, issued two ordinances on 15 February 1377:[1]

(i) The king, to celebrate the jubilee of his reign, and in consideration of the dissensions which have arisen out of his regalian right, renounced the right to present to all benefices due to him under the regalian right which had fallen vacant before 15 February 1376.

(ii) The king for the same reason quashed all his presentations to benefices, made by virtue of the regalian right before 15 February 1376, which had not yet taken effect.

It is clear that both sides were prepared to make certain limited concessions or promises of moderation, but were unwilling to give up any general principles for the future. It was a deadlock between two unlimited prerogatives. Moreover, Edward died in June 1377. This 'still-born concordat' of Bruges had not solved the relations of Crown and Papacy.

In 1377 Richard II succeeded to the throne, and in 1378 came the Great Schism in the Papacy, with Urban VI and his successors at Rome and Clement VII and his successors at Avignon. The Great Schism on the whole rather improved Anglo-papal relations; the English felt a certain proprietary pride in 'our Urban', as against the wicked schismatic Frenchmen who supported the anti-pope, while the rather precarious position of the popes made them on the whole anxious to please. In 1381–2 there were renewed attempts to arrive at a concordat, but they broke down.[2] A few years later a new crisis arose (c. 1388–93). On the one hand, in the Parliament of Cambridge in 1388 there were fresh complaints against the seeking of provisions; on the other hand, the pope began to show

---

[1] Rymer, III, 1072; Perroy, *Schisme*, 44.　　[2] Perroy, *Schisme*, 278–81.

himself difficult about appointments to bishoprics.[1] In 1390 the Statute of Provisors was renewed, with redoubled penalties. In reply, the pope solemnly annulled the statute of 1390, together with its predecessors of 1307 and 1351.[2] Moreover, it was feared that the pope was threatening to take proceedings against certain bishops for executing royal mandates on behalf of royal nominees to benefices, and worse still, arbitrarily to translate certain English bishops, even to places outside the realm, and so deprive the king of his counsellors.[3] It was to meet these threats that the 'great statute of Praemunire' was made in 1393; England was to be kept watertight against such dangerous papal citations and bulls. But the pope did not in fact carry out these threats, and the statute of 1393 seems to have been a dead letter until it was invoked against Cardinal Beaufort in the fifteenth century and again by Henry VIII in the sixteenth century.

The crisis of 1388–93, however, did not prevent negotiations for a concordat from going on, and at last in November 1398 the terms of a concordat were agreed upon, as follows:[4]

(i) As regards the appointment of bishops, when a vacancy occurs, the pope shall allow time for the election to be notified to the Curia, and shall then provide the elect, if the king writes for him, or else some other liege subject acceptable to the king.

(ii) As regards provisions in cathedral and collegiate chapters, the pope and the bishop shall take turns in appointing to the next vacancies, until each shall have had three turns, the pope providing cardinals or other Englishmen [cardinalibus vel aliis Anglicis]; after that the bishop shall go on appointing. But no cardinals shall be provided to elective dignities or benefices involving cure of souls or residence, and no aliens except cardinals shall be provided at all within the kingdom.

---

[1] Perroy, Schisme, 306–8. [2] Ibid. 319; CPL, IV, 277.
[3] Perroy, Schisme, 331–3; W. T. Waugh, art. cit. EHR, xxxvII (1922), 178–9; compare these threatened translations with the translations for political reasons in 1388, 1397, 1399 (above, pp. 24–5).
[4] Perroy, Schisme, 349–51, 419–20.

(iii) As regards provisions to benefices in the patronage of ecclesiastics, outside cathedral and collegiate churches, the pope and the ecclesiastical patron shall appoint alternately until Easter 1400. But before Easter 1400 had come round, Richard II had been deposed, and the concordat was never put into permanent effect. It only remains to be said that in practice, after 1400, the appointment of bishops by agreement between the Crown and the Papacy continued, and while the provision of Englishmen to other benefices continued to a very limited extent, the provision of aliens became almost unknown.

The remarkable feature about the period from 1372 to 1399 is the combination of protests and conflicts with continued negotiations for a concordat, to which were added in the last few years the diplomatic attempts at bringing the Schism to an end, even by threatening withdrawal of obedience. There is a contrast between the intransigence of the claims and theories on both sides, and the easy *modus vivendi* in practice. The conflicts did not stop the negotiations; in spite of high words on both sides, a concordat always remained the desideratum, not rupture.

What is the significance of the long diplomatic and legal duel between the Crown and Papacy throughout the fourteenth century, with the period of Provisors and Praemunire as its peak? It is important to understand what this struggle is, and what it is not.

In the first place, on a higher plane, it represents the clash of rival legal claims. In other words, it belongs to the same order of things as the long struggle between the archbishops of Canterbury and York, or the struggle between an exempt monastery or chapter and the bishop who is trying to control it. It illustrates the medieval zeal for legal rights, and while to us it may seem to have been carried sometimes to grotesque lengths, that zeal represents one of the finer features of the medieval mind, and one that has done a good deal to mould western civilization and society. To defend the legal rights of one's office or community was one of the highest and noblest duties that a man could undertake and suffer for. When the monks of Durham, in the course of a legal struggle with their bishop in 1300, were besieged in their cathedral church, the chronicler tells us that they 'rejoiced that they were found worthy to suffer contumely for the Name of Jesus'.[1] Such a phrase must have seemed as natural and fitting to them as the texts which we put on our war memorials seem to us. Medieval men felt as deeply about a just lawsuit as modern men feel about a just war. It was everyone's duty to uphold his legal rights. So the pope felt it his duty to uphold the 'liberties of the Church', liberties on which the salvation of souls might depend; the king felt it his duty to uphold the 'rights of the Crown', as he had sworn to do in his coronation oath.

On a lower plane, it was a conflict of two rival systems of patronage or rival interests, the pope's protégés versus the king's protégés, and this in a period when patronage counted for so much. There were, however, complications and a certain artificiality of situation, since the pope's protégés and the king's might be the same persons, for, as has been pointed out, a man might owe some preferments to the king, some to the pope. It is this that helps to explain the surprising ease with which Crown and Papacy managed in practice to co-operate.

On the other hand, the struggle was not a movement for breaking away from the spiritual authority of the Papacy, for 'shaking off the papal yoke'. It was quite different from the radical challenge to or denial of papal authority by, say, the Anonymous of York in the early twelfth century or by Wyclif in the late fourteenth century. This border warfare between the Crown and the Curia did not imply any disbelief in the pope's spiritual authority, any more than the royal writs of prohibition directed against the bishop's courts implied that the king doubted episcopal authority. Hence it

---

[1] *Gesta Dunelmensia*, in *Camden Miscellany XIII* (Camden Third Ser. XXXIV, 1924), 33; cf. Acts, v. 41.

was not insincere or even inconsistent for the king to protest vigorously against what he regarded as papal encroachments on the royal rights, while at the same time—by the same post, so to speak—he made full use of the pope's *plenitudo potestatis*, by asking for favours such as dispensations or even provisions. The king would probably have argued that papal provisions only encroached on the Crown's rights when they were exercised against the king's wishes.

Again, although contemporary protests paint a lurid picture of the evil effects of papal provisions on the English Church, the agitation against provisions cannot seriously be regarded as a movement for reform. It was too limited, too interested. Only a man like Grosseteste, who was opposed to the exploitation and misuse of benefices in every form, could claim to be a reformer in this respect. As I have tried to explain, papal provision was only one element in a vast system of patronage; pope, king, prelates, lay magnates, all had a share in promoting the clergy and all must share the blame for any defects. On the whole, I think that papal provisors were probably neither better nor worse than those appointed by the king or other patrons, and if one had been introduced into a roomful of fourteenth-century archdeacons, canons and so forth, in most cases it would have been difficult to guess which had been promoted by papal appointment, which by royal or episcopal. It was not going to make any real difference to the salvation of souls whether the archdeaconry of Richmond or the deanery of Salisbury was held by a cardinal or by the Keeper of the Privy Seal. It would have made little improvement, if any, if the whole system of papal provision had been entirely abolished; it would only have smoothed the way for others, for royal nominees for instance. Indeed, from 1400 onwards, the most unpopular feature of papal provisions, the provision of aliens, practically disappeared.[1] Yet it would be a bold

---

[1] Among the few important exceptions were Cardinal Prosper Colonna, provided to the archdeaconry of Canterbury in 1424; and the Italian bishops of Hereford, Worcester and Salisbury in early Tudor times (cf. above, p. 56).

thing to claim that the condition of the Church in England was for that reason better in the fifteenth century than it was in the fourteenth. The real tragedy about papal provisions was that it was a great opportunity lost; it might have been used as an instrument of reform, by giving to the Church prelates who would not have been promoted by the normal means. Thus in the thirteenth century the Papacy did give the English Church men like Langton, St Edmund and Pecham, and an attempt was even made to give us St Bonaventure as Archbishop of York. In the fourteenth century, though we can still find a chronicler praising John XXII for saving the English Church from unworthy appointments, yet, on the whole, papal provision had become a matter of compromise: the pope was generally ready to give the king the bishops he wanted, and to go shares over the prebends and dignities. It was not that the Church in the later Middle Ages was too intransigent and exorbitant, but rather that it was too ready to compromise.

The legislation of Provisors and Praemunire in effect aimed at defending the rights of the Crown and the laity against ecclesiastical encroachments, but it cannot be considered as being genuinely a defence of the rights and liberties of the English Church, for it was the Crown which was likely to benefit. Grosseteste, who was a critic of the abuse of provisions, as well as a champion of ecclesiastical rights, would have strongly disapproved of the Statute of Provisors, which simply had the effect of transferring so much ecclesiastical patronage to the lay power.

As has been remarked, after 1400 the provision of aliens to English benefices almost ceased, and papal provision, so far as it survived, was simply one of the several ways by which Englishmen got English benefices. Thus the papal provision of aliens to English benefices, contrary to the popular notion, cannot be seriously considered as one of the causes of the Reformation, for by the time of Henry VIII the invasion of English benefices by aliens was as much a thing of the remote past as the slave trade or the rotten boroughs are to the present day.

In considering the relations of Church and State during the fourteenth century the remarkable fact emerges that although the two were so closely connected and overlapping, yet fundamentally each side respected the independence and integrity of the other. Thus while on the material plane, in such things as the use of benefices to support civil servants, the State grossly exploited the Church, it made no attempt to interfere with or exploit the doctrinal and spiritual functions of the Church. The government might ask for prayers and processions for the success of a campaign, or try to damp down an awkward controversy; for this reason John Lutterel, Occam's opponent, was forbidden to go to the Curia in the 1320's, and attempts were made for a time to silence Wyclif's opponents; but that was as far as they would go. Whatever else may be said of the medieval clergy, they cannot be described as a kind of government police or a body of government propagandists. A medieval bishop did not at all fill the role of a Minister of Culture in a modern totalitarian government. And on the other hand, the Church, while pushing its claims and privileges to the utmost, and often claiming a theoretical supremacy over the State, in fact did not interfere with purely secular politics. It would be very difficult to find an example, in English history at any rate, of the secular government doing something that it did not want to do, or forbearing to do something that it wanted to do, simply because of clerical dictation. The most that one might find is that the clergy may add their weight and moral support to some existing movement, as with Langton's support of the opposition to John, or that the pope may protest (without avail) against some piece of foreign policy like the alliance of Edward III with Lewis the Bavarian. The relations of Church and State were thus very different from that 'clericalism' which a modern anti-clerical might imagine to have prevailed.

Is it possible to summarize the effects of what we have so far been considering, the system of patronage, and the relations of the English Church, the Papacy and the Crown? At first sight, all this may seem to the observer a rather sordid story of 'scrambling at the shearers' feast'. But in fact, as we shall see in the later chapters of this book, the fourteenth-century English Church had other, more spiritual and intellectual activities. In the same way, judging simply from official records, one might suppose that, for instance, the universities of the present day were mainly concerned with getting and spending money or with administrative *minutiae*, but we know in fact that they have higher activities as well. As I have already said, it is not enough to criticize, we must try to understand, and the important thing to realize is that all this was not an arbitrary and meaningless system of corruption. The people who governed the medieval Church and State, from popes and kings downwards, were not usually fools or knaves; they really wanted their administrative systems to work, and they were struggling with very difficult conditions. If their methods seem to us sometimes rather grotesque and incompetent, it is worth remembering that we today are probably unconsciously tolerating and using methods and systems that may seem grotesque and incompetent to future historians. This is no reason for refusing to exercise moral judgment about the past, but it is a reason for judging with tolerance and sympathy.

Can we then estimate the effects of fourteenth-century conditions on the Church in any detail? In the first place, with regard to the parochial clergy, the net result of patronage, pluralism and the general exploitation of benefices for the higher purposes of Church and State was that the working clergy were poorly paid. There were two distinct classes among the clergy: one lot of people, the 'sublime and literate persons' who were so necessary for the running of Church and State, took most of the revenues, and another lot of people did most of the pastoral work. It was probably not very easy to pass from one class to the other. This division was not necessarily based on social origins. It was possible for a man of the humblest origins, with sufficient academic or administrative ability, to rise to the top of the ecclesiastical tree—as did Grosse-teste in the thirteenth century and William of Wykeham in the fourteenth. But it would perhaps be more difficult to find examples of men who had spent a considerable part of their career as an acting parish priest ending up as a bishop. The poverty of the working clergy was not necessarily a fatal flaw. We know from the experience of all countries and all denominations that it is possible to have a poorly paid clergy who are nevertheless efficient, zealous and devoted. It was perhaps a more serious drawback that the Church was in fact so much a career open to talent, and that the abler clerks could be so quickly and easily skimmed off and sent into academic or administrative life. But the defects of the lower clergy in the Middle Ages were due much more to faulty recruitment and the lack of any systematic training comparable to the seminaries of the post-Tridentine world. That men of this period were acutely conscious of the need for instructing the clergy we shall see later.

With regard to the cathedral clergy, the dignitaries, archdeacons and canons, the difficulty is that before we can say much about them, we need much more research. We need reliable lists of dignitaries and canons—a new version of Le Neve's *Fasti*—and we need to analyse the various chapters, to see what sort of men they contained, both as residentiaries and non-residents. It seems clear, however, even now, that these cathedral benefices were heavily raided for the benefit of royal and papal officials. This certainly meant a certain diversion of wealth; how far it seriously affected the efficient working of the Church is another matter. The turning of archdeaconries into sinecures was likely to have the most serious effect. But the work of Miss Edwards on the English secular cathedrals shows that the residentiary canons were a more consider-able and active body than has been thought, and that 'the history of the secular cathedrals is not a steady decline from an ideal'.[1]

With regard to the bishops, here too there is need for more research, for instance, by the study and publication of the bishops'

[1] K. Edwards, *The English secular cathedrals*, 330.

registers; it is unfortunate that for most dioceses the publication of the registers has not got far into the fourteenth century. The registers will tell us something, if not of the bishops' personalities, at any rate of their activities, their itineraries, how much time they spent in their dioceses and how much time in London. We may find that they were more active in diocesan affairs than one is apt to think. It is interesting to notice that a typical civil servant bishop, John Thoresby of York, is chiefly remembered for the excellent 'catechism' that he published. The large amount of diocesan legislation put out by the bishops, not by means of diocesan synods as in the thirteenth century, but by the issuing of episcopal 'mandates' or pastoral letters, is also impressive.[1] One of the aristocratic bishops in the later part of the century, William Courtenay of Hereford, London and Canterbury, has been described as 'one of the ablest and most honourable of English medieval churchmen', to whom insufficient justice has been done.[2] At a time when convocation was tending to become a machine for meekly meeting the king's requirements, Courtenay in 1373 courageously protested against clerical taxation without redress of grievances,[3] and he also showed his courage in leading the opposition to Wyclif at a time when the latter still had influential support. As we have seen, there was in the course of the century a tendency for the scholar-bishops to be pushed out of the key positions in the Church in favour of administrators and aristocrats, but we must not exaggerate the evil effects of this, for it is not certain that scholars necessarily made the best bishops. In the reign of Edward II there were still plenty of distinguished scholar-bishops, like Thomas Cobham and Roger Mortival, but they lacked the force of character and political ability to deal with the political situation, and political leadership passed to more unscrupulous bishops like Orleton, Airmyn and Burghersh.[4]

---

[1] E.g. Bishop Grandisson issued about thirty-five mandates between 1328 and 1361.
[2] K. B. McFarlane, *John Wycliffe and the beginnings of English nonconformity* (London, 1952), 71.
[3] *Ibid.* 57; M. V. Clarke, *Medieval representation and consent*, 29.
[4] K. Edwards, *art. cit. EHR*, LIX (1944), 311–47, especially 347.

On the whole I think that the episcopate of the fourteenth century, while it did not consist simply of corrupt 'Caesarian prelates', as it has so often been misrepresented, did suffer something from the prevailing system of exploitation, patronage and lay control. After the promise of the thirteenth century, one might have expected to find more men of the calibre of Langton, Grosseteste, Pecham or Winchelsey, but that was not to be; bishops of the stature of Courtenay were rare in the fourteenth century. It was not a question of wickedness in high places, but perhaps of a certain mediocrity in high places.

It is an interesting symbol of the way in which the hierarchy was tamed and controlled by the State that it was in the course of the later Middle Ages that the principal residence of the Archbishop of Canterbury came to be fixed, not at Canterbury, nor at any of the manor houses in his diocese, but at Lambeth, within a stone's throw of the seat of civil government at Westminster, so that to this day, we use the name of 'Lambeth', not of 'Canterbury', as a synonym for the authority and policy of the Primate. In some countries, the civil capital also became in time an archbishopric and in effect the ecclesiastical capital, as happened for instance with Paris and Vienna. That did not happen in England, either before or after the Reformation. With characteristic outward conservatism, London remained a suffragan of Canterbury, but in fact, from the later Middle Ages onwards, the province of Canterbury was governed from a suburb of the civil capital.

Bishops might be pastoral-minded, busy in sending out mandates, or they might be remote and preoccupied with politics and administration; parish priests might get on well or badly with their parishioners. But the one class that seems to have been generally unpopular was the bureaucracy concerned in carrying out the coercive jurisdiction of the Church, the archdeacons and their servants, summoners, apparitors and the like. Everyone will remember what Chaucer has to say about them, and we shall see how they were denounced, along with the corresponding officials of the lay courts, by the author of the *Memoriale presbiterorum*, himself a stickler for the Church's rights. It is difficult to know how far the whole class of these officials can fairly be condemned. Moral correction must always be unpopular, even at the hands of the most disinterested and saintly pastors; one remembers what trouble Grosseteste got into over his inquiries into the sins of laymen. But it looks as though there was a certain streak of corruption and oppression running through both ecclesiastical and lay officialdom at this time, and the fact that this was noted about lay as well as about ecclesiastical officials, and noted by an ecclesiastical lawyer, suggests that this was not just a figment of anticlerical prejudice. There are few things that can make or mar the well-being of a community so much as the behaviour of minor officials. This was perhaps the point at which absenteeism and pluralism did most harm, by leaving subordinates too much to their own devices; it was precisely these evils that could have been checked by the full-time attentions of a zealous bishop or archdeacon. It was here that the claims of Westminster or Avignon bore most heavily on the rank and file of the faithful. On the other hand we must not imagine that all the laity were injured innocents; the complaints about successful tithe-evasion, whether among city merchants or peasants, or the petty persecution of neighbours, show that the clergy had no monopoly of abuses.

PART II

INTELLECTUAL LIFE AND
CONTROVERSY

CHAPTER VI

SCHOLASTIC INSTITUTIONS AND THE GEOGRAPHY OF LEARNING

THE UNIVERSITIES

THE rise of the universities, constituting as it did the creation of a new organ in the Church, was one of the most important features of thirteenth-century church history, and one to which ecclesiastical reformers looked for the transformation of the Church. Here again therefore is a good opportunity for observing the effect of the thirteenth century upon the fourteenth. The two English universities of Oxford and Cambridge were well established by 1300; how did they continue to shape during the next hundred years?[1]

One important development was the foundation of colleges. As Dr H. E. Salter and others have pointed out, the older historians of Oxford and Cambridge have erred in exaggerating the importance of the colleges in the medieval universities. They tended to think of the medieval university, like the modern university, as a federation of colleges. It must be emphasized that during the first and in some ways most vital and constructive century of the universities' existence at Oxford and Cambridge, there were practically no colleges at all, and that even when they did come into existence, until the end of the Middle Ages the vast mass of both graduates and undergraduates lived and worked outside the colleges in the numerous halls and hostels and hired lecture rooms scattered about the city. The medieval colleges in fact only catered for a tiny

---

[1] For the University of Oxford in this period, see H. E. Salter, *Medieval Oxford* (*OHS*, c, 1936), chapter v; H. Rashdall, *The Universities of Europe in the Middle Ages*, ed. F. M. Powicke and A. B. Emden (Oxford, 1936), iii; K. B. McFarlane, *John Wycliffe*, chapter i; for Cambridge, J. B. Mullinger, *The University of Cambridge from the earliest times to the Royal Injunctions of 1535* (Cambridge, 1873); Rashdall, *op. cit.* iii, 274 ff.; J. R. H. Moorman, *The Grey Friars in Cambridge 1225–1538* (Cambridge, 1952).

minority of graduates, rather like the research institutes of the present day. Dr Salter estimates that even as late as 1360 the six existing Oxford colleges together only contained about forty M.A.s, twenty-three B.A.s, and ten undergraduates.[1] A turning point came with the foundation of New College in 1379, with a lavish scale of numbers and endowments.

But we must not go to the other extreme and underestimate the importance of the colleges. The first half of the fourteenth century saw a notable activity in the foundation of new colleges; the experiments of the late thirteenth century had clearly aroused interest and were being imitated. At Oxford, to the three late thirteenth-century colleges of University, Balliol and Merton, were added Exeter (1314), Oriel (1324-6), and Queen's (1341), while Balliol was enlarged and to some extent reorganized in 1340. The monastic colleges were also growing; to the houses of friars, which went back to the early thirteenth century, were added the Benedictine Durham College and Gloucester College at the end of the thirteenth century, and the monks of Christ Church, Canterbury, after experimenting with sending students to Paris and hiring a hall in Oxford, obtained a permanent house of studies with the foundation of Canterbury College in 1361. The efforts of the Benedictines to establish themselves at Oxford, in the face of great constitutional and economic difficulties involved in the collaboration of many independent houses and the maintenance of monks at a distance from home, well illustrate the importance which all classes of the community, even the most conservative, by now attached to the training of the schools.

At Cambridge the multiplication of colleges in the first half of the fourteenth century is even more striking. To the single thirteenth-century foundation of Peterhouse there were added King's Hall (c. 1316), Michaelhouse (1324), Clare (1326), Pembroke (1347), Gonville Hall (1349), Trinity Hall (1350), and Corpus Christi (1352). This galaxy is all the more striking because of the lull of nearly a

---

[1] Salter, *Medieval Oxford*, 97.

hundred years which followed until the foundation of God's-house in 1439.

The founders of these fourteenth-century colleges form an interesting group of men. A number of them were civil servants: Walter de Stapledon, founder of Exeter College, was Treasurer (and reformer) of the Exchequer; Adam de Brome, founder of Oriel College, was a Chancery clerk; Robert de Eglesfield, founder of Queen's College, Oxford, was a clerk of the king and chaplain to the queen; William of Wykeham, founder of New College, was of course the most outstanding civil servant of the age; Hervey de Stanton, founder of Michaelhouse, Cambridge, was a judge and Chancellor of the Exchequer. Such men must have derived most if not all of their wealth from their ecclesiastical preferments, even Stanton the judge being a prebendary, and thus these foundations constitute a rather unexpected and wholly commendable by-product of that system of royal exploitation of benefices which we have already considered. This period of collegiate foundations by civil servants was also the period when graduates were becoming more prominent in the civil service. The Curia, like the cloister, was learning to appreciate the schools. It should be noted that throughout the later Middle Ages the aristocratic churchmen of the type of Arundel and Beaufort were much less generous toward the universities than the civil servant churchmen, or laymen like Duke Humphrey and Henry VI.

At Cambridge we find some interesting examples of lay initiative, two colleges being founded by noblewomen (Clare and Pembroke) and one (Corpus) by a guild whose head was Henry Duke of Lancaster. Henry was the author of *Le livre de Seyntz Medicines*, one of the most interesting and attractive religious treatises of the period, and especially remarkable as the work of a devout layman.[1]

The chief importance of the colleges was that in providing fellowships they created a new type of academic benefice, which

[1] See below, p. 231.

enabled a secular graduate to go on to the lengthy course of study necessary for the Doctorate of Divinity or Canon Law. Hitherto in the thirteenth century the friars had had a great advantage over the seculars, since they were supported by their order and so could stay up indefinitely to study and teach theology. This is reflected for instance in academic statistics between 1282 and 1302, when the theologians who were members of the religious orders were about double the numbers of the secular theologians.[1] With the increasing number of colleges, the secular Masters, at least those who were lucky enough to get fellowships, were now on an equal footing with the friars. This is perhaps reflected in academic output and prestige; whereas in the thirteenth century, after the time of Grosseteste, it seems to be the great friar schoolmen, such as Pecham and Kilwardby, who are most prominent, the fourteenth century sees a much larger number of outstanding secular Masters like Bradwardine and the group of other Mertonians, and Fitz-Ralph and Wyclif. The career of Wyclif would hardly have been possible without college maintenance and college preferment. The role played by Merton College, Oxford, is particularly remarkable. Three, if not four, of the Archbishops of Canterbury between 1328 and 1366 had been Fellows of Merton, and we shall see later how much intellectual achievement could be kept up for two or three generations by a small and intimate coterie, such as a college then was, led by two or three outstanding personalities.[2] Clearly, the fourteenth-century colleges had an importance out of all proportion to their size.

College fellowships were the one type of benefice which was never exploited or diverted by outside powers during the Middle Ages. We have seen how the most lucrative ecclesiastical benefices from bishoprics downwards were earmarked for high officials in Church and State, but, so far as I know, no Chancery official, no Auditor of the papal Court, ever helped himself to a college fellow-

---

[1] A. G. Little and F. Pelster, *Oxford theology and theologians c. 1280–1300* (OHS, xcvi, 1932), 73 ff., 249 ff.　　　[2] See below, p. 136.

ship or headship. Nor do we find in the Middle Ages that subtler form of abuse, not unknown in modern times, by which dons are borrowed and used as public servants. Wyclif once described himself as *peculiaris regis clericus*,[1] but he could hardly be described as a civil servant. Nor again do we find in the Middle Ages the Crown exerting pressure on colleges to elect its nominees to fellowships and headships, as happened in Tudor and Stuart times. Perhaps this immunity was partly due to the small value of fellowships and even headships, which consisted mostly of allowances in kind, food, clothing and rooms, and for which residence in college was still insisted on. But medieval kings and magnates were not above taking the humblest pickings, such as monastic corrodies, for their servants, and perhaps the immunity of the colleges was partly due to the genuine respect, the rather pathetic respect, accorded to intellectual prowess in the Middle Ages.

THE GEOGRAPHICAL DISTRIBUTION OF HIGHER STUDIES

One of the most interesting problems in English history is to account for the reason why Oxford and Cambridge were the only universities in England until the nineteenth century. The thirteenth century saw a certain degree of centralization in higher studies, like everything else. In the twelfth century there had been many schools, cathedral schools and others, scattered all over the country, such as those at London, Salisbury, Exeter, Lincoln, Northampton, Bury St Edmunds, any of which might perhaps be called a potential university; and it is surprising that no universities developed, for instance, at London or Lincoln, which had important schools. France by the end of the Middle Ages had some fifteen universities, and even Scotland, a poorer and more thinly populated country, had three. The fact that until the nineteenth century Oxford and Cambridge were the only universities for the whole of England

[1] H. B. Workman, *John Wyclif* (Oxford, 1926), I, 237-9.

gave them a quite extraordinary scarcity value, and if there had been four or five English universities from medieval times onwards, the social and intellectual history of England might, for better or worse, have been very different. It cannot be said that this restriction was due to the lack of suitable urban communities and to the small scale of English town life. Oxford and Cambridge before the nineteenth century were small towns; if you could house universities there, you could house them almost anywhere, and certainly such towns as London, York or Lincoln were more commodious and presented closer analogies with Paris, Cologne or Bologna.

It was in the early fourteenth century that the restrictive decision was made; I think that at the beginning of the century the monopoly of Oxford and Cambridge was not yet a foregone conclusion. The turning point was probably the Stamford secession of 1333–4, when the attempt of certain Oxford masters to set up a university there was suppressed with the aid of the Crown; that seems to have been the last attempt to break away. Robert Stratford, one of the comparatively new class of influential graduate civil servants, and brother of the archbishop, seems to have taken a leading part in having the Stamford schism suppressed.[1]

While, however, Oxford and Cambridge were establishing their monopoly in a strict and technical sense, there is some evidence that in the early fourteenth century the universities were not the only centres of higher studies. The other possible centres were the cathedrals. Like so much else, this role of the cathedrals goes back to and beyond the Lateran Councils of 1179 and 1215. By canon law every cathedral was to have a school, and every archbishop's cathedral was to have a theological school for clerks—archbishops being more plentiful in southern lands than in the north. In England it was the Chancellor of the cathedral who was responsible for the cathedral school.[2] In the twelfth and perhaps the early thirteenth

---

[1] For the Stamford secession and its suppression, see Rashdall, *op. cit.* III, 89–90; *Collectanea I* (*OHS*, v, 1885), 3–56; *Oxford Formularies*, I, 84–111.

[2] On cathedral schools, see K. Edwards, *English secular cathedrals*, 187–208.

century the cathedral schools were still a reality, but they subsequently declined, partly perhaps because of the rise of the universities, partly perhaps because of the tendency to treat the cathedral dignities, of which the chancellorship was one, as sinecures. But at some cathedrals at least scholastic activity appears or reappears in the early fourteenth century.

At St Paul's, London, Bishop Richard Gravesend (1280–1303) ordered that every chancellor of the cathedral must be a Doctor or Bachelor of Divinity and must deliver lectures or find a lecturer, a stipulation which was renewed in 1308; special revenues were assigned for the purpose.[1] We find Robert Winchelsey, the future archbishop, then Archdeacon of Essex, lecturing at London (c. 1285–92).[2] Later on, Thomas Wilton, Chancellor of St Paul's, was dispensed (c. 1320–22) from residence and lecturing at St Paul's, because he was studying at Paris; he was at that time chaplain to a cardinal, and had probably been at Paris since about 1311.[3] Some of his *Quaestiones* survive, and he seems to have been quite a noted figure, as *Thomas Anglicus*, in the scholastic controversy of the period, with allegedly Averroist tendencies.[4] An even more notable schoolman, Bradwardine, was Chancellor at St Paul's 1337–48, and presumably should have lectured there. And Richard Kilwington, Dean of St Paul's 1353–61, was a protégé of Richard de Bury, a friend of FitzRalph, and a writer and preacher of some importance.[5]

At Salisbury the leading figure was Bishop Simon of Ghent (1297–1315), a very interesting man with a reputation for learning and sanctity, who translated the *Ancren Riewle* into Latin, and composed a *Meditatio de statu prelati*,[6] a charming meditation on his own

---

[1] *Registrum Radulphi Baldock*, ed. R. C. Fowler (C and YS, 1910–11), 88–9.
[2] Wharton, *Anglia Sacra*, I, 12; Little and Pelster, op. cit. 103; EHR, LV (1940), 625–6. Magdalen College, Oxford, MS. 217 contains *Questiones Roberti de Wynchelse disputate apud London' cum ibi legeret*; these were not elementary lectures for ordinands (as one might expect at a cathedral school), but highly technical discussions of the doctrine of the Trinity.
[3] CPL, II, 82, 153, 206, 213, 225.   [4] De Wulf, III, 166–7, 175.   [5] See below, pp. 161–3.
[6] Bodleian, MS. Laud. Misc. 402, and Brit. Mus., MS. Royal 5 C III, fo. 301; K. Edwards, art. cit., Church Quarterly Review, CXXXVIII (1944), 66.

unworthiness for his office. We also have a sermon which he preached as Chancellor at Oxford on Ash Wednesday 1293. It is a sermon on penitence, which combines a highly artificial style with moral earnestness and a deep sympathy for the difficulties of those whom he is addressing, the crowd of young 'clerks', herded together, with so many privileges and so little discipline. Thus he makes a quaint comparison between the temptation of Eve, and a knot of undergraduates being tempted to rebel against the university statutes:

For the serpent said: 'Why are you forbidden to eat of every tree of paradise?' And Eve answered: 'Lest by chance we die.' But the serpent said: 'By no means, but you shall be like gods.' Is not that just the way some go on nowadays, seducing others? 'Why are you forbidden to go into taverns, to play after curfew, to go into the houses of layfolk?' One will reply: 'Lest by chance I am excommunicated or imprisoned or some such ill befall me.' 'By no means,' says another, 'let us go and play; don't let us give it up for such reasons.' And so they draw many after them and deceive them. I have heard this year about some who have in this way persuaded others to play and led them into thieving, have gone to the tavern and then drawn them to the brothel, have persuaded them to a trial of strength and have ended up with manslaughter. I have even found this to be true, that some have led their friends to the tavern, and when they have got there, others have tried to cut their throats....For who are more obstinate nowadays than clerks? Who is there among the laity that is not kept from evil by the fear of punishment or loss? Who that does not fear the sentence of excommunication? But clerks fear neither the temporal nor spiritual penalty nor excommunication....Remember, O clerk, chosen to God's lot. Your friends perhaps have worked hard to maintain you in the schools, that you may profit yourself and others. Now you are neither profiting yourself nor others, nay you are only hurting them and wasting your parents' money in evil uses. Those who used to have hope of your promotion have now given you up in despair.[1]

Simon of Ghent was clearly a man with a strong sense of pastoral duty. In 1300 he ordered the chancellor of Salisbury Cathedral to

---

[1] Little and Pelster, *op. cit.* 205 ff. The Chancellor's anxieties are echoed in contemporary letters between students and their parents or patrons.

give lectures on pastoral theology,[1] and by way of practical encouragement to learning, he collated scholars to prebends at Salisbury and so built round him a very remarkable group of learned men; in his time the Salisbury chapter included four ex-Chancellors of Oxford and other Oxford theologians.[2] Ghent was succeeded by one of his learned protégés, Roger Mortival. As we shall see later, William of Pagula, the author of one of the most popular manuals of pastoral theology, at the beginning of the fourteenth century, may have had some connexion with this Salisbury group.[3]

At Wells Bishop Ralph of Shrewsbury (1329–63) had been Chancellor of Oxford immediately before his appointment as Bishop; we find him in 1335 and 1337 insisting on the chancellor of the cathedral lecturing or providing lectures in theology or canon law from October to July, that is to say, during the university terms.[4]

At Lincoln, under Bishop John Dalderby (1300–20), himself an Oxford theologian, we find two ex-Chancellors of Oxford as deans, Roger Mortival and Henry de Mamesfeld.

At Exeter Bishop John Grandisson (1327–69), who had studied at Paris, attracted and patronized learned men. In 1331 he gave Richard FitzRalph a retaining fee and the promise of a benefice, as FitzRalph was meaning to settle in the diocese, and although Fitz-Ralph's preferments were to lead him far afield, for a time during the winter of 1347–8, when newly consecrated Archbishop of Armagh, he stayed with Grandisson at Exeter, to help him in his diocesan work.[5] About the same time, Thomas Buckingham was Chancellor of Exeter Cathedral (c. 1346–50). He was a fellow of

[1] *Registrum Simonis de Gandavo*, ed. C. T. Flower and M. C. B. Dawes (*C and YS*, 1934), I, 41–2.
[2] Simon of Ghent, William de Bosco, Henry de la Wyle, Roger Mortival, Walter Burdun, Richard of Winchester, John of Winchelsea, James Berkeley; cf. Little and Pelster, *op. cit.* 80; K. Edwards, *art. cit.*, *Church Quarterly Review*, cxxxvIII (1944), 72.
[3] See below, p. 195.
[4] *Register of Ralph of Shrewsbury*, ed. T. Scott Holmes (*Somerset Record Soc.*, 1896), 341; Wilkins, II, 578; *Calendar of the MSS of the Dean and Chapter of Wells*, ed. W. H. B. Bird and W. P. Baildon (*Royal Commission on Historical MSS*, 1907–14), I, 239, 240, 545, 548.
[5] Grandisson, *Reg.* 616, 1022.

Merton, and an important theologian, whose commentary on the Sentences was printed at Paris in 1505. He was interested in the same questions of predestination and freewill as Bradwardine, and his *Quaestiones* on these subjects, if the manuscript reading is correct, seem to show that Exeter cathedral school was the scene of lively theological controversy. These *Quaestiones* are described in a New College manuscript (MS. 134) as 'Questions treated by Thomas of Bukingham, lately chancellor of the church of Exeter, showing that a middle, Catholic way can be found between the errors of Pelagius, Cicero and Scotus, and that the eternal pre-destination, preordination, prevolition and concourse of God is consistent with the freewill and merit of the creature'.[1] In the fifty-third question he describes his controversy with a certain 'reverend doctor' at Exeter, who might conceivably be FitzRalph:

Here I will insert a question which was discussed for a long time at Exeter[2] among certain Doctors. And the question was in this form: whether all, adults and children, who died before Christ, died in mortal sin and without the grace of present justification and remission and gratification, being bound to perpetual loss of the vision of God?

The man who seems to hold the affirmative part, supported it with the sayings of the saints and with various reasons, and appears to answer the authorities and reasons which are contrary to him. But to anyone who collects and sums up what the said man has to say about the question and the contrary reasons, it seems that the Doctor says many things opposed to the sayings of the saints and unheard of in the schools, from which many things I will collect a few, and refute them if I can.

Buckingham then gives thirteen articles from the teaching of the 'reverend doctor', which he proposes to refute:

These articles, saving always the reverence of him who holds them, seem as it were wholly erroneous and repugnant to the writings of the

[1] De Wulf, III, 172, 175; M. D. Chenu, 'Les Quaestiones de Thomas Buckingham', in *Studia medievalia in honorem...R. J. Martin* (Bruges, n.d.), 229–41; F. M. Powicke, *The medieval books of Merton College* (Oxford, 1931), 113.

[2] The MS. clearly reads *Exonie*, not *Oxonie*; it may of course be a scribe's error for *Oxonie*, but the fact that Buckingham was chancellor at Exeter gives some likelihood to the reading *Exonie*. Note also that further on he submits his sayings to the correction of 'my prelate', which seems to suit Exeter better than Oxford.

saints and the principles of the schools, and I count the contrary position as Catholic and faithful, which I hope to declare by proof (*probabiliter*); and first of all with my whole heart I submit all my sayings to the correction of the Church and of my prelate, whose teaching in all things I wish to follow; to no one do I impute error or falsehood, because if these things were not said, or if they were said and finally corrected, that is all I ask for; and lest anyone believe these things in the future, I write them down....

After meeting the 'reverend doctor's' arguments point by point, Buckingham concludes:

Now having, as I hope, truly dealt with the reasons of the Reverend Doctor, it remains to declare my own position, nay the common opinion, with reasons and the testimony of the saints; and because the Doctor against whose sayings I have taken up my speech, calls his conclusions 'appearances', I, desiring rather the ancient Truth than a novel appearance, empty and fallacious, elicit certain truths, according to the articles which have to be gone through.[1]

In a letter to the king in 1349, Bishop Grandisson explains the difficulty of keeping a cathedral stocked with theologians capable of preaching and lecturing, what with the competing claims of the Crown, the Papacy, friends and relatives to preferment:

Wherefore, most honoured Lord, please to understand that all my time I have been so burdened and charged with provisors of the Court of Rome, until this pestilence, that except by doing something out of my own pocket for certain persons, I have been unable to advance any of my men, except by way of permutation or other ways, with great anguish of heart; and now, dearest Lord, with your leave, as God wills that I live and am able to advance those to whom I have been for a long time past bound and obliged, and also Masters of Divinity, who can preach and lecture, to the honour of God, in the church of Exeter, of whom there is now great lack, for there is no one residing here; I have by God's grace firmly in purpose to deliver myself, and to fill up the said church, before any more provisors come, as I have heard that there are already some making preparations; and namely, as long as I am living for a short while in this wicked life; so that I may be at my

---

[1] New College, Oxford, MS. 134, fo. 395 v, 396, 399 v; and see below, p. 263.

judgment before God excused for the fact of having, before this time, perchance too much, for carnal or other unworthy reasons, advanced those of my family or others. Wherefore, most righteous Lord, do not take it ill that I do not do your command on this occasion, as I have done on other occasions, for the said reasons. For I know well that your clerks can get from the Court of Rome, and also from your own gift, enough advancement, as is right and reasonable. And for the love of God, most honourable lord, be not displeased, if my conscience distrains me in the time which now is short. For if I had advanced any of the aforesaid to whom I am so held and promised, I would willingly do your command.[1]

On another, and earlier, occasion Grandisson had written, this time to the pope, explaining the difficulty of providing for theologians and relatives at Exeter:

Owing to the slenderness and smallness of the income of the ministers of the said church [of Exeter], there is a very small number of canons in comparison with the other cathedral churches of England; wherefore persons notably literate and useful for the edification of souls and for the defence of the rights of the said church have been wont to be appointed by the bishop's predecessors by ordinary right [iure ordinario]; and now he has been unable to appoint and promote any theologian or anyone of his own family. For certain self-seekers, 'whose presence in the said church would be fruitless, useless, burdensome or rather pernicious, owing to their known conditions and circumstances', have by 'suggestion, suppression, importunity and exquisite colour' obtained papal provision to prebends and dignities, and so the bishop has irreparably lost all facility, nay all hope of making provision in the said church by his own right; so now he prays the Pope to provide a prebend or dignity for his nephew, J. de Northwode, and for his master, Richard FitzRalph, a distinguished Doctor of the Sacred Page, who at present— shame it is to say—holds no benefice.[2]

Evidence about lectures at cathedrals seems lacking in the later fourteenth century, but there is evidence that early in the fifteenth century, John Orum, Chancellor of Exeter and canon of Wells, was lecturing at Wells on the Apocalypse.[3]

---

[1] Grandisson, Reg. I, 307–8. Buckingham must have ceased to reside in 1349.
[2] Ibid. I, 106; the date is probably 1331, not 1328–9; cf. CPL, II, 355.
[3] Bodleian, MS. Bodley 859, fo. 261–289v.

I have dwelt on all this scholastic activity at the cathedrals in some detail, because although the evidence is scrappy and may seem small beer, it does represent a very interesting experiment in what we should call 'university extension'. It should be noted that in every case the initiative seems to have come from a bishop who was a university graduate and in several cases an ex-chancellor of his university; such a man seems to be making a genuine attempt to put into practice in his cathedral the traditions and methods he had seen at the schools, even down to the dates of the lecturing terms. And perhaps one can see why the experiment apparently petered out, as a tragic result of the way in which the scholar bishops were, if not extinguished, at least pushed out of the more important sees.

So far we have been considering the secular cathedrals. The monastic cathedrals also take part in this extension of higher studies. By the early fourteenth century they were beginning to get a regular supply of monk graduates, trained at the universities, and capable of providing claustral lectures and sermons at home in their cathedrals. In this connexion it is necessary to make a distinction between two levels of instruction given in the monasteries at this period, in accordance with demands of canon law and the legislation of the general chapters.[1] On the one hand there was the elementary instruction given to the novices *in primitivis scientiis*, in grammar and logic, a kind of rudimentary arts course, from which outsiders were excluded. On the other hand there were the lectures in the cloister in theology or canon law, which were ordered to be delivered where possible by the monks themselves, and to these outsiders seem to have been admitted (as they were to the theological lectures given in the friars' convents); this at any rate was so at Christ Church, Canterbury, where the chantry priests attached to the Almonry and to the Black Prince's chantry were expected to attend the lectures.[2] At Christ Church, Canterbury, there is in fact

[1] Pantin, *Chapters*, I, 28, 75, 117; II, 84, 205, 231; III, 53, 83; *Downside Review*, XLVII (1929), 201 ff.
[2] British Museum, MS. Cotton Galba E IV, fo. 89; *Literae Cantuarienses*, ed. J. B. Sheppard (*RS*, 1887–9), II, 427.

a wealth of evidence about these claustral lectures in theology; at first the monks employed Franciscans as lecturers (from 1275 to 1314), and thereafter a succession of their own monks, the first of whom had studied at Paris.[1] It is edifying to find Archbishop Walter Reynolds (of all people) in 1324 exhorting the monks of Christ Church to be more generous to their monk-lecturer and to give him a stipend, like the lecturers in other churches, together with a quiet study and an assistant, as is only reasonable, since 'auditors flock in great numbers [copiosius affluant] to your schools, and so your lecturers have a heavier burden'—which probably implies the admission of outsiders.[2]

At Worcester Cathedral the monks not only provided their own monk-lecturers but were able to export them to St Augustine's, Canterbury, and Ramsey.[3] The Worcester monks also deserve an honourable mention as a race of indefatigable takers of lecture notes; from Worcester we have a valuable series of note-books of Oxford lectures and disputations, in theology and arts, as well as sermons, from the late thirteenth to the mid-fifteenth century.[4]

At Durham and at Norwich precise evidence about claustral lectures is lacking, but I think we can infer their existence, because both monasteries had a good supply of monk graduates, including two very eminent ones, Uthred of Boldon (from Durham) and Adam Easton (from Norwich). Both these houses were also at pains to provide monk preachers; at Durham there was the celebrated preacher, Robert Rypon at the end of the century,[5] and at Norwich the monks recalled Adam Easton from Oxford (c. 1357–63), for the express purpose of organizing the monks as preachers in the cathedral, in place of the friars who had hitherto been employed there.[6]

---

[1] *Gervase of Canterbury*, ed. W. Stubbs (*RS*, 1880), II, 281; A. G. Little, *The Grey Friars in Oxford* (*OHS*, xx, 1891), 66.
[2] *Registrum Hamonis de Hethe*, ed. C. Johnson (*C and YS*, 1914–18), 341–2.
[3] Pantin, *Chapters*, I, 181–5.
[4] Worcester Cathedral, MSS. F.65, F. 73, F. 116, F. 118, Q. 31, Q. 46, Q. 71; Bodleian, MS. Bodley 962; cf. Little and Pelster, *op. cit. passim*.
[5] Cf. G. R. Owst, *Preaching in medieval England* (Cambrige, 1926), index, *s.v.* Rypon.
[6] See below, p. 175.

While Durham and Norwich produced preaching monks, at another monastic cathedral, Rochester, there was a tradition of preaching bishops: John Sheppey (1353–60), formerly prior of Rochester; Thomas Trillek (1364–72), who at least collected sermons; and above all the celebrated Thomas Brunton (1373–89), a former monk of Norwich.[1]

How far did the friars contribute to this extension of learning? Their higher studies, in the form of their *studia generalia*, were naturally concentrated in Oxford and Cambridge, but there was one other town at least which they helped to make a centre of intellectual activity, namely York, where the house of the Austin Friars had one of the finest and most interesting libraries in the country, and where John Waldeby, one of the best preachers of the age, was busy from *c.* 1354 giving courses of sermons.[2] York was also the scene of a disputation on the Immaculate Conception in 1355, between the Dominican William Jordan and the Franciscan John Mardisley,[3] which reminds one of Buckingham's disputes at Exeter. One would like to know more about these intellectual tournaments in the provincial capitals of fourteenth-century England.

Norwich also was an important centre of the friars' activities, including lectures. The Franciscan school there was sufficiently active to attract foreign students; the manuscript note-book of an Italian Friar, Nicholas of Assisi, contains notes of lectures and disputations attended at Norwich *c.* 1337, as well as lectures at Oxford in 1339–40.[4] The phenomenal number of Carmelite and East Anglian schoolmen known to us from the writings of John Bale and Leland suggests that other regions and other religious orders may have had many schoolmen who are unknown to us through lack of a patriotic historiographer.

[1] See below, p. 182.　　　　[2] Gwynn, *English Austin Friars*, 114–21.
[3] T. Tanner, *Bibliotheca Britannico-Hibernica* (London, 1748), 509.
[4] V. Doucet, 'Le studium franciscain de Norwich en 1337 d'après le MS Chigi B.V. 66 de la Bibliothèque Vaticane', in *Archivum Franciscanum Historicum*, XLVI (1953), 85–98.

One other place was, perhaps rather unexpectedly, important as an intellectual centre: the Roman Curia, whether at Avignon or at Rome. The Curia was bound to be a great meeting-place of men and a clearing-house of ideas. So many had to go there, from all parts of Christendom and on all sorts of business; and some who went on business found time to indulge in the pleasures of controversy and study. Some even had to go there on the business of controversy, for the Curia was a court of appeal in the theological as well as in legal matters.[1] Thus one English controversialist who was active at the Curia was John Lutterel, who after being Chancellor of Oxford (1317-22) had evidently quarrelled with the university and was deprived of his chancellorship.[2] He was at the Curia in 1323-6 and took a leading part in delating, examining and reporting to the Pope on William of Occam's doctrine. Perhaps his hostility to Occam was the reason for his quarrel with the university. King Edward II, who objected to having English university disputes ventilated beyond the seas, tried to prevent his going to the Curia, and to recall him when there.[3] We also find Lutterel at the Curia c. 1333-4 taking part in the discussions on the doctrine of the Beatific Vision.[4] We have already seen how Lutterel was originally urged by a friend to come to the Curia in the hope of preferment; though he received more than one prebend, he never attained a bishopric. Another less fortunate English visitor to the Curia was the Dominican Thomas Waleys, who opposed Pope John XXII's views on the Beatific Vision; the process against him was one of the *causes célèbres* of the fourteenth

---

[1] For an account of the leading French theologians and canonists connected with Avignon, see *Histoire Littéraire de la France*, XXXIV, XXXV (1915, 1921).

[2] For Lutterel, see *Snappe's Formulary*, 44, 70, 304, 325; De Wulf, III, 163-4, 174; F. Hoffmann, *Die erste Kritik des Ockhamismus durch den Oxforder Kanzler J. Lutterell* (Breslau, 1941); A. Pelzer, 'Les 51 articles de G. Occam censurés en Avignon en 1326', in *RHE*, XVIII (1922), 240ff.

[3] Rymer, II, 494; *Calendar of Close Rolls* (1323-7), 373; *Calendar of Patent Rolls* (1321-4), 329, 336; cf. *CPL*, II, 472; see also below, p. 163.

[4] In a letter to a friend (cited above, p. 20), Lutterel refers to discussions at the Curia at which he was present, and propounds his own view on the subject; Cambridge University Library, MS. Ii iii 10, fo. 91v.

century.[1] English theologians at the Curia seem to have taken a large part in this controversy over the Beatific Vision; of a committee of theologians consulted in 1333, five out of fourteen members were apparently Englishmen, and of another committee in 1335, six or seven out of sixteen seem to have been English.[2] At this period, in fact, it seems to have been impossible for any visitor to the Curia with a reputation for theological learning to escape being drawn into the affair; thus Thomas Poucyn, coming to the Curia in 1334 on business, as Abbot-elect of St Augustine's, Canterbury, was not allowed to depart until he had given his opinion, and the St Augustine's chronicler proudly tells us how he courageously supported Waley's opinion against the pope, both by lecturing [legendo] and writing, the necessary books being supplied to him out of the papal library.[3]

Perhaps the two best examples of men whose intellectual interests and work were profoundly influenced by their sojourn at the Roman Curia were Richard FitzRalph and Adam Easton. FitzRalph's first visit to the Curia was in 1334–5, just when the controversy about the Beatific Vision was at its height. The dying Pope John XXII consulted FitzRalph, who as ex-Chancellor of Oxford was already a man of some importance, and we may probably identify FitzRalph among the eighteen leading theologians of · Europe consulted by the new Pope Benedict XII, in preparation for his bull on the subject.[4] FitzRalph's second visit was to the Curia from 1337 to 1344 in litigation on behalf of the chapter of Lichfield; it was precisely then, as he tells us, that he seriously turned from philosophy to theology, and was commissioned to explain the Catholic faith to the Armenian envoys, which he did in his great *Summa de erroribus Armenorum*, perhaps his most

[1] See below, p. 145.
[2] H. Denifle and E. Chatelain, *Chartularium Universitatis Parisiensis* (Paris, 1891), II, no. 975, 995.
[3] Thorne's *Chronicle* in Twysden, *Scriptores Decem*, col. 2067.
[4] A. Gwynn, 'The Sermon-diary of Richard FitzRalph, Archbishop of Armagh', *Proc. of Royal Irish Academy*, XLIV (1937), Section C, No. 1, 32–4; Denifle and Chatelain, *op. cit.* no. 995; for FitzRalph's career, see below, pp. 151 ff.

important work. His next visit to the Curia was *c.* 1349–51, this time representing the king; it was on this occasion that he found other churchmen with the same grievances that he had against the mendicants, and in particular he joined forces with the Archbishop of Trau in Dalmatia, forming a curious Armagh–Trau axis against the friars; it was this that led on to his best-known work, *De pauperie Salvatoris.* Thus FitzRalph's two major works were occasioned by visits to the Curia on legal business.

Adam Easton, the Benedictine monk-scholar from Norwich and Oxford, spent many years at the Curia, both at Avignon and Rome, first as proctor for his order and later as cardinal.[1] It was there that he read writers like Dante, Marsilius of Padua and John of Jandun (writers at that time probably hardly known in England); it was there that he undertook the study of Hebrew, with a view to a better understanding of the political theory of the Old Testament; and it was there that he came to know the great Swedish mystic St Brigit of Sweden and took up her cause. Marsilius, the *Hebraica veritas,* and the Revelations of St Brigit represent a curious cross-section of the varied interests a man might find at the Roman Curia—an aspect of the 'sinful city of Avenon' unsuspected by the petitioners of the Good Parliament.

[1] See below, p. 177.

CHAPTER VII

TOPICS OF CONTROVERSY

IT cannot be too much stressed that the fourteenth century was throughout an age of continuous controversies, that there was a close connexion between theology and politics, and that we can only understand such a thing as the Wycliffite controversy, for instance, by considering it as one episode, admittedly the most extreme, in a long series of controversies. It may be useful therefore to attempt to analyse or list the various ingredients of controversy during this period. Here, as in other respects, the fourteenth century was very much a development of the thirteenth; many of the topics had their origin in the previous age.

APOSTOLIC POVERTY

The controversy about Apostolic Poverty goes back to the thirteenth century and especially to the attacks upon the mendicants by William of St Amour and Gerard of Abbeville and their defence by St Thomas Aquinas, St Bonaventure and John Pecham.[1] The controversy took two forms. On the one hand there was the internal split among the Franciscans, between the Conventuals and the Spirituals, over the interpretation of the Franciscan ideal of poverty. On the other hand there was the external war between the rival claims of the mendicants, that is, those religious who lived by begging alms, and the possessioners, that is, those religious who lived on their endowments. Could it be said that one of these two represented the more perfect, the more expedient, or even the only lawful form of life? Such questions involved the discussion not only of the practice of mendicancy among the friars, but also of the

---

[1] Knowles, *Religious Orders*, I, 221–4, 245–7; P. Glorieux, 'La polémique contra Geraldinos', in *RTAM*, VI (1934), 5 ff.; and 'Contra Geraldinos, l'enchaînement des polémiques', *ibid.* VII (1935), 129 ff.; D. L. Douie, *The nature and effect of the heresy of the Fraticelli* (Manchester, 1932).

exact degree of poverty practised by Christ and the Apostles. There were extremists on both sides; some of the possessioners, for instance, appear to have believed seriously that any form of mendicancy was unlawful. It was obviously impossible for the Church to come down definitely on one side or the other, in the sense of outlawing either form of life. Early in our period, however, Pope John XXII did intervene with two important bulls: *Ad conditorem* (1322), which abolished the legal fiction by which the property of the Franciscans was vested in the Holy See; and *Cum inter nonnullos* (1323), which declared it heresy to assert that Christ and the Apostles had not owned any property.[1] This legislation affected the Franciscans more directly than the other medicant orders.

SECULARS AND MENDICANTS

There was also the controversy between the secular clergy and the mendicants, over the question of the friars' privileges and the rights of the secular clergy, a controversy also going back into the thirteenth century. At the beginning of our period Pope Boniface VIII in his bull *Super Cathedram* (1300) had carefully regulated the relations of the friars and the seculars.[2] The friars were to have the right to preach in their own churches, and elsewhere by invitation of the parish priest or the bishop; they were to have the right to choose a certain number of confessors, to be licensed by the bishop to hear the confessions of the laity; they were to have the right to bury laymen in their churches; and they were to give a quarter of all offerings and legacies received to the parish priest. The bull was a statesmanlike compromise, which aimed at making use of the friars, while respecting the rights of the bishops and parish priests. Unfortunately, the truce was not observed, and Jean de Pouilly, c. 1312–18, attacked the friars' privileges, and argued, or was

[1] Knowles, *Religious Orders*, I, 246–7; Douie, *op. cit.* 153 ff.; *Histoire littéraire de la France*, XXXIV, 446 ff., 454 ff.
[2] A. G. Little, *Studies in English Franciscan history* (Manchester, 1917), chapter III and especially p. 114; Knowles, *Religious Orders*, I, 182–8.

accused of arguing, that the pope had no powers to dispense the faithful from the obligation to confess to their own parish priests, as being contrary to the divine and natural law. Pope John XXII issued the bull *Vas electionis* in 1321, condemning Jean de Pouilly, and confirming the right of the friars to hear confessions.[1]

It should be noted that this controversy arose partly out of the famous decree of the Lateran council of 1215, *Omnis utriusque sexus*, requiring annual confession to the parish priest; the responsibility and machinery for the hearing of confessions, on which so much spiritual and moral welfare depended, was a topic that preoccupied the fourteenth-century Church, as we shall see in another connexion when we come to consider the religious literature of the period. The seculars were confident that they had divine right and responsibility on their side; the friars were confident that they had superior technical training.[2]

Again, this controversy seemed to involve the opponents of the friars in a critical attitude towards the *plenitudo potestatis* of the Holy See, questioning the pope's power to alienate the rights and duties of bishops and priests, and so it has been suggested that here we may see one of the sources of Gallicanism.[3]

Finally this controversy raised the question whether anyone enjoying a right or privilege (such as the friars), forfeited it through abusing it. A specialized form of the controversy between the seculars and the friars, transposed from the parochial to the academic sphere, can be seen in the struggle between the universities and friars, at Oxford *c.* 1303–20, and at Cambridge *c.* 1303–6, which helped to strengthen the general feeling of the secular clergy against the friars.[4]

---

[1] *Histoire littéraire de la France*, XXXIV, 233–55; J. G. Sikes, 'John de Pouilli and Peter de la Palu', in *EHR*, XLIX (1934), 219–40; J. Koch, 'Der Prozess gegen den Magister Iohannes de Polliaco und seine Vorgeschichte (1312–21)', in *RTAM*, V (1933), 391 ff.

[2] For the arguments for and against the friars, see Little, *Studies*, 116–22.

[3] K. Schleyer, *Die Anfänge des Gallikanismus im 13. Jahrhundert* (Berlin, 1937); K. Schleyer, 'Disputes sur les états de perfection', in *RTAM*, X (1938), 279 ff.

[4] Rashdall, *Universities*, III, 66–78; A. G. Little, 'The Friars *v.* The University of Cambridge', in *EHR*, L (1935), 686–96; Knowles, *Religious Orders*, I, 190–1.

Throughout these controversies the Papacy on the whole supported the friars on the question of privileges, such as the right to hear confessions, and was against them on the question of the more extreme interpretation of poverty. As one might expect, the Papacy was more interested in the friars as a means for the saving of souls than as an experiment in asceticism.

CHURCH ENDOWMENT

There was also the question of church endowment which was connected with the controversy over poverty already mentioned. Is the endowment of the Church necessary or desirable? Did it exist in the Old Testament or in the Apostolic age, and if not, why not? Has the Church too much wealth? This point of controversy is perhaps connected with the medieval legend that when Constantine endowed the Church, an angel was heard to cry in the air: *Hodie venenum effusum est in ecclesia Dei.* This legend is quoted and discussed by such writers as Langland, Wyclif and Uthred of Boldon, and is perhaps hinted at by Dante in his passage about Constantine's 'fatal marriage dower', and it seems to go back at least to Odo of Cheriton in the early thirteenth century.[1]

A further question arose over endowments: could things once given to God and the Church ever be taken back? In other words, could rights or possessions be forfeited by the Church on account of abuse of them? and what rights have founders or their heirs over endowments given to the Church? This question of forfeiture and founders' rights comes up in the Statute of Westminster II (1285), and in the parliamentary protests against the papal provision of aliens to English benefices during the fourteenth century; if the endowments or benefices are misused, it is argued, they may revert to their founders.[2] And the founders' rights are the basis of the

[1] Cf. *Piers Plowman*, C Text, Passus XVIII, 220; H. B. Workman, *John Wyclif* (Oxford, 1926), II, 99.

[2] K. L. Wood-Legh, *Studies in Church life under Edward III* (Cambridge, 1934), 8; *Statutes of the Realm*, I, 91–2; *Chronicles of...Edward I and II* (RS), I, 164–5; cf. the remarks of the 'monk of Malmesbury', *ibid.* II, 198, quoting *Decretum*, II pars, causa xi, qu. iii, c. 63 on the forfeiture of privileges.

Statute of Provisors; it is as 'patron paramount' of the realm that the king steps in and protects ecclesiastical patrons against papal provision (incidentally annexing their patronage). The same notion of founders' rights was also exemplified from time to time in the royal administration and royal visitations of hospitals, free chapels and monasteries of royal foundation.[1] It was the question of forfeiture that led FitzRalph to discuss the nature of lordship as part of his arguments against the mendicants. And of course the notion of forfeiture and reversion of endowments to founders lay at the root of the Wycliffite claim that the State had the right and duty to correct a delinquent Church, and of the later Lollard schemes for the disendowment of the Church.

Thus ideas and claims which really had their roots in primitive feudal institutions like the *Eigenkirche* and lay investiture, came to life again, if indeed they had ever been even dormant, with terrific effect in the fourteenth century. These theories about endowment and forfeiture were the latter-day equivalent of the Investiture question in the realm of theory, just as the elaborate system of patronage, examined in an earlier chapter, was the practical equivalent of the earlier forms of lay investiture.

THE RIGHTS OF THE STATE

Closely connected with the topic of endowment, is the question as to what rights the State has, and under what circumstances, to tax the Church, or to impose a capital levy, or to confiscate Church property. This question, of course, went back to the bull *Clericis laicos* (1296), but it was hardly a cause of difficulty in the first quarter of the fourteenth century, that golden age of Anglo-papal fiscal relations, when obliging popes levied clerical tenths for the king's use to the tune of about £230,000.[2] But the question of clerical taxation became a vital issue after the outbreak of the Hundred Years War, and was fought out on two planes.

[1] Cf. Wood-Legh, *op. cit.*, chapters I and II; Pantin, *Chapters*, III, 34 ff.
[2] See above, p. 79.

On the political plane, there was a protracted duel between Parliament and Convocation, so well described by Miss Clarke;[1] had Parliament the power to tax the clergy, or was it necessary for the latter to give their consent in Convocation? Again and again the lower clergy tried to resist taxation, and at first they were supported by the bishops, as in 1341, but later, as in 1356 and 1370, the bishops, who after all were many of them civil servants, joined the Crown and Parliament in urging the lower clergy to give in.

On the theoretical plane, the question had been discussed by no less a person than William of Occam, who wrote a treatise (c. 1338–40) for Edward III: 'An rex Angliae pro succursu guerrae possit recipere bona ecclesiarum?' The answer was in the affirmative.[2] In 1370 we find the bishops arguing that the clergy were bound by natural law to contribute to the relief of the realm, and in 1371 two Austin friars appeared in Parliament to present eleven articles to the same effect; by the laws of God and nature, the clergy could not refuse taxation, but were bound to help in time of necessity and common danger, and these arguments were supported by citations from the Decretals and the Fathers.[3] It is probably to this Parliament that belongs the speech reported by Wyclif, about the parable of the owl and the feathers: the other birds had given the owl some of their feathers, but when the hawk swooped down on them, they took back their feathers, in spite of the owl's denial. 'Thus when war breaks out, we must take from the endowed clergy their temporal possessions, since property belongs to us and to the realm in common.'[4] These arguments may owe something to the Stoic and early medieval view of private property as a conventional arrangement superimposed upon the more natural condition of common ownership.[5] Langland, it will be remembered, depicts

[1] M. V. Clarke, *Medieval representation and consent*, chapter III.
[2] R. Scholz, *Unbekannten Kirchenpolitischen Streitschriften* (Rome, 1911–14), 432 ff.; *Guillelmi de Ockham Opera politica*, I, ed. J. G. Sikes (Manchester, 1940), 223–71.
[3] V. H. Galbraith, 'Articles laid before the parliament of 1371', in *EHR*, XXXIV (1919), 579.
[4] M. V. Clarke, *op. cit.* 31.
[5] R. W. and A. J. Carlyle, *A history of medieval political theory in the west* (Edinburgh and London, 1903), I, 23 ff., 135 ff.

the friars as 'proving it by Seneca that all things under Heaven ought to be in common',[1] a significant reference to Stoic doctrine.

The same question was involved, in a more extreme form, in the seizure and later suppression of alien priories, and in the seizure of aliens' benefices, a measure which made a great impression abroad. It was apparently the seizure of the cardinals' benefices in England, much more than the Statute of Provisors, that so incensed the Papacy in 1352.[2]

THE TWO SWORDS

There was also the long-standing topic of the relation of Church and State, of the two swords, spiritual and temporal, and the question which of the two was superior. At first sight this seems rather an academic and unreal topic, at least in England, with all the careful negotiations and compromises going on between the two powers, behind the high claims. Nevertheless this question of supremacy of Church or State was brought up, among other things, by the renewal of the pope's claim to the tribute due from England by reason of King John's submission, and it formed the main theme of that conference of 1374, real or imaginary, so picturesquely described by the continuator of the *Eulogium Historiarum*, when the Black Prince is supposed to have called the Archbishop of Canterbury 'an ass'.[3] Both Uthred of Boldon and Adam Easton wrote to uphold the supremacy of the spiritual power.

DOMINION

The subject of dominion or lordship raised a number of questions, such as, what is the nature of dominion? Does it only belong to those in Grace? What right has the Church to exercise it? 'Dominion by Grace' is one of the fourteenth-century theories most

---

[1] *Piers Plowman*, C Text, Passus XXIII, 273 ff.   [2] See above, p. 87.

[3] *Eulogium Historiarum*, ed F. S. Haydon (*RS*, 1863), III, 337–9; we should probably regard this account as a political pamphlet rather than as sober history; cf. Gwynn, *English Austin Friars*, 218; Perroy, *Schisme*, 35; J. Tait in *DNB*, *s.v.* Whittlesey.

familiar to students of history; it is only necessary to remind the reader here that it began as a papalist argument in the hands of Giles of Rome at the beginning of the century,[1] and ended as an argument against the Church's claims in the hands of Wyclif. Wyclif, like Hobbes, had a knack of taking a familiar doctrinal weapon and turning it round in the opposite direction. It is wrong to suppose that the theory of dominion by Grace was discredited by its adoption by Wyclif; we find it, for instance, taken for granted by his opponent Uthred of Boldon, and perhaps also by Adam Easton.

MONASTIC LIFE

Another controversy consisted of discussions concerning the monastic life. Thus the rival claims of the various religious orders to greater antiquity or perfection were dealt with in a whole series of historical tracts, accompanied by lists of monastic saints and writers, in which the polemics between the orders were mixed with a certain amount of straightforward edification and antiquarianism.[2] The subject was closely connected with the question of mendicancy already mentioned. Another subject of discussion was the legitimacy of the religious state and the religious vows of what Wyclif called 'private religions'. Their legitimacy was of course questioned by Wyclif; it would be interesting to know if it had been fundamentally questioned before. At any rate the attacks of William of St Amour in the mid-thirteenth century had caused the mendicant apologists, St Thomas Aquinas and St Bonaventure, to discuss the question of perfection and evolve a classic treatment of the subject. In the fourteenth century at least one English writer, Uthred of Boldon, dealt with the monastic vows and religious perfection in two remarkable treatises.[3]

[1] Gwynn, *English Austin Friars*, part II, chapter IV.
[2] *Medieval studies presented to Rose Graham*, ed. V. Ruffer and A. J. Taylor (Oxford, 1950), 189–215.
[3] *Studies in medieval history presented to F. M. Powicke*, ed. R. W. Hunt, W. A. Pantin and R. W. Southern (Oxford, 1948), 363–85; cf. below, p. 173.

PREDESTINATION AND GRACE

A lively interest was taken in this period in a group of interrelated problems concerning predestination, God's foreknowledge and human freewill, grace, and justification.[1] The problem of predestination, of course, preoccupied Bradwardine, and Buckingham (who tried to steer a middle course), and also FitzRalph, who devoted to it three of the nineteen books of his *Summa de erroribus Armenorum*; and of course it played a fundamental part in the development of Wyclif's thought. This problem was not only raised by the ever-present influence of St Augustine, but also, it should be remembered, any serious discussion of the authority and infallibility of Scripture (and this was an age when men were much concerned with Scripture) involved the question of prophecy and therefore God's foreknowledge of future contingencies and the reconciliation of this with man's freewill. If a prophet foretells a certain action, is the human agent of that action free to perform it or not? FitzRalph expressly pointed out this connexion between Scripture and predestination. The discussions about grace and justification included among other things the question of the salvation of unbaptized persons, which so much exercised such different types of thinkers as the Benedictine Uthred of Boldon and the poet Langland.

THE IMMACULATE CONCEPTION

The doctrine of the Immaculate Conception was a frequent subject of discussion in this period, all the more because on the one hand it fitted in with the contemporary preoccupation with questions of grace and justification, and on the other hand there was a rivalry between the Franciscans and Dominicans on the matter—well typified by the debate between Friar Jordan and Friar Mardisley at York. FitzRalph touched on this doctrine, once in his Oxford

---

[1] P. Vignaux, *Justification et prédestination au XIV siècle* (Paris, 1934).

lectures, taking a rather negative view, and again in a sermon in 1342, taking a more positive view.[1]

ANTI-INTELLECTUALISM

Another feature of this period is a marked reaction against the excessive intellectualism and excessive subtlety of scholasticism. This represents a very old tradition, going back in some form to those Fathers, such as St Ambrose, who were fond of contrasting Gospel simplicity with sophisticated pagan philosophy; God had revealed Himself to fishermen, not philosophers. *Non in dialectica complacuit Deo salvam facere plebem suam.* The same thought is echoed centuries later in the words of Pascal's memorial: 'Dieu d'Abraham, Dieu d'Isaac, Dieu de Jacob, non des philosophes et sçavans.' Somewhere in the early Middle Ages this contrast became transposed into an internal contrast, within the limits of Christianity, between the simple, direct knowledge and experience of the mystic, and the subtleties of the schoolman. It is most familiar in the well-known outburst in the *Imitation of Christ*: 'I had sooner feel compunction than know its definition.... At the last judgment, we shall not be asked how many books we have read, but how we have lived.' Among the English mystics this attitude was most marked in Richard Rolle. Closely connected with this reaction against the intellectualism of the schools were two other phenomena. On the one hand, a thinker like FitzRalph seems to undergo a definite 'conversion' from philosophy to theology. FitzRalph boasted in later life that he had 'destroyed the English sophisms of Occam and Burley',[2] and he tells us, in the course of a long autobiographical passage put in the form of a prayer to Christ, that he underwent his 'conversion' during his six years' stay in the Court of Rome (*c.* 1337–43):

Nor were You, the Solid Truth, absent from me those six years [at the Court of Rome], but, in Your Holy Scriptures you shone upon me

---

[1] A. Gwynn, *The Sermon-diary of Richard FitzRalph*, 41.
[2] A. Gwynn, 'Archbishop FitzRalph and the Friars', in *Studies*, xxvi (1937), 66.

as in a certain radiant mirror; whereas in my former years, in the trifles of the philosophers, you had been hidden from me as in a certain dark cloud. For previously, I used to think that through the teachings of Aristotle and certain argumentations that were profound only to men profound in vanity,—I used to think that I had penetrated to the depths of Your Truth, with the citizens of Your Heaven; until You, the Solid Truth, shone upon me in Your Scriptures, scattering the cloud of my error, and showing me how I was croaking in the marshes with the toads and frogs. For until I had You the Truth to lead me, I had heard, but did not understand, the tumult of the philosophers chattering against You, the pertinacious Jews, the proud Greeks, the carnal Saracens, and the unlearned Armenians. . . . At last, O Solid Truth, You so shone upon me from above, that I burned to seize and to hold You, the Truth, Jesus promised to us in the Law and Prophets. And when in the turmoil of lawsuits a certain spell of serenity had smiled upon me, I sought You in Your sacred Scriptures, intimately and importunately, not only by reading, but also with prayer, until You came to meet me joyously in Your ways.[1]

The other feature connected with the anti-intellectualist or anti-scholastic trend was the deliberate use of Scripture instead of scholastic arguments. FitzRalph did this in his *Summa*, where no doubt it was in any case necessary in dealing with the Armenians.[2] Adam Easton spent twenty years studying Scripture (including the study of Hebrew) as an approach to the problem of Church and State, and in presenting his articles in defence of St Brigit of Sweden to the pope, he claimed that 'they speak according to the manner of speaking of Holy Scripture and of the holy doctors, especially the ancient ones'.[3] Thomas Netter of Walden made the same use of Scripture, and Wyclif's appeal to Scripture was an important part of his system. Of course theology had always been conceived of as based on Scripture, as *pagina sacra*, but these men

---

[1] L. J. Hammerich, *The beginning of the strife between Richard FitzRalph and the Mendicants* (Copenhagen, 1938), 20; Bradwardine also, in an autobiographical passage, describes himself as undergoing a dramatic intellectual change; but this was not so much a conversion from philosophy to theology, as the adoption of a particular view of the doctrine of grace; T. Bradwardine, *De causa Dei contra Pelagium*, ed. H. Savile (London, 1618), 308.
[2] A. Gwynn, in *Studies*, XXII (1933), 606. [3] Bodleian, MS. Hamilton 7, fo. 248.

seem disposed to take that more literally than usual. And on the Continent it was at this time that Nicholas de Lyra, *Doctor planus et utilis*, was laying great emphasis on the literal sense of Scripture.

Throughout these controversies one can distinguish certain degrees of intensity. First there were the more polite and academic controversies, such as that between Buckingham and the unnamed doctor at Exeter, or between Bradwardine and the 'Pelagians'. These men were not merely debating, they seriously regarded their opponents' views as unsound and dangerous, but the controversy did not lead to any official action or legal process, though Bradwardine expressed the wish that the pope would make a pronouncement.[1] To this type belong Wyclif's early controversies such as those with Uthred of Boldon or Binham, over monasticism; opponents were still addressed as 'my reverend doctor'.

The second type of controversy was more embittered and violent, such as that between Uthred of Boldon and the Friars, over questions of Grace and Justification, where Uthred complained of the attacks and libellous writings put out against him by 'false brethren', who by canon law deserved excommunication and by civil law beheading! And the matter was formally referred to the judgment of the Archbishop of Canterbury.[2] Similarly with the dispute between FitzRalph and the friars, the matter was taken up to the Court of Rome.[3] John Lutterel's attack on Occam was also fairly violent, and may have lost Lutterel his Oxford chancellorship. But in these cases, while there was much heat and bitterness, neither side was seriously at this stage in danger of a heresy charge.

The third and most desperate stage came when the controversy was felt to be a 'war to the knife' and each side felt that its very existence was at stake, as in the later stages of the Wyclif controversy. The reason for the English bishops' slowness to condemn Wyclif (for which they were rebuked by the pope), and for the government's readiness to intervene on his behalf, was probably because for

---

[1] Bradwardine, *op. cit.* 872.　　[2] See below, pp. 168–9.　　[3] See below, pp. 162–3.

a long time the attacks of Wyclif seemed to belong to the second rather than to the less familiar third category of controversies.

Our knowledge of fourteenth-century controversies comes from a variety of sources. Not only do we have formal scholastic writings, such as treatises and *quaestiones*, but a good deal of light comes from such unexpected sources as official correspondence, letters between the king and the pope, petitions preserved in the Parliament Rolls, manifestos of various sorts, including an interesting genre of imaginary letters, already referred to, like the letter of 'Peter son of Cassiodorus' at the time of the Parliament of Carlisle, or the letter supposed to be sent from the pope to the king of England, beginning 'Ventrem suum dolet alma mater ecclesia'; and certain of the chroniclers specialize in comments on ecclesiastical affairs. All these sources contain between them an interesting body of doctrine and claims touching on theology, political theory and law.

CHAPTER VIII

PERSONALITIES

THE MERTONIANS

In considering the personalities who played a part in fourteenth-century intellectual life and controversy, it is only possible here to select a few individuals or groups. In the first place there is a very remarkable series of writers who were Fellows of Merton College, Oxford, in the first half of the fourteenth century.[1]

During the first quarter of the century, the series starts with Walter Burley (c. 1305), the earliest and one of the most influential of the group; he was a logician and commentator on Aristotle with a European fame, being later known as *Doctor planus et perspicuus*, and had taught at Oxford, Paris and Toulouse. Such an international scholastic career, which had once been common enough, was now beginning to be uncommon, at least among seculars. A slightly junior contemporary was John Mauduit (c. 1309–19), an astronomer.

During the second quarter of the century, we find at Merton the great Thomas Bradwardine (c. 1323–35), the *Doctor profundus*, remembered chiefly as a theologian for his work *De causa Dei contra Pelagianos*, but also a writer on mathematics and dynamics; Richard Camsale (c. 1305–26), a logician; John Dumbleton (c. 1338–47), also a logician; Thomas Buckingham (c. 1324–40), a theologian; William Heytesbury (c. 1330–46), a logician and physicist; Simon Bredon (c. 1330–41), an astronomer; John Ashenden (c. 1336–53), also an astronomer.

---

[1] For the fourteenth-century Mertonians, see Powicke, *Medieval books of Merton College*, 23–8; R. T. Gunther, *Early science in Oxford* (*OHS*, LXXVII–VIII, 1922), I, 96 ff., 389 ff., II, 42 ff., 380 ff.; Lynn Thorndike, *History of Magic and Experimental Science* (New York, 1934), III, 141 ff., 325 ff., 370 ff.; P. Duhem, *Etudes sur Leonardo de Vinci* (Paris, 1906–13), III, 405 ff., 451 ff., 493 ff.; G. Sarton, *Introduction to the History of Science* (Baltimore, 1947), III, 116 ff., 563 ff., 736 ff., 1412; De Wulf, III, 164–75. I have to thank Mr A. B. Emden for help with regard to the dates of the Mertonians. The dates in brackets are approximate, giving the tenure of fellowships, as far as is at present known.

About the middle of the century, we have Richard Swineshead (*c.* 1344–55), a celebrated writer on logic, mathematics, and physics, known as the *Calculator*; William Rede (*c.* 1344–57), a mathematician and astronomer; Richard Billingham (*c.* 1344–61), a logician; Reginald Lambourn (*c.* 1353–7), an astronomer; Ralph Strode (*c.* 1359–60), a logician; John Chilmark (*c.* 1384–93), a logician and physicist. At the end of the century Queen's College seems to take over the leadership, with Robert Alington (*c.* 1379–86) and John Sharpe (*c.* 1391–1404).

The group of subjects in which these men were interested is remarkable and well-defined: it covered logic (especially the branch of logic known as *sophismata*), physics and dynamics, mathematics and astronomy, and these were often combined with theology. This combination of interest in natural science and theology goes back to the thirteenth century, where one finds it, for instance, in Grosseteste and Pecham; it was a healthy phenomenon, perhaps partly due to the university curriculum, which forbade men to study theology without previously graduating in arts, so that every theologian had at least a perfunctory knowledge of the arts, rather in the way that in modern times the older generations of scientists had all had some training in the classics. The particular kind of problems discussed and methods employed by these men, such as the *sophismata*, the *Calculationes*, the 'intension and remission of forms', and a curious application of mathematics and physics to theology, are technical matters which need to be dealt with by a specialist.[1] Here it is sufficient to point out that their work is extremely important and cries out to be studied, because it is men like Swineshead and Heytesbury, so violently derided by the humanists at the time of the Renaissance, who appear to be among the most important links between medieval science and modern science.[2]

[1] A. C. Crombie, *Robert Grosseteste and the origins of experimental science 1100–1700* (Oxford, 1953), chapter VII; A. Maier, *An der Grenze von Scholastik und Naturwissenschaft* (Essen, 1943); A. Maier, *Die Vorläufer Galileis im 14. Jahrhundert* (Rome, 1949).

[2] Duhem, *Etudes sur Leonardo de Vinci*, III, 450, 525.

Roughly speaking the years 1300–60 represent the heyday of the Merton school, while the years 1380–1400 represent a similar period for Queen's College. Why do we find this crowding of at least fifteen outstanding men into sixty years at Merton, followed by a halt about 1360? This cannot be put down to the Wycliffite controversy, which has been made to answer for so much, in fact too much, in Oxford history. We must look for more positive and personal factors. The great Mertonian period was probably due to two or three outstanding personalities, such as Burley, Bradwardine[1] and Rede, who encouraged the rest for two or three generations, and when they went the movement died out. While it lasted, the position of Merton was perhaps comparable to that of Oriel in the early nineteenth century or that of Balliol in the late nineteenth century. It may be noted that it was just at the time of its intellectual pre-eminence that Merton gave several archbishops to Canterbury. There was nothing escapist or introvert about the schoolmen of this period, nothing of the ivory tower; their energies very easily ran into practical politics, as can be seen from the careers of Occam, FitzRalph or Wyclif.

The secret of Merton's success was not, I think, that the College officially took up a particular line of work, as a college or institute might nowadays decide to specialize in medicine or social studies or oriental languages. It was rather that the college was an informal coterie of friends, encouraging each other, rather like the academies of the fifteenth-century Renaissance, or, to take an example closer in time, the group of scholars in Richard de Bury's household. The very personal and affectionate relationship involved is reflected in Bradwardine's letter *ad suos Mertonenses* which accompanied his great book *De causa Dei*: they are *in doctrina discipuli, in caritate amici, in Christo conservi*.[2] A college, being a *societas* or fellowship of men living and working together, was an ideal instrument for such an intellectual movement, more so than a larger body like a

---

[1] Bradwardine is quoted by some of the other Mertonians as '*Doctor noster*', A. Maier, *Die Vorläufer Galileis*, 96n.   [2] Bradwardine, *De causa Dei*, 876.

faculty. This perhaps accounts for the influence of the early medieval colleges out of all proportion to their size. In some ways, I think, the medieval colleges were influential just because they were small coteries rather than the great high-powered educational organizations they have since become; they were nearer to the seminar or 'the small back room' than to the correspondence college. The great achievement of a spontaneous and informal movement of this kind is not without relevance to the present day, when there is a tendency to think that the advancement of this or that branch of knowledge can be laid on at the command of the planner. Hitherto European learning has prospered because men have wanted to find out about things, not because they have been told to do so. It is significant that the few medieval experiments in the 'planning' of learning from above, like the well-intentioned attempt of the Council of Vienne to promote the teaching of eastern languages, were not successful.

I have just mentioned another circle of scholars, smaller and even more informal than the Mertonians, though partly overlapping with them, namely the scholars whom Richard de Bury, Bishop of Durham (1333–45), kept in his household, where we are told he had them disputing before him every day after dinner.[1] These scholars were Bradwardine, Burley, Maudit (Mertonians, as we have seen); FitzRalph, the Dominican Robert Holcot, and Richard Kilwington, later Dean of St Paul's and a friend of FitzRalph, all these being Doctors of Theology; in addition there were two civil servants who later became bishops, Richard Bentworth and William Segrave, and also, apparently, the celebrated canonist, John Acton. It is interesting to note that Richard de Bury's circle provided a common meeting place for theologians, lawyers and civil servants; we must not think of these different classes as living in separate compartments and necessarily antagonistic to each other.

---

[1] For Richard de Bury and his group of scholars see *Hist. Dunelm. Scriptores Tres*, 128; J. de Ghellinck, 'Un bibliophile au XIV siècle: Richard d'Aungerville', in *RHE*, xviii (1922), 491–500; N. Denholm Young, in *TR Hist. Soc.* (iv) xx (1937), 160–5.

Richard de Bury's circle of scholars illustrates the importance of patronage among scholars as among so many other classes of contemporary society. One way in which relations of scholars and their patrons can be traced is in the dedication of works. Walter Burley, for instance, dedicated the same work, his commentary on the *Politics* of Aristotle, to two successive patrons, first to Richard de Bury, for obvious reasons, and secondly in 1343 to Pope Clement VI, whose style of lecturing (*artificiosum multumque ordinatum*) he had so much admired at the University of Paris.[1]

THE FRIARS

We have seen how one feature of the thirteenth century—the growth of the universities and in particular of the secular colleges within the universities—produced an important crop of fourteenth-century secular schoolmen like the Mertonians. Another feature of the thirteenth century had been the establishment of the friars in England, and particularly at the universities. What contribution did the friars make to fourteenth-century English scholarship? Can we say that here too the thirteenth century finds its fulfilment in the fourteenth century?

At the beginning of the fourteenth century the English—or perhaps we should here say the British—Franciscans included two outstanding schoolmen: John Duns Scotus (d. 1308) and William of Occam (d. 1349).[2] Both received some part of their training at Oxford, though both spent a large part of their careers on the Continent, and became in fact European figures; both, as is well known, exercised an enormous influence on the development of late medieval scholastic thought. Later in the century the Franciscans produced two important controversialists, Roger Conway (d. 1360),[3] who defended the mendicant claims against the attacks

---

[1] A. Maier, 'Zu Walter Burleys Politik-Kommentar', in *RTAM*, XIV (1947), 332–6. Cf. the relations of Nicholas Trivet and Thomas Waleys to literary patrons, below, pp. 143, 146.

[2] For Scotus and Occam, see De Wulf, II, 332–52, III, 27–51; Knowles, *Religious Orders*, I, 235, 238 and references there given.

[3] *DNB*; Little, *The Grey Friars in Oxford*, 239–40; Gwynn, *English Austin Friars*, 90.

of FitzRalph, and William Wodeford (died *c.* 1390),[1] who was perhaps the ablest of the orthodox opponents of Wyclif in this century, defending both the mendicant ideal and the orthodox doctrine of the Eucharist.

The fourteenth-century English Franciscans also left their mark in quite a different field, namely Middle English religious verse. Friar William Herebert (died *c.* 1333)[2] has left a number of English lyrics, translations of well-known Latin hymns and antiphons, which he apparently made or collected for use in preaching. This is an early example of those hymn translations which have played such a large part in English hymnology. These English hymns, however, were probably not meant for singing, but for insertion in sermons. It was a favourite device for preachers in this period, whether preaching in English or in Latin, to summarize the main points which they wished to drive into the memories of their hearers in the form of rhyming phrases,[3] so that there was a close practical connexion between preaching and poetry.

Another English Franciscan, John Grimstone, has left a commonplace book of pulpit material, written in 1372, containing 143 topics arranged alphabetically; interspersed throughout are a number of English lyrics, either composed or collected by Grimstone.[4] These lyrics are fine specimens of religious poetry; they dwell, as one might expect, with great feeling on the nativity and passion of Our Lord, and several are on the favourite theme of Christ's appeal to man:

> I am Jesu, that come to fight
> Withouten shield and spear,
> Else were thy death i-dight[5]
> If my fighting ne were.

[1] *DNB*; Little, *op. cit.* 246–9; Gwynn, *op. cit.* 226–8, 233.

[2] *Religious lyrics of the fourteenth century*, ed. Carleton Brown (Oxford, 1924), xiii–xiv, 15–29.

[3] The Dominican Thomas Waleys discusses and criticizes the use of rhyme, in his treatise on preaching, T. M. Charland, *Artes praedicandi* (Paris, 1936), 372–6. The Franciscan John of Wales regards rhyme as an aid to memory, *ibid.* 154n. Cf. also Owst, *Preaching in medieval England*, 272 ff.

[4] Carleton Brown, *op. cit.* xvi–xix, 69–92.　　　　　[5] *i-dight*: prepared.

Since I am come and have thee brought
A blissful boot of bale,[1]
Undo thy heart, tell me thy thought,
Thy sins great and small.

Love me slew,
And love me drew,
And love me laid on bier.
Love is my peace,
For love I chose
Man to buyen dear.
Ne dread thee nought,
I have thee sought
Bothen day and night,
To haven thee,
Well is me,
I have thee won in fight.

Sinful man, bethink and see
What pain I bear for love of thee.
Night and day to thee I grede,[2]
Hand and foot on rood i-spread.
Nailed I was to the tree,
Dead and buried, man, for thee;
All this I bear for love of man,
But worse to me that he ne can
To me turn but once his eye,
Than all the pain that I drye.[3]

And there is man's answer:

Gold and all this worldis win
Is nought to Christis rood;
I would be clad in Christis skin
That ran so long in blood,
And go to His Heart and take mine inn,
There is a fulsome food.
Then give I little for kith or kin,
For there is all good.[4]

[1] *boot of bale*: remedy for woe. [2] *grede*: cry aloud. [3] *drye*: suffer.
[4] Carleton Brown, pp. 82 (no. 63), 84 (no. 66), 88 (nos. 70, 71).

If preaching turned some friars to poetry, it seems to have turned others to the study of classical antiquity. The English Dominicans in the early fourteenth century produced an interesting group of men, who combined an interest in preaching and in scripture with a love of moralization and a desire to understand and make use of the history and literature of classical antiquity. One of these Dominicans was Nicholas Trivet (c. 1258–1328),[1] a man of good family, whose father was an itinerant justice. He was a versatile writer; he wrote a useful chronicle (for which he is chiefly remembered), an exposition of the Mass, commentaries on various books of the Old Testament, and commentaries on St Augustine's *City of God*, on Boethius, on Seneca the Elder's *Declamations* and Seneca the Younger's *Tragedies*, and on Livy. He studied and taught at Oxford and at Paris, and we know that he was lecturing in theology in London in 1324. He was evidently much appreciated as a commentator and interpreter of classical literature by some of the leading men at the papal Curia at Avignon in the early fourteenth century, where, at a time when Petrarch was still a child, there was beginning to make itself felt that revived interest in the classics which may be called 'pre-humanism'. Thus the Cardinal Bishop of Ostia, Nicholas Alberti, hearing that Trivet had already commented on Boethius and the *Declamations* of (the elder) Seneca, wrote (c. 1314) to ask him to go on to comment on the *Tragedies* of (the younger) Seneca. Again it was at the command and at the payment of Pope John XXII that Trivet wrote what seems to be the earliest known commentary on Livy (c. 1316–19).

Trivet's interests as a commentator lie predominantly in historical and grammatical matters; he points out the difference between Livy's account and that of other writers, and he paraphrases Livy's text into easier Latin. He is a collector of data rather than a critic or a philosopher. 'When a class of students or a superior wants an explanation of the obscurities of a classical text, Trivet will explain where a dative case is needed, what the modern word-order would

---

[1] For Trivet, see *DNB*; Knowles, *Religious Orders*, I, 234 and references there given.

be, or who the Etruscans were. He will not venture to compare an ancient government with a modern one, the strategy of Hannibal with that of the Bruce, or the character of a Punic general with that of an English leader of his own generation.'[1] Similarly in commenting on the *De civitate Dei*, his interest is less with the philosophical or theological ideas discussed by St Augustine than with the book as a great quarry of classical lore to be set forth and explained; he calls his commentary an 'explanation of the extraneous histories and poetical sayings which are touched upon by Augustine in the books on the City of God'.

This work of commentary was a humble but necessary task. Intelligent and busy men in the fourteenth century, from popes and cardinals downwards, wanted to read writers like Seneca and Livy, but they found them hard going, both because of the unfamiliar style and because of the historical and mythological allusions. It was the purpose of men like Trivet to make such classical writers intelligible and attractive to their contemporaries, and it is difficult to see what progress the revival of classical studies could have made without such preliminary work.

Trivet applied the same textual interest that he had in the classics to the study of scripture. He was one of those medieval scholars who were interested in Hebrew; his commentary on the psalter often refers to the Hebrew text, of whose meaning he was obviously anxious to get as accurate as possible an understanding.[2]

Another of this group of English Dominicans was Robert Holcot (d. 1349).[3] He was an Oxford graduate, and one of the scholars in the household of Richard de Bury. Indeed, the *Philobiblon* is ascribed to Holcot's authorship in some manuscripts, and it seems very likely that he at any rate helped Richard de Bury in the

---

[1] R. Dean, in *Medievalia et Humanistica*, III (1945), 87 ff.

[2] B. Smalley, *The study of the Bible in the Middle Ages* (2nd edn., Oxford, 1952), 346–7.

[3] For Holcot, see *DNB*; J. de Ghellinck, *art. cit.*, *RHE*, XVIII (1922), 301, 494–5; B. Smalley, 'Some Latin commentaries on the sapiential books in the late thirteenth and early fourteenth centuries' in *Archives d'histoire doctrinale et littéraire du moyen âge*, XVIII (1950–1), 117–21.

writing of it, 'devilled' for him in fact. Holcot is chiefly remembered for his commentaries on the Sapiential Books—Wisdom, Ecclesiastes, Ecclesiasticus and Proverbs; Holcot on Wisdom was one of the best-sellers of the age, the sort of book you would have been sure to find in every respectable late medieval library.

Holcot has the same interest in classical lore that we find in Trivet and in the *Philobiblon*. In his scriptural commentaries he is fond of bringing in continually bits of classical learning, from Seneca, Valerius Maximus, Suetonius, Ovid or Virgil, to improve a moral. In his *Sermo finalis* (part of his scholastic acts at Oxford),[1] he compares the theological course to the mythical Atalanta:

> In this manner, my beloved, in the Church Militant it seems to be laid down by the revelation of Phoebus [i.e. God] concerning this noble maiden (that is to say, theological wisdom) and those who wish to enter into marriage with her, that is to say that no one, however studious he may be, shall contract the marriage of inception (the Doctor's degree) with her, unless he has promised that he will run with her and lecture fully on the four books of the Sentences in a cursory lecture.

Another feature of Holcot is that 'he carries on and enlarges the practice of discussing political questions in the framework of the Sapiential books';[2] in particular he quotes Aristotle's *Politics* for this purpose.

Thomas Waleys (died *c.* 1349)[3] was another English Dominican with varied interests, which included classical antiquity. He is now chiefly remembered for the part he played in the controversy over the theological views which Pope John XXII, as a private theologian, put forward on the subject of the Beatific Vision.[4] In a sermon preached at Avignon in January 1333 Waleys violently

---

[1] Ed. J. C. Wey, 'The "sermo finalis" of Robert Holcot', in *Medieval Studies*, XI (1949), 219.

[2] B. Smalley, *art. cit.* 120.

[3] Knowles, *Religious Orders*, I, 249; T. Käppeli, *Le procès contre Thomas Waleys O.P.* (Rome, 1936); B. Smalley in *Archivum Fr. Praedicatorum*, XXIV (1954), 50.

[4] *Histoire Littéraire de la France*, XXXIV (1914), 391 ff.; *Dictionnaire de Théologie Catholique* (1910), II, 657–96.

attacked the pope's views and the pope's supporters, and expressed some theological opinions of his own which were themselves attacked. A pamphlet war followed, and Waleys was imprisoned at Avignon for a number of years. He regarded the Franciscans as chiefly responsible for his persecution—he had already crossed swords with them over the poverty of Christ, and the controversy may have been complicated by rivalry between the orders. Waleys was evidently distinguished as a preacher; it was a sermon, as we have seen, that got him into trouble, and he wrote a treatise on the art of preaching at the request of Theobald Orsini, Archbishop of Palermo.[1] This must have been after his imprisonment, so that it seems clear that Waleys regained both his liberty and his prestige as a preacher.[2]

Like Trivet, Waleys wrote a commentary on part of St Augustine's *De civitate Dei*; he concentrates on explaining the historical allusions and linguistic meaning rather than the philosophical ideas. He also left moralizations on various books of the Old Testament, which, like Holcot, he illustrates with stories and quotations drawn from ancient history and the classical writers on natural history. Thus he takes the opening verse of the book of Judges: 'After the death of Joshua, the children of Israel consulted the Lord saying: Who shall go up before us against the Chanaanite, and shall be the leader of the war?' He uses this as a peg on which to hang a discussion of the right conduct of ecclesiastical elections, which he curiously illustrates from natural history:

And indeed [he writes] as Solinus tells us, among the elephants it is the largest who leads the file, that is the herd; about whom St Ambrose tells us in the *Hexameron* that the king elephant excells in greatness and meekness; from which it seems that the animals have an instinct given them by nature, whereby the one endowed with the best natural gifts rules the rest. If only things were like that nowadays in the Church,

---

[1] T. M. Charland, *Artes praedicandi*, 94, 328–403.
[2] He was probably released some time after 1342; he was evidently back in England by 1349, when he petitioned successfully for a papal provision for a friend who was supporting him (*CPP*, 1, 146). Waleys was then old and paralysed.

how good it would be and what a wonderful time we should have! But nowadays those who are altogether unworthy in God's judgment are promoted in the Church, not by God's counsel, but by that of their relatives and carnal friends.[1]

Another fourteenth-century English Dominican, John Bromyard,[2] was the author of one of the most celebrated of medieval aids to preaching, the *Summa praedicantium*, a vast encyclopaedia of subjects suitable for the use of preachers, arranged alphabetically. He also is fond of quoting classical writers. In his prologue he comments on and defends this practice. It is right, he says, to quote pagans and their works as witness to the truth, and to extract edification out of a moralization of the pagans' fables: *fas est et ab hoste doceri*, and we can enrich the Hebrews with the spoils of the Egyptians—a line of argument which of course goes back to the Fathers.

The interest in classical antiquity that these friars showed was not a novelty. Here, as in so much else, the men of the fourteenth century were exploiting and developing something inherited from the thirteenth century. This particular enthusiasm can be traced back to a thirteenth-century Franciscan, John of Wales, who died between 1285 and about 1300.[3] John's largest and best-known work is the *Summa Collationum*, a large collection of edifying material, carefully classified, for use not only in preaching but also in private conversation—the evangelist at the breakfast table. In this he draws on classical sources as well as on the Scriptures and the Fathers. But perhaps his most interesting works are his *Compendiloquium* and his *Breviloquium de virtutibus*. In the first he deals with 'the lives of the illustrious philosophers, their moral sayings and imitable examples',

---

[1] New College, Oxford, MS. 30, fo. 47v; and see below, p. 266.

[2] He has generally been identified with the John Bromyard who was Chancellor of Cambridge University in 1383 (cf. *DNB*); but as the *Summa praedicantium* is cited in the sermons of John Sheppey, 1336–53 (New College, Oxford, MS. 92), it seems likely that the author must be an earlier John Bromyard, O.P., who was presented to the Bishop of Hereford to be licensed to hear confessions in 1326, *Registrum Adae de Orleton* (*C and YS*, 1908), 350. I owe this point to Mr G. Mifsud.

[3] A. G. Little, *Studies in English Franciscan History*, 174–92.

beginning with men like Diogenes, Socrates and Plato and ending with Cicero, Seneca and Boethius; the latter is the only Christian philosopher included. In the second treatise he takes the four cardinal virtues, Justice, Prudence, Temperance and Fortitude, and illustrates each by anecdotes and sayings of the philosophers and heroes of the ancient world. He draws heavily on such writers as Valerius Maximus, Cicero and Seneca.

The most striking thing about John of Wales's work is his enormous admiration for the moral virtues of these pagan philosophers and heroes. He has chapter after chapter on their mortification, continence, contempt of riches, patience and so forth. The result is that a picture emerges of Diogenes or Socrates that is curiously like that of an ideal friar. John is never tired of holding up his good pagans as an example to his readers; if this is what they, with all their limitations, could do, what ought not Christians to attain? From one point of view, all this is parallel to the rediscovery of the ethical and political teaching of Aristotle; from another point of view, it represents the enthusiasm and the curiosity of the antiquary. John of Wales was really reviving the humanism of the twelfth-century in an up-to-date, systematic form; in particular he makes great use of the *Policraticus* of John of Salisbury, and seems to have been responsible for popularizing that work.[1] John of Wales's classical interest seems to have passed in the fourteenth century mainly to Dominicans, as we have seen, but there was at least one fourteenth-century English Franciscan in this tradition, John Ridewall or Ridevaux (*c.* 1330) who wrote a moral commentary on the Mythology of Fulgentius,[2] while at the end of the century we find the Benedictine chronicler, Thomas Walsingham, writing a similar commentary on Ovid's *Metamorphoses*.[3]

This wave of interest in classical antiquity and classical learning and literature among the friars of the late thirteenth and fourteenth

---

[1] B. Smalley, *art. cit.* 113.
[2] H. Liebeschütz, *Fulgentius Metaforalis* (Leipzig, 1926), especially 31 ff.
[3] F. W. Hall, 'An English commentary on Ovid', in *Classical Quarterly*, xxi (1927), 151 ff.

centuries is a remarkable phenomenon, which deserves more study. It may seem at first sight a very unexpected by-product of the evangelical zeal of the Poor Man of Assisi or the *Domini canes*. Yet this classical interest seems to be connected none the less with the pastoral aims of the friars and in particular with their revival of the art of preaching.[1] Medieval men took the classics very seriously, and classical antiquity and classical literature were valued as an inexhaustible quarry for edifying material. Diogenes in his tub, the love-affairs of the gods, the habits of elephants—all were grist to the preacher. But it would be a mistake to suppose that the classics were only so much jam to hide the powder of edification. These friars and their contemporaries did come to have a genuine interest in classical history and literature, and a genuine admiration for the moral virtues of the ancient world. Different as was their approach from that of Valla or Poggio or Petrarch, it represented an important stage in the development of the Renaissance.

So far we have been considering Franciscan and Dominican scholars. In the thirteenth century these two orders may be said to have monopolized the friar's scholarship in England. But in the fourteenth century the two other orders of friars, the Carmelites and the Austin friars, who had already established themselves at Oxford and Cambridge, began to produce important scholars, though on a smaller scale. Among the English Carmelites the outstanding scholar of the century was certainly John Baconthorpe, the *Doctor resolutus*, who died in 1346.[2] Among the Austin Friars two scholars stand out: Geoffrey of Hardeby, who defended the mendicant ideal against FitzRalph in his *De vita evangelica (c.* 1357–8);

---

[1] This connexion may be illustrated by the fact that one of Bishop Sheppey's collections of sermons (Merton College, Oxford, MS. 248) contains extracts from Aesop's fables and some *Flores moralium antiquorum* (ranging from Pythagoras to Ovid, Galen and Boethius), collected for the use of preachers; though the compiler adds a warning against the excessive use of fables in sermons, 'lest those who ought to be stirred by holy words to the sorrow of penitence and devotion to God, be dissolved in laughter by such trifles'.

[2] Knowles, *Religious Orders*, I, 241; B. M. Xiberta, *De scriptoribus scholasticis saec. XIV ex ordine carmelitarum* (Louvain, 1931), 167–240; De Wulf, III, 110.

and John Waldeby, who about the same time made a name for himself as a preacher at York.[1] We know more about the intellectual life of the Austin Friars at York than we do about most communities at this time, thanks to the happy survival of the catalogue of their extremely interesting library.[2]

It is clear that the friars made a most important contribution to fourteenth-century English scholarship. Other aspects of the friars' life were to be the subject of sharp criticism and controversy from their opponents—their theory and practice of poverty, their privileges, their relations with the secular clergy. Even in the field where they were most successful, the improvement and development of pastoral technique, as preachers and confessors, they were involved in controversy. But their worst enemies could hardly deny their eminence in the schools. We are apt to take all this for granted. It is worth remembering that in three out of the four orders, this concentration on scholarship was something of a revolution or a deviation. It is well known that St Francis mistrusted learning as a source of intellectual pride, and it seems a far cry from the schools to the groups of hermits in which both the Carmelites and the Austin Friars originated. With the Dominicans, it was different; it was their peculiar glory that they had from the first seen themselves as a studying and teaching order, with an intellectual vocation: *contemplari et aliis contemplata tradere*. The fact that the other orders came to take the same line comparatively quickly was of incalculable importance to the Church, to the universities and to the orders themselves. When St Bernard had preached on conversion to the scholars of Paris, his preaching, if successful, would have emptied the schools. To the friars, on the contrary, conversion meant an intensification of the life of the schools.

---

[1] Gwynn, *English Austin Friars*, 90–5, 114–23, 124–9.
[2] *Ibid.* 130 ff.; printed in *Fasciculus J. W. Clark dicatus* (Cambridge, 1909), 2 ff. The books that belonged to Friar John Erghome are particularly notable.

RICHARD FITZRALPH

Richard FitzRalph (*c.* 1300–60), Archbishop of Armagh, and hence known and cited in the history of medieval thought as 'Armachanus', is the outstanding figure in the mendicant controversy. FitzRalph's early career shows that he was one of those churchmen who made their name and fortune in the schools.[1] He was born *c.* 1300 at Dundalk in Ireland, came to Oxford *c.* 1315, became Doctor of Theology in 1331, and was a Fellow of Balliol, and Chancellor 1332–4. He went to Paris *c.* 1329–30, taking with him a nephew of Bishop Grandisson of Exeter, to whom he was acting as tutor; and in 1334–5 he went, perhaps as representative of the university, to the Roman Curia at Avignon, where he was consulted by Pope John XXII on the question of the Beatific Vision. FitzRalph at this stage owed much to the patronage of Bishop Grandisson of Exeter, a scholar and a patron of art and one of the most interesting bishops of his age. FitzRalph was tutor to Grandisson's nephew, and in May 1331 Grandisson gave him a pension and the promise of a benefice;[2] it was evidently intended that FitzRalph should settle in the Exeter diocese. A little later, Grandisson got a faculty from the pope to provide FitzRalph with a canonry,[3] and it was probably the combined influence of Grandisson and Bradwardine that secured for him papal provision to the deanery of Lichfield in 1335. As we have already seen, FitzRalph was one of the clerks attached to the household of Richard de Bury, probably in 1334. All this is significant because it shows how the patronage system, which is apt to appear rather cynical and corrupt to modern eyes, could be used by scholars to promote scholars, and in particular we see how a bishop like Grandisson would keep his eyes open

---

[1] For FitzRalph's career, see the series of articles by Fr. Aubrey Gwynn, S.J., in *Studies*, XXII (1933), 389ff., 591ff.; XXIII (1934), 395ff.; XXIV (1935), 25ff., 558ff.; XXV (1936), 81ff.; XXVI (1937), 50ff.; A. Gwynn, *English Austin Friars*, 66–73, 80–9; L. J. Hammerich, *The beginning of the strife between Richard Fitz-Ralph and the Mendicants*; A. Gwynn, 'The Sermon-diary of Richard FitzRalph', 1–57.

[2] Grandisson, *Reg.* II, 616; cf. I, 233.

[3] *Ibid.* II, 719; *CPL*, II, 355; cf. the letter to the pope quoted above, p. 116.

to recruit a rising young Oxford man for his diocese. Our knowledge of details like this is only too rare.[1]

The summit of FitzRalph's career is represented by the period when he was Dean of Lichfield (1335–46) and Archbishop of Armagh (1346–60); he attained both offices by papal provision. FitzRalph did not forget his patron Grandisson; when appointed Archbishop of Armagh, he went to Exeter for consecration, and spent the winter of 1347–8 as a kind of episcopal apprentice, helping Grandisson with the work of his diocese,[2] before going over to Ireland, which he reached about April 1348. A striking feature of FitzRalph's career is the long periods of residence he made at the Roman Curia at Avignon: 1334–5, when being consulted by John XXII and Benedict XII on the Beatific Vision; 1337–44, when representing the Lichfield chapter in a lawsuit against the Archbishop of Canterbury; 1349–51, when sent by King Edward III to ask for an extension of the Jubilee Indulgence of 1350; and 1357–60, during his controversy with the friars. FitzRalph testifies to the fairness of his treatment in the Roman Curia; he had fifteen decisions in his favour in seven years.[3] This aspect of FitzRalph's career is again a warning against superficial judgment; at first sight he seems to be an absentee, a confirmed litigant, a papal provisor, in fact all that is deplorable according to text-book standards; yet in fact we know him also as a zealous diocesan, an acute and courageous thinker and writer, and a man of deep piety, perhaps the nearest approach that the fourteenth century produced to the type of Grosseteste and Pecham.

FitzRalph is one of the most important English theological writers of the fourteenth century. A good deal of his writings survive, though very little has so far been published in modern times. His writings are interesting both for their content and for the various occasions that produced them.

[1] Cf. Nicholas of Sandwich's patronage of William Rede, Powicke, *Medieval books of Merton College*, 28.   [2] Grandisson, *Reg.* II, 1022.

[3] In a sermon preached in 1349; quoted in Gwynn, 'The Sermon-diary', 36; *Studies*, XXII, 597; cf. also below, p. 154.

In the first place there are his lectures on the Sentences, belonging to his Oxford days, c. 1328–9.[1] Secondly there is his *Summa de erroribus Armenorum*, composed perhaps c. 1340–44 at the Roman Curia, and later dedicated (c. 1347) to Pope Clement VI.[2] If one wonders how the Dean of Lichfield came to be involved with the Armenians, one must remember that this was an age of widening horizons, when, for instance, Franciscan missionaries were penetrating as far as China; the Holy See had for a long time been interested in a variety of missions to and negotiations with the East, and, among other things, negotiations were at this time going on with the Armenians for reunion with Rome. Hence FitzRalph had conversations with an Armenian archbishop at the Roman Curia, and was commissioned by the pope to write a *Summa*, to explain the Catholic faith to the Armenians, in nineteen books. Books I–XIII deal with the Incarnation, the Roman Primacy and the Sacraments; then follow some topical questions, such as Book XIV on the Beatific Vision, and Books XV–XVII on God's foreknowledge and freewill; Books XVIII–XIX deal with the Koran and with the Jews; and the whole work ends with a remarkable autobiography in the form of a prayer addressed to Christ, which belongs to the same literary genre as Augustine's *Confessions*, and Bradwardine's *De causa Dei*, where part of the work is addressed to God. FitzRalph's autobiographical prayer is a combination, so characteristic of the period, of a highly elaborated form with genuine religious feeling. It is divided and subdivided after the manner of a sermon: Christ has been to FitzRalph the Way, the Truth and the Life, *Via tuta*, *Via recta*, *Via laeta*, *Veritas lucida*, *Veritas valida*, *Veritas solida*.[3]

Christ was the *Via tuta*, the safe Way, to FitzRalph, when he was an exile, fleeing from his persecutors, when those persecutors met him in the streets and did not recognize him, when he escaped unharmed from the hands of robbers. Christ was the *Via recta*, the

---

[1] Gwynn, *English Austin Friars*, 80, 132.   [2] *Ibid.* 67; *Studies*, XXII (1933), 599.
[3] Hammerich, *op. cit.* 18–22.

straight Way, when FitzRalph was fleeing and hiding from the royal servants at the ports, who had received writs ordering his arrest. Christ was the *Via laeta*, the joyful Way, when He gave FitzRalph exultation as well as tribulation, and brought him to the Roman Curia. Christ was the *Veritas lucida*, the clear Truth, when the justice of FitzRalph's cause was made clear and the calumnies of his adversaries were exposed before the Auditors of the Apostolic Palace, and he found favour in the eyes of all. Christ was the *Veritas valida*, the strong Truth, when sixteen appeals that were made in succession against FitzRalph were broken like reeds, and he triumphed over his powerful adversaries, and so, after six years' servitude, he was set free (as the old law had commanded) in the seventh year. Christ was the *Veritas solida*, the solid Truth, for during those six years FitzRalph underwent that conversion from philosophical trifling which has already been described.[1]

Thirdly, there is the treatise *De pauperie Salvatoris*, written *c.* 1350–6, which discusses the theory of lordship and property (books I–V) and the privileges of the friars (books VI–VII);[2] the writing of this arose out of the controversy with the friars, as we shall see later.

Fourthly, throughout his career FitzRalph was active as a preacher; he was a great preacher in what was a classic age of great preachers, and he regarded the 'office of a devout preacher' as peculiarly his vocation. Fortunately, he has left us a remarkable document in the form of a sermon-diary, recording nearly a hundred sermons preached between 1335 and 1359, giving the dates, places, types of audience and occasions; this has been described by Father Aubrey Gwynn. FitzRalph was ready to

---

[1] See above, p. 132. The six years would be *c.* 1337–43; the 'persecutors' and 'adversaries' must refer to the Archbishop of Canterbury, against whom FitzRalph was litigating at the Curia.

[2] R. L. Poole, in an appendix to his edition of Wyclif's *De dominio divino* (Wyclif Society, 1890), edited books I–IV of the *De pauperie* (277 ff.) with the table of contents of books V–VIII (264 ff.); cf. Gwynn, *English Austin Friars*, 67–9, 83.

preach various types of sermon, devout, outspoken, severely moral, controversial, before any audience, whether in the papal Curia, or at St Paul's Cross, at Lichfield cathedral, or his diocese of Armagh, sometimes in English, sometimes in Latin, according to the type of audience.[1]

FitzRalph is pre-eminently associated with the great outburst of controversy between the secular clergy and the friars, c. 1350-60, which was fought in several different quarters. One scene of the controversy was the Roman Curia. Already, as we have seen, the Holy See had defined the privileges of the friars in relation to the secular clergy, as to preaching, hearing confessions, and so forth, on several occasions, notably in the bulls *Super cathedram* (1300) and *Vas electionis* (1321). In 1349 the friars put forward a *Propositio* in the Roman Curia, asking the pope for a mitigation of the existing settlement in their favour. In July 1350, FitzRalph put forward a counter-proposition, beginning *Unusquisque*,[2] in the opposite sense, asking for a restriction of the friars' privileges. FitzRalph delivered this proposition 'on behalf of the prelates and curates of the whole Church', in the form of a sermon preached before the pope, and was supported by the Archbishop of Trau in Dalmatia, a curious alliance which shows the widespread nature of the anti-mendicant feeling. Apparently the pope was sufficiently impressed to appoint a committee of theologians, including FitzRalph, to inquire into the matter, and FitzRalph followed this up by setting to work on his treatise *De pauperie Salvatoris*.[3]

The scene next shifted to Ireland, where in his diocese of Armagh FitzRalph became involved with friars c. 1354-6, as is reflected in his sermons for this period.[4] FitzRalph had extremely severe views in moral theology, on such questions, for instance, as restitution and alms-giving; thus he held that a man who bequeathed his money to charity after his death, instead of giving it away during his life,

[1] Gwynn, 'The Sermon-diary', 1-57.
[2] Printed in Hammerich, *op. cit.* 53-73.
[3] Wyclif, *De dominio divino*, ed. Poole, 273.
[4] *Studies*, xxv (1936), 83-4.

was still guilty of avarice and would not escape damnation.[1] He was much concerned also with such evils as usury and crimes of violence, and particularly the prevailing feuds between English and Irish in the March of Ireland: 'that an Englishman should claim the sanction of the *lex marchie* for the killing or robbing of Irishmen, without further question, is to him a manifest violation of the law of God.'[2] It was his moral severity that brought FitzRalph into conflict with the friars, for he believed that they were too indulgent as confessors, and that they exceeded their powers in absolving excommunicates. Speaking before the pope in 1357, he said:

For I have in my diocese of Armagh, as I suppose, two thousand subjects, who every year are involved in sentences of excommunication, on account of the sentences passed against wilful homicides, public robbers, incendiaries and the like; of whom scarcely forty in a year come to me or to my penitentiaries; and all such men receive the sacraments like other men, and are absolved or are said to be absolved; nor are they believed to be absolved by any others except by the friars, without doubt, for no others absolve them.[3]

The problems connected with the correct administration of the sacrament of penance had been raised by the decree of the Lateran Council of 1215, *Omnis utriusque sexus*, making annual confession to the parish priest obligatory, and this legislation was further elaborated by the English bishops throughout the thirteenth century; the need for properly trained confessors was urgently felt. These problems continued to dominate the fourteenth century in several ways. Thus, on the one hand, the regulation of confession lay at the root of this controversy between seculars and friars; and on the other hand, the same topic of penance loomed large in the manuals for the instruction of parish priests and in the

[1] *Studies*, xxv (1936), 87–8, xxvi (1937), 63.
[2] Gwynn, 'The Sermon-diary', 31; cf. *Studies*, xxv (1936), 90.
[3] *Fasciculus rerum expetundarum*, ed. E. Brown (London, 1690), ii, 468; cf. *Studies*, xxv (1936), 83, 94–5.

moral treatises for the laity, as we shall see in later chapters. It is significant that at least one of these manuals for the instruction of parish priests, namely the *Memoriale presbiterorum* (*c.* 1344) anticipated FitzRalph in complaining of friars and others who were too lax and exceeded their powers as confessors.[1]

In England the controversy between the secular clergy and the friars was of long standing. The points at issue are well illustrated in a petition presented by the rectors of the London churches to the Provincial Council of the province of Canterbury, probably held in 1309 in London. They first of all complain of the way in which the friars abuse their privileges in respect of preaching, confessions, and burials, and then go on to complain about the effect which the friars have upon those laymen who go to them for confession and counsel. 'By these circumventions of the friars the hearts of laymen are hardened and turned against their parish churches and their rectors, and these laymen presume to work wonderfully and contemptuously against the liberties of the Church.' Thus these 'hardened' laymen who are the friars' penitents neglect to attend their parish churches, neglect to pay tithes on their business dealings, make their wills with the help of laymen instead of the parish priests, claim the control and care of the churches and churchyards and of their relics and sacred ornaments, assign burial-places in the churches and churchyards without consulting the parish priests, saying that the latter are only concerned with the chancels and the divine services; they interfere with the trees in the churchyards, and pull down the houses built there to accommodate the parish priests. Thus the parish priests suffer at once from the neglect and interference of these laymen (who are presumably the churchwardens), and are reduced to beggary, while the friars grow rich and erect grand buildings. The parish priests end by begging the help of the bishops of the province against their powerful enemies; otherwise untold evil will follow, and this will be put down to the 'holy simplicity' (*sancta rusticitas*) of the prelates. Holy simplicity is all

[1] Cf. below, pp. 209, 211.

very well and may edify the Church, but it is harmful if it fails to resist delinquents.[1]

There is much more in all this than professional rivalry and the clash of vested interests; it reveals in a most interesting way some of the fundamental problems which the vigorous development of town life had created for the Church. On the one side there are the numerous and often small parish churches with their ancient organization and rights, and on the other hand the endemic anti-clericalism of the city merchants, their generosity combined with thrift and possessiveness; reluctant to pay tithes,[2] desiring to control 'their' churches. In fact we have here the bourgeois equivalent of the old *Eigenkirche*, the proprietary church owned by a lord; and like the feudal patrons of the early Middle Ages, the merchants, while giving with one hand, try to hold on with the other. This problem is complicated by the presence of the friars, who had so much to offer the devout laity; and the friars seemed to be allying themselves with the laity against their rectors, rather as, at a higher level, they seemed to be allying themselves with the politicians who sought to tax and disendow the Church.

Turning to the situation in England in FitzRalph's time, we find here c. 1354–5 in two west country dioceses, Exeter and Hereford, evidence of friction between the bishops and the mendicants, analogous to what had occurred at Armagh. The bishop of Exeter was John Grandisson, FitzRalph's patron; he had been a student at Paris at the time when Jean de Pouilly had been attacking the friars' privileges, and it may be that FitzRalph first acquired his interest in the mendicant controversy from Grandisson.[3] Bishop Grandisson was very active in issuing mandates concerning the hearing of confessions, and in appointing penitentiaries to hear confessions on the

---

[1] Cambridge University Library, MS. Gg. IV. 32, fo. 125–9; cf. *Victoria County History, London*, I, 200.

[2] Cf. the complaints of John Sheppey in his sermon at St Paul's Cross (1337), New College, Oxford, MS. 92, fo. 178v; and A. G. Little, *Personal tithes, EHR*, LX (1945), 67–88.

[3] Gwynn, *English Austin Friars*, 81.

bishop's behalf. He complained on more than one occasion, for instance in 1342 and again in 1354, that the friars were acting as bishop's penitentiaries without authorization, and so in 1354 he revoked the faculties granted to the friars. This seems to have been part of a drive against bogus penitentiaries.[1] In the same way at Hereford, Bishop Trilleck, who in 1354 admitted eleven Franciscans as confessors, in 1355 revoked all faculties and excluded all friars.[2]

In the Convocation of Canterbury in May 1356 a bill of complaints was presented against the friars, as slanderers of the clergy and flatterers of magnates, and as over-indulgent confessors; this evidently represents the same uneasiness as the bishops felt, but in a more extreme form. The clergy of the province of Canterbury complain, in rather incoherent phrases, that

these religious, to whom the quest of beggary ought to provide a living, go about with loosened reins, flowing with delights, on noble palfreys of their own, with saddles and reins most exquisitely ornamented, beyond the manner of the greater prelates of England; they frequently visit the courts of magnates and public and populous places; and not fearing the censures of the archbishops, bishops and other prelates of the province of Canterbury and of the English Church and of the laws and canons, they become the most biting detractors, the adulators of magnates and their confessors; they handle secular and spiritual affairs touching our lord the King and other nobles and magnates of the land, to the prejudice of the clergy and the English church, to whom in these days they are clearly more hostile than the laity; they are astute and one-sided middlemen, corrupt and disguised under the veil of religion; they frequently even become mediators of contracts of marriage, illicitly and of their own free will, and deceitful agents of business; and by their blandishments they acquire the goodwill of the lords and ladies of the realm of England to such an extent, that very many churches in the realm of England to which they are opposed are outrageously oppressed in their legal rights; and what is more to be wept

[1] Grandisson, *Reg.* I, 557; II, 953, 1128, 1143–7, 1208; *Studies*, XXVI (1937), 54–5.
[2] *Registrum Iohannis de Trillek*, ed. J. H. Parry (C and YS, 1911–12), 20, 232; *Studies*, XXVI (1937), 55–6.

over, being the confessors of such noble lords and ladies, nay rather the betrayers and notorious deceivers of their souls, they convert to their own gain the compensation for wrong-doing which by earthly and heavenly law ought to be restored to the injured parties, and a pillow of flattery is put under the sinner's head as he sleeps in his sin; loaded with goods, they stuff their ruddy cheeks and blow out their bellies; and when they are deservedly rebuked for fomenting sin in this manner, they daily prepare intolerable plots against the English church, and secretly commit things concerning which it is not expedient to speak at present, since they hold such sway. Wherefore your clergy pray that for the salvation of the English church you would cause to be applied some timely remedy against these insolencies of the said mendicants, in this present council or by provision of the Apostolic See.[1]

What was at the root of this bitter and rather unedifying controversy? Undoubtedly there was some element of resentment at injury to vested interests in the objections of the secular clergy, whether it was the London rectors finding their tithes and offerings and legacies falling off, or the clergy of the province alarmed at the social success and power of the friars in high places. But the matter cannot be dismissed as simply as that. The objections of a zealous bishop like Grandisson or FitzRalph were genuine and sincere. And it is significant that the petition of the London rectors against the friars in 1309 is found copied into a book that was evidently compiled by or for a devout and zealous London priest, who took his pastoral duties seriously.[2] There were clearly two sides to the question.[3] On the one hand the bishops and the secular clergy undoubtedly had the responsibility for the cure of souls and especially for the sacrament of penance, and it seemed to them that some of the friars at least were exceeding their powers and using them irresponsibly and laxly, to the ruin of souls, and that they therefore deserved to lose their privileges, which they had only gained from

---

[1] Public Record Office, D.L. 42/8 (Selby Register), fo. 79v; and see below, p. 267.
[2] Cambridge University Library, MS. Gg. IV. 32 contains several treatises for the instruction of priests, on the hearing of confessions, a collection of prayers, etc.
[3] Cf. A. G. Little, *Studies in English Franciscan History*, 116–20.

the Papacy by false pretences. On the other hand, the friars felt some justifiable dissatisfaction with the low standards of the secular clergy, dissatisfaction which Pecham had expressed on more than one occasion in no uncertain terms;[1] the friars undoubtedly had a superior training for their work, and were men of picked ability, capable of dealing with any penitent from a king to a condemned criminal. It is significant that in the Exeter diocese the friars were the only penitentiaries who understood the Cornish language.[2] The modern system whereby every secular priest is given a thorough intellectual and moral formation in a seminary is a product of the Counter-Reformation, and it is difficult for us to realize how haphazard was the selection and training of the rank and file of the secular clergy in the Middle Ages. Judged by modern standards, the friars as a body were properly trained in a way that the secular priests as a body were not. The development of town life in particular since the twelfth century, together with the rise of a new and cantankerous type of educated or half-educated laity, had produced serious problems, and it is difficult to see how the Church could have met the crisis adequately, without the aid of the friars. Yet as we have seen, there were bishops and others in the early fourteenth century who were trying hard to raise the standard of the secular clergy, by such means as the cathedral schools and manuals of instruction, and this must have made the more serious members of the secular clergy all the more unwilling to be written off as obsolete and inferior to the friars.

We have already seen the developments that had been taking place at the Curia, in Ireland, and in the west of England. The scene now shifts to London. FitzRalph came to England in the summer of 1356 and spent the winter in London. He was invited to preach at St Paul's Cross by the Dean of St Paul's, Richard Kilwington, an old friend and companion of his in Richard de Bury's household

---

[1] *Registrum epistolarum Fratris Iohannis Peckham*, ed. C. T. Martin (*RS*, 1885), III, 948, 953, 957.
[2] Grandisson, *Reg.* II, 1146.

twenty years before; one can see again the ties of personal friend-
ship and patronage having their effect. Between June 1356 and
March 1357 FitzRalph preached a number of sermons, some in
London at St Paul's Cross, some at Deddington near Oxford; in
these he attacked the friars, both on the questions of poverty, such
as Christ's poverty and the practice of mendicancy, and on the
question of the friars' privileges.[1] In March 1357 the friars drew up
a list of twenty-one 'errors' in FitzRalph's teaching on the poverty
of Christ, on mendicancy and on the privileges; and in a sermon of
12 March 1357 at St Paul's Cross, on the text *Nemo vos seducat
inanibus verbis*, FitzRalph answered the friars, point by point.[2]

Given such publicity, the controversy aroused general interest;
it was about the same time that the king issued an injunction to
restrain FitzRalph and Kilwington from preaching against the
friars, and also forbade both FitzRalph and his opponents to cross
the seas, that is to say, to go to the Curia.[3] This royal intervention is
interesting. It was perhaps partly inspired by a desire to protect the
friars, from whom the royal confessors were drawn, and to prevent
disturbances in the kingdom, if popular feeling was inflamed too
much. But there are also parallels before and after. Thus thirty
years before, the king had tried to prevent John Lutterel, Occam's
adversary, from going to the Roman Curia; and twenty years later,
there were several royal interventions to protect Wyclif, such as an
injunction to restrain his Benedictine opponents, Gaunt's appearance with Wyclif at St Paul's in 1377, and the message from
the queen-mother to stop the bishops' condemnation at Lambeth
in 1378. It would, I think, be a mistake to see in these interventions
by the lay power in theological controversies any attempt at
ideological dictation of the sort that was to become common in the
sixteenth and seventeenth centuries; it is not likely that Edward III
took much interest in the details of the poverty controversy or the

---

[1] *Studies*, XXVI (1937), 56; Gwynn, 'The Sermon-diary', 45–7, 54–5.
[2] *Studies*, XXVI (1937), 58; Gwynn, *English Austin Friars*, 86–7.
[3] Gwynn, *English Austin Friars*, 88; Rymer, III, 352.

terms of the bulls *Super cathedram* and *Vas electionis*. What was probably felt to be at stake was rather the Crown's patronage and still more the Crown's responsibility for preserving the peace. Jurisdiction over breaches of the peace was a matter about which the Crown was very sensitive and very jealous of any encroachment. The dislike of having dirty linen washed in public was another motive for trying to prevent disputes being taken abroad. Edward II had written to John Lutterel in 1322, at the time of his quarrel with the University of Oxford, pointing out that

grave dissensions and discords have arisen, under pretext of which, if by the perilous presumption now begun, they are divulged in parts beyond the seas, that is to say in universities or other public places, scandals and other grave perils may very likely arise, not only for you and the said masters and scholars and the said university, but also for our kingdom and its inhabitants.[1]

The final scene of the controversy was at the Roman Curia again. In spite of the king's prohibition, FitzRalph did succeed in getting to Avignon, and there on 8 November 1357 he preached his famous proposition, the *Defensorium curatorum*, before the Papal Consistory, and this led to formal litigation in the Curia. On the one hand, there survive some legal documents, putting the case for the secular clergy, including those of France as well as those of England, and some tracts written by FitzRalph and by his friend Richard Kilwington, Dean of St Paul's. On the other hand, the friars produced their answers. The Franciscan Roger Conway wrote his *Defensio religionis mendicancium* in reply to FitzRalph's *Defensorium curatorum*, to which FitzRalph replied with *Replicaciones*, to which in turn Conway, rejoined with three *Quaestiones* concerning the poverty of Christ and temporal dominion. Moreover an Austin friar, Geoffrey Hardeby, regent master at Oxford *c.* 1357–8, and later influential at the court of Edward III, wrote the treatise *De vita evangelica* in answer to FitzRalph's *De pauperie Salvatoris*. Thus a formidable literary battle went on. In the end, the decision at the

---

[1] Rymer, II, 494; see also above, p. 120.

Roman Curia went against FitzRalph; on 1 October 1358 and on 14 July 1359 the pope issued two bulls, confirming the teaching of *Vas electionis* and the friars' privileges, but without condemning FitzRalph's teaching on lordship and grace. In 1360 FitzRalph died at Avignon.[1]

There are some curious by-ways of the mendicant controversy to be noticed. Here is one example. A remarkable compilation is contained in the British Museum MSS. Royal 6 E VI and VII, entitled *Omnebonum*; it is an alphabetical encyclopaedia, consisting of articles dealing with canon law, theology, history, geography and natural history; it is exquisitely illuminated, and seems to be unfinished. It was apparently written by a Cistercian monk, named James, in or near London, c. 1350–60.[2] His articles reflect certain peculiar and personal enthusiasms and aversions. He obviously followed eagerly the mendicant controversy, and shows a strong animus against the friars; his article *Fratres* is taken largely from William of St Amour and FitzRalph, he has a good deal to say about the friars' methods under the article *Adulacio*, and under the article *Christus* he is careful to explain that Christ and the Apostles did not beg. On the positive side, the writer has a great admiration for FitzRalph, and gives us the whole text of FitzRalph's most devotional sermon, *Veni Domine Jesu*; he is interested in the controversy over the Beatific Vision and in devotion to the Holy Name, about which he quotes St Bernard and Richard of St Victor. In his combination of piety and controversy and in his miscellaneous erudition, the product no doubt of a good library, the writer seems characteristic of the period.

Another, more picturesque, product of the controversy is Richard Helmslay, a Dominican, of Newcastle upon Tyne, who caused a stir in 1379–80 by preaching in Newcastle against the rights of the secular clergy, and attacking the secular clergy in general. In

---

[1] *Studies*, xxvi (1937), 61–7; Gwynn, *English Austin Friars*, 89, 90–4.
[2] Gwynn, 'The Sermon-diary', 15; D. L. Douie, *The nature and the effect of the heresy of the Fraticelli* (Manchester, 1932), 200.

preaching he used an *exemplum* about a certain sick king (i.e. the people, who are sick with sins) who had a very skilled physician (the four orders of friars); but another physician (the secular clergy), jealous of the king's physician, wrote a letter to the king, warning him against taking his physician's medicine (this letter represents other preachers, such as monks, hired to deceive the people). But the king saw through this jealous ruse, took his own physician's medicine (i.e. the friars' spiritual care) and recovered. But what attracted most attention was Helmslay's ingenious interpretation of the decree of the Lateran Council obliging everyone to confess to his parish priest; strictly speaking, he argued, this decree, *Omnis utriusque sexus*, only applied to those who were literally *utriusque sexus*, that is to say, hermaphrodites! The indignant clergy of the diocese of Durham cited him to Rome, and a contemporary correspondent tells us that Helmslay was known throughout the Roman Curia as *Frater Ricardus utriusque sexus*. In the end, he was ordered to make a public recantation of his teaching, at Durham and at Newcastle.[1]

TWO MONASTIC WRITERS:
UTHRED OF BOLDON AND ADAM EASTON

Uthred of Boldon and Adam Easton are the two outstanding writers and controversialists among the ranks of the English Black Monks in the second half of the fourteenth century. Monastic scholars of this type represent the fourteenth-century outcome of a notable thirteenth-century experiment, namely the establishment of colleges for monk-scholars at the universities, such as Gloucester College and Durham College, Oxford.[2] This had been a difficult undertaking, but was now beginning to pay a dividend and to

---

[1] Bodleian, MS. Bodley 158, fo. 142v; Durham Cathedral Muniments, Registrum II, fo. 205.

[2] For Gloucester College, Oxford, see *Snappe's Formulary*, 337–86; *Oxoniensia*, XI–XII (1946–7), 65–74; for Durham College, see *Collectanea III* (*OHS*, XXXII, 1896), 3–76. For the Black Monks' policy with regard to studies, see Pantin, *Chapters*, subject index, *s.vv.* Lectures, Studies, University.

produce a new type of monk, '*le moine universitaire*'. The English Black Monks had for some time voluntarily anticipated the legislation of Benedict XII (1336), which required one out of every twenty monks to be sent to university. Inevitably some slack or impoverished houses fell below their quota, as complaints in the provincial chapters show, but there is also evidence that there was, especially from the greater and better-ordered houses, a steady flow of monk-students to the universities, and that when these returned home as monk-graduates, they played a dominant part both in their own house and in the provincial chapters. The intellectual achievement of the monk-scholars is more difficult to assess, and will continue to be so until more work has been done on the surviving scholastic literature of the period. The monks cannot claim to have produced so many outstanding schoolmen as the friars, and they came late to the schools, but it would be a mistake to regard the monk-scholars merely as not very successful imitations of the friars. The two monk-scholars about whom we know most, Uthred and Easton, show themselves to be writers and thinkers with a very definite character of their own. Another important point about them is that whereas FitzRalph represents the opposition of the secular clergy to the mendicants, these two represent the attitude of the 'possessioners', of the endowed religious orders, and particularly of the Benedictines, towards the mendicants. The opposition of the monks came much more slowly than that of the seculars—there had been no Benedictine equivalent of William of St Amour—but it was none the less marked when it did come.

I. UTHRED OF BOLDON.[1] Uthred of Boldon was probably born between 1315 and 1325, and died in 1397. He took the Benedictine

---

[1] For Uthred's career and writings, see Tanner, *Bibliotheca*, 743; *Studies in medieval history presented to F. M. Powicke*, 363–85; *Bulletin of the Institute of Historical Research*, III (1925), 46; M. D. Knowles, 'The censured opinions of Uthred of Boldon', in *Proceedings of the British Academy*, XXXVII (1951), 305–42; M. E. Marcett, *Uthred de Boldon, Friar William Jordan and Piers Plowman* (New York, 1938); Pantin, *Chapters*, III, 318. There is an unpublished thesis (Ph.D., Manchester, 1936) by C. H. Thompson on 'Uthred of Boldon and his writings', which includes an edition of the *De dotatione* and other treatises.

habit at Durham in 1341 and was apparently professed in 1342. He was at Durham College, Oxford, from 1347 until probably about 1367, becoming a Doctor of Theology in 1357. The last thirty years of his life, *c*. 1367–97, were spent back in the north, partly as Subprior of Durham, partly as Prior of the nearby cell of Finchale. He was employed a good deal on the business of the provincial chapter of the English Black Monks, taking part, for instance, in the difficult and important visitation of Whitby in 1366, and he had sufficient name as a theologian to be sent by the king on a delegation to Avignon in 1373, to discuss papal provisions and papal subsidies. A picturesque but probably unreliable passage in the *Eulogium historiarum* represents him as taking part in a conference of lords, prelates and doctors in 1374,[1] where he is described as upholding the pope's temporal power, on the grounds that Peter has the 'two swords', while two friars, a Franciscan and an Augustinian, are made to deny the pope's temporal power. Even if the incident is fictitious and in the nature of a pamphlet, it at any rate shows that he was a public figure and a name to use, and it seems to represent his views accurately. Uthred was clearly valued by his order as a man of practical ability and zeal as well as for his scholarship, and like Wyclif he illustrates the way in which a fourteenth-century scholar could be drawn into public life; but on the whole he led a retired and rather academic life.

Uthred's writings, so far as they are known to us, consist of some twenty-one works, the majority of which survive. Some of his most important works were the product of controversy, sometimes with the friars, sometimes with Wyclif and the Wycliffites, and perhaps these two phases of controversy overlapped, that is to say, he may have been still skirmishing with the friars when he started fighting with Wyclif, who may have appeared to him at first as an extreme left-wing ally of the friars in the attack on the possessioners.

To the controversy with the friars, *c*. 1366–8, belong two works. First there is a short and undated *quaestio* concerning mendicancy,

---

[1] *Eulogium Historiarum*, III, 337; cf. above, p. 129.

in which Uthred argues that mendicancy is an impediment to the preaching of the Word of God. This is a direct attack on the friars, and probably represents a continuation of the controversy begun by FitzRalph.[1]

The other and more serious controversy with the friars took place between Uthred and William Jordan, a Dominican, *c.* 1366–8; it is described in Uthred's treatise *Contra iniustas querelas fratrum.* Apparently the friars had drawn up twenty-eight articles, containing the 'errors' which, they alleged, Uthred had been maintaining publicly in his lectures and determinations. Uthred is extremely indignant: the friars, he says, have attacked him behind his back instead of in the schools; they have misrepresented his teaching; they are illiterate [*laici ydiote*] and ignorant of logic, however learned they may be thought at home; they represent the 'perils from false brethren' spoken of by the Apostle; and according to the civil law they deserve to be beheaded for such libellous attacks. He proceeds to deny, or explain away, or defend the twenty-eight articles.[2]

Perhaps the most interesting feature is that the articles under dispute are not concerned with the obvious topics that divided the monks and the friars, such as poverty and mendicancy, but with more purely theological topics, especially grace and justification, and so they illustrate those theological preoccupations which can also be seen in Bradwardine and Buckingham, and in other theologians of this period on the Continent. Among other things, Uthred is seen here to be much interested in the question of the salvation of unbaptized persons, in which he resembles the poet Langland, and he elaborates a peculiar theory that everyone in the instant of death is given a 'clear vision' of God and a free 'election'

[1] Paris, Bibliothèque nationale, MS. Lat. 3183, fo. 160v. I owe this reference to Father Stephen Forte, O.P.

[2] M. E. Marcett, *op. cit.* 25–37, prints the treatise in full; Knowles, *art. cit.*, prints the articles, together with a valuable historical and theological discussion of them. Something like Uthred's theory of the 'clear vision' has been revived more than once in modern times.

between good and evil, and on this alone depends a man's salvation or damnation. Uthred's argument springs from a generous and charitable motive, a desire to demonstrate that everyone is given a fair chance, but the doctrine as he works it out is a dangerous one, for it would seem to reduce all the moral and spiritual life of a man, before the instant of death, to a triviality. To judge from Uthred's explanations, the friars had not in fact misrepresented his teaching so much as he makes out. It was clearly his theory of the 'clear vision' that was most attacked by them. This controversy became so violent that it was brought before the Archbishop of Canterbury, who after imposing silence on both parties in February 1368, in the following November condemned a whole series of thirty articles as erroneous; twenty-four of these correspond to the 'errors' ascribed to Uthred, the others may perhaps represent the teaching of Jordan.[1] The archbishop did not condemn Uthred by name, and his reputation and career do not seem to have suffered by this setback. But clearly tempers were rising, imputations of heresy were being made, and men were getting away from the purely academic and friendly disputes of the schools, to something more like the violence and desperation of the Wycliffite controversy, to the real heresy hunt.

Another group of Uthred's writings deals with church endowment and the relations of Church and State; these seem to be mainly directed against the Wycliffite attacks, but perhaps also partly against the friars.

The treatise *De dotatione ecclesie sponse Christi*[2] deals with the question whether it is right for the Church to be endowed with possessions, lordships and rents. First Uthred produces the arguments against endowment, mainly on historical grounds, as that there was no endowment of the Church under the natural law or under the law of Moses or in the early Church, and that there was

---

[1] Wilkins, III, 75; Knowles, *art. cit.* 340–1.
[2] Durham Cathedral Library, MS. A. IV. 33, fo. 69; Bodleian, MS. Bodley 859, fo. 277. I have based my summary of this treatise on the Bodley MS.

no such endowment at Rome until the third century, or in England until the time of King Lucius in the second century; moreover, endowments have evil effects. On the other hand the arguments in favour of endowment are stated, and here Uthred makes it clear that he accepts in some form the doctrine of Dominion by Grace. Adam forfeited dominion, Christ regained it; He alone is the true and principal lord, and He restores dominion to men who are regenerated through the Church. Therefore kings would be guilty of ingratitude if they did not endow the Church, which is the source of their dominion. With regard to the ecclesiastical exercise of lordship, Uthred argues that as the priesthood are more spiritual, therefore they are more discreet and suited to govern. He seems in effect to be equating ecclesiastics with the Aristotelian natural rulers or citizens, and provides an interesting theoretical justification of the age-old preponderance of clerics in government and administration, in fact for the 'Caesarian prelates' who were beginning to be attacked by Wyclif and Langland. Uthred goes on to enumerate the advantages of church endowment: it gives men greater freedom for contemplation and divine worship, it assists the relief of the poor, it gives the Church power against her enemies, such as heretics, it makes the building and ornamentation of the churches possible, and it increases the respect of the laity for the clergy. This treatise may possibly have originated as a defence of the possessioners against the mendicants rather than against the Wycliffites.

Another treatise in this group is the *Contra garrulos ecclesie dotationem impugnantes*.[1] This is directed against those 'false brethren' and 'pseudo-apostles' who incite temporal lords to chastise ecclesiastics and confiscate their goods in order to reduce

---

[1] Durham, MS. A. IV. 33, fo. 99. I have based my summary of this and the following treatise on the Durham MS. I am grateful to the Dean and Chapter of Durham for kindly depositing this MS. in the Bodleian Library for my use and for allowing parts of it to be photographed, and to the late Mr John Meade Falkner, who originally showed me the MS. (which was then in his possession) and allowed me to examine it, a few years before his death in 1932.

them to the poverty of Christ. This is more clearly aimed against the Wycliffites and their allies, such as John of Gaunt, though perhaps the mendicants may also be included. The curious epithet *garruli* may perhaps be intended as a translation of the word Lollard. Uthred produces seven arguments in defence of endowments. These include among other things the argument that the possessions in question are given primarily to God and the Church (as shown by the phrase used in charters, *Deo et ecclesie*), and only secondarily to God's servants, the churchmen; hence it is not right to deprive the owner for the misdeeds of His servants. Arguments are also brought forward to prove that things once given to God can never be taken back. Most interesting of all is the final argument, in which Uthred discusses the rights of patrons of churches, and this brings him into the realm of legal theory as well as into that of theology. He argues that a lord has no more right over things given by him or his predecessors to God and the Church, than he has over things given by other lords who are his equals or superiors; in neither case has he any right to confiscate goods so given, for the fault of the Church's servants. (The phrase about 'equals or superiors' may possibly leave a loophole for the rights of the king, as 'patron paramount', over gifts made by his inferiors.) Uthred bases his argument on the nature of Frankalmoin, 'pure and perpetual alms', which must mean that the donor reserves to himself no rights in what he is giving. He has to meet the objection that patrons do in fact exercise some rights over vacant churches, such as custody, the *congé d'élire*, and the confirmation of elections, and also the seizure of temporalities in certain cases where the prelate has committed a crime. These are explained away as being safeguards for the benefit of the churches concerned, not as arbitrary rights over them. This discussion is particularly interesting in view of the importance attached to founders' rights in medieval thought. Uthred also discusses whether a man can grant away anything in perpetuity, and whether a man can alienate property from his natural heir. Here again Uthred shows, incidentally, that he

171

takes for granted the doctrine of Dominion by Grace, as when he argues that there can be no lawful buying or selling, alienating or commuting, unless both parties have baptismal grace, and hence that if the heir is an unbaptized infant, the inheritance temporarily reverts to the next of kin until the heir is baptized.

A third treatise in this group is the *De naturali et necessaria connexione ac ordine sacerdotalis officii et regalis*,[1] dealing with the relations between the priestly and royal powers. Among the chief points which Uthred discusses are, first, the question which of the two powers is the higher (decided in favour of the priestly power); secondly, whether the king's power of punishment and coercion applies to the priesthood as well as to the laity (which is denied), and thirdly, whether the priesthood's power of binding and losing, setting up and deposing, applies to all men, high and low (which is affirmed). This treatise, at any rate in the form in which we now have it, must have been written some years after 1378, since it refers to the Great Schism as having lasted for 'many years', and discusses the problem of how to get rid of the 'false head', that is to say, the anti-pope: could the royal power remove the 'false head'? Here we have an important contemporary idea, that of calling in the lay power to deal with a delinquent Church, an idea that appears both in Wyclif's and in Langland's thought. Uthred is opposed to this: the true solution is for the cardinals and the clergy to be called together, and to trust in Christ for guidance.

Uthred was a senior contemporary of Wyclif; they knew each other at Oxford, and Wyclif, while combating Uthred, at first treated him with respect. Wyclif's *Determinatio* against Uthred, dated by Workman in the autumn of 1374,[2] is a reply to Uthred's teaching, that is to say, Uthred apparently had the effect of drawing Wyclif out. But it is difficult to establish the precise chronological relationship of Uthred's and Wyclif's works, especially

---

[1] Durham, MS. A. IV. 33, fo. 24.
[2] J. Wyclif, *Opera minora*, ed. J. Loserth (Wyclif Society, 1913), 404–30; cf. Workman, *John Wyclif*, I, 231, 257.

as published, written works must have been preceded by oral disputations in the schools. We have already seen how Uthred's written polemic against the friars had arisen out of his teaching in the schools.

Uthred's other theological works included treatises on the Church Militant, on the Eucharist, and on predestination (this last work has not survived). He also wrote two important treatises on the monastic life,[1] mainly defending it against Wycliffite attacks, but with some side blows against the mendicants. The first of these is the treatise *De substancialibus regule monachalis*, which defends the lawfulness of the three 'substantials' or vows of poverty, chastity, and obedience. Uthred outflanks the Wycliffite objection to the monastic orders as 'private religions', by arguing that monasticism is not merely something lawful, but is deeply rooted in the nature of man as a rational being. All men, as rational beings, are bound to practise some degree of poverty, chastity and obedience, which thus constitute a kind of primitive, natural rule imposed on all men at creation. The later monastic rules are an aid to the fulfilment of this. Thus all men are in a sense monks; to adapt Aristotle's phrase, we might say that man is by nature a monastic animal.

The other treatise *De perfectione vivendi in religione* deals with the problem whether perfection lies in the life of seculars or the life of regulars, that is, of those living the monastic life. To a certain extent, this is the age-old problem of the relative claims of the active and contemplative life. Uthred gives the traditional orthodox teaching that personal perfection consists in interior dispositions, such as faith, hope and charity, and not in external observances, and that it may therefore be attained in any state of life. As regards the claims of different ways of life to be regarded as the state of perfection, Uthred seems to think that the highest form consists of a mixed life, both active and contemplative at once, as practised by Christ and the Apostles. He ends the treatise with a very learned panegyric of the monastic life, quoting largely from

[1] *Studies in medieval history presented to F. M. Powicke*, 368–85.

the *Ecclesiastical Hierarchy* of the pseudo-Denys, of which he quotes five different translations and three commentaries.

Finally, the work by which Uthred was probably most widely known in the later Middle Ages, to judge from the number of manuscripts, was his *Meditatio*, a long meditative prayer, dwelling on God's mercy and man's ingratitude. It is satisfactory to know that this indefatigable controversialist also composed among other things a treatise 'On loving one's enemies', now unfortunately lost. Uthred was also remembered among the Durham community for a proverbial saying which seems to echo that distrust of excessive intellectualism felt by so many men in the later Middle Ages, as we have already noted. Half a century after his death, we find the Prior of Durham writing to a monk-scholar, reminding him of

that proverb of Master Uthred, which I gave as a special charge to you and all the scholars sent to the University from the time I took over the government of the Priory: namely that it is no good losing the substance for the sake of the accidents. The substance I call celebrating and hearing Mass, saying the Divine Office at the proper hours, and fulfilling as a first duty the other things that belong to the monastic life; and as a secondary matter, as opportunity allows, to give oneself up to books and learning.[1]

I have discussed Uthred's writings at some length, in order to give a picture of the various topics in which a leading controversialist of the later fourteenth century would become involved. But Uthred was more than a mere controversialist; he seems, like Mabillon, three centuries later, to be one of those who are stimulated by controversy into producing a constructive piece of work. This at any rate is true of his two monastic treatises, and here too he shows a remarkable serenity and rationality in his manner of treatment, as when demonstrating the rational and natural character of monasticism. I think this is, among other things, an interesting by-product of the Aristotelian revival of the thirteenth century, and it

[1] *Hist. Dunelm. Scriptores Tres*, Appendix, cclxiii.

contrasts favourably with the shrillness and violence of his own earlier polemics against the friars, and still more with the violence and bitterness of the later stage of the Wycliffite controversy.

2. ADAM EASTON. Adam Easton, monk of Norwich and afterwards cardinal, began his career like Uthred as a monk scholar, but with a much more adventurous and dramatic conclusion.[1] He was born probably about 1325, became a monk of Norwich Cathedral Priory, and was at Gloucester College, Oxford, from some time before 1355 until 1366. He incepted as D.D. in 1363–4, and was *Prior studentium* (head of Gloucester College) in 1366. During the middle of his Oxford career, at some date between 1357 and 1363, he was temporarily recalled to Norwich to organize preaching by the monks in the cathedral, and to silence the mendicants. When Gloucester College wrote to ask for him to be sent back to Oxford, the Prior of Norwich explained that he was indispensable at home:[2]

To the venerable fathers and lords, the Prior and the whole company of Black Monks studying at Oxford, from your humble servants the Prior and convent of Norwich, reverences and honours due to such fathers, with all prompt desire to please. By the tenor of your reverend letters, we understand the deplorable infertility of the sons of mother university studying at Oxford, to such an extent, as you assert, that out of the whole order of Black Monks there are scarcely to be found three bachelors studying theology at the present time; among whom your most gracious goodness considers our brother and your fellow, Adam Eston, to be senior, and out of the militia of scholastic labour, in the course of his studies to be nearest to the doctor's reward. Wherefore you have asked us, with sincere affection, to send him back next year and effectually restore him to the maternal bosom of the schools, whence we have recalled him for a short time for a certain cause. Indeed reverend fathers and lords, with the greatest desire we would like to accede to your wishes, as we ought, if we were not hindered by the reasons given below.

[1] For Easton's career and writings, see Tanner, *Bibliotheca*, 266; *DNB*; Pantin, *Chapters*, III, 28 n., 320.

[2] Pantin, *Chapters*, III, 28.

For of old, in our cathedral church, situated as it is in such a populous city and country, it has been the custom to have many sermons of God's word preached to the people at certain times; and this duty used to be undertaken, at the cost of entreaties and gifts, yet with some difficulty, by the mendicant friars, who are the enemies of our order, and indeed of all churchmen, loosing their backbiting mouths at everyone. However, with unanimous deliberation, considering it a shame and a detriment to us that these preachings in our own church should be undertaken by friars, we have decided altogether to exclude all friars, and so far have imposed that laborious work upon our own brethren. But because that harvest is laborious and great, and our labourers are wearied and few, we have thought it necessary to set up our said brother [Eston] as a subtle and experienced reeve over these reapers who are thus wearied; lest the sheaves of the word of God, bound up in bundles, be incautiously sown amongst biting, envious men and the mouths of those that speak iniquity. Who also, our said brother, may baffle the backbiting mouths of those that rise up against us, and impose silence upon these Sadducees. For certain matters against sound doctrine and the liberty of the Church were brought forward by certain friars, whom by true doctrine he has restrained from their erroneous way, and will shortly, God willing, completely triumph over them. For blessed be the Most High, his doctrine enjoys special favour among clergy and people. But if his absence came to be known at present, we fear that they [the friars] would at once come up like mice out of their holes, and we have no one else to resist them in wisdom or learning, but they would proudly make broad their fringes exceedingly.

Wherefore, lest these things or worse happen, it seems to us necessary either to recall our brother Thomas de Brinton, or to keep our brother Adam for a short time. We hope indeed soon to exalt them both to the pinnacle of the doctorate, God willing, and with the intervention of your gracious help. May it please your reverend fatherhood and the lordship of your whole venerable company to have us favourably excused in these and in other altogether necessary things. For we would shudder greatly, God knows, to offend such a company, or to delude with feigned excuses such a congregated flower of the order. May the wisdom of God the Father enlighten your scholastic acts, to the exaltation of the universal Church and the special honour of the whole order. Amen.

This letter was probably written during the last stages of the struggle between FitzRalph and the friars (c. 1357–60), when the English Benedictines subscribed money to support FitzRalph, who was 'fighting against the friars in the cause of God, as we believe', to quote the St Albans chronicler.[1] It should be noted that the friars are accused of teaching not only against 'sound doctrine', but also against the 'liberty of the Church'. This probably refers to some dispute about church endowments or the taxation of the clergy; we have seen how two friars supported the taxation of the clergy in the Parliament of 1371.[2] It is interesting to notice that a cathedral city, as well as the universities, could be a centre of lively theological controversy.

After leaving Oxford Easton went to the Roman Curia, probably accompanying Cardinal Langham, a fellow Benedictine, in February 1369. He was proctor at the Curia for the English Benedictines in 1373. In 1376 he wrote from the Curia to the Abbot of Westminster, asking for copies of Wyclif's writings,[3] and it may well have been Easton who was responsible for the papal condemnation of Wyclif in 1377. At the time of the much disputed election of Urban VI in 1378, Easton was present in Rome and was in fact among the crowd, and he has left an interesting account of his conversation with one of the cardinals after the election.[4] He is an important witness in favour of the validity of Urban's election, for he tells us that the cardinals had agreed to elect Urban before the conclave began. In 1381 he was made a cardinal, perhaps as being a strong English supporter of the Urbanist cause, or as a distinguished theologian, or as both, and he afterwards became involved in the stormy politics of the Great Schism. In 1385 he was one of those suspected of conspiracy by Urban VI, and was imprisoned, tortured and deprived of his benefices. He was reinstated in 1389, and died in 1397; his fine tomb still stands in his titular church of St Cecilia in Trastevere.

---

[1] *Gesta abbatum mon. S. Albani*, II, 405; Pantin, *Chapters*, III, 255.
[2] See above, p. 128.　　　　　　　　[3] Pantin, *Chapters*, III, 76.
[4] L. Macfarlane, 'An English account of the election of Urban VI, 1378', in *Bulletin of the Institute of Historical Research*, XXVI (1953), 75–85.

Like Uthred, Easton was a prolific writer; he is credited by Bale and others with about twenty-one works, most of which are now lost. His most important work seems to have been his *Defensorium ecclesiastice potestatis*,[1] dealing with the spiritual and temporal powers and their relationship. In his introduction Adam tells us that this book was the result of twenty years' study. He was interested in the conflicting views of political theorists. Some men, he says, extol the power of kings, giving them the right to take away the goods of a delinquent Church, denying the Church any coercive power over its subjects, and saying that the clergy should be reduced to apostolic poverty; others claim that the pope is the monarch of the whole world. In order to deal with these problems, Easton had turned to the study of Scripture, and this in turn necessitated learning Hebrew, with the aid of a Jewish scholar, a truly monumental and original approach to political science. While at the outset of his studies Easton had evidently had in mind the attacks of William of Occam, Marsilius of Padua and John of Jandun, the immediate occasion of his writing the *Defensorium* was the news of the attacks of a certain 'notable doctor' on the rights of the Church, which I think means the news of Wyclif's attacks; as we have seen, Easton was corresponding with the Abbot of Westminster about this in 1376. The book was probably written between 1376 and 1378, and was dedicated to Urban VI; it was perhaps partly as a reward for this that Easton was made a cardinal.

The *Defensorium* was a vast work in six books, of which only the prologue and the first book survive, occupying 366 folios in one manuscript; it is possible that the whole work was never completed. The work was written in the form of an imaginary dialogue between a bishop and a king, supporting the claims of Church and State respectively. In the first book Uthred undertakes a historical examination of three topics, the priesthood, the royal power, and dominion (or lordship); he discusses the nature and relationship of

---

[1] For the *Defensorium* see *EHR*, LI (1936), 675–80. Mr Leslie Macfarlane is making a study of Easton and his writings, especially the *Defensorium*.

these three powers, as exercised in God's government of the world, in the angelic hierarchy, in man's state of innocence before the fall, under the law of nature after the fall, under the Mosaic Law, and under the Christian dispensation. At every stage he is at pains to demonstrate the superiority of the priestly over the temporal power. The book thus has an elaborately worked-out and symmetrical plan, but from time to time the argument leads to excursions into such varied topics as predestination and the problem of evil, an analogy between the cardinals and the higher orders of angels, powers of legislation, the jurisdiction of infidel kings, the monarchies and empires of the ancient world, papal taxation, and evangelical poverty. To Easton the Old Testament seems to have appealed as providing a fascinating field for political analysis and speculation, rather as the Greek city state or the New World have appealed to political thinkers in other ages.

The remaining books are known to us only from the summary given in Easton's prologue: in Books II and III he proposed to combat the views of Marsilius, of John of Jandun and of the *Dialogus* of William of Occam; in Book IV, to deal with the kingship and priesthood of Christ, with references to the mendicant controversy; and in Books V and VI to show that the pope is monarch of the world and that emperors and kings need his confirmation and approval.

The *Defensorium* is interesting as showing an English monastic writer wholeheartedly defending the highest papal claims in temporal as well as in spiritual affairs. Easton tells us that his aim was to 'remove ambiguities from the hearts of kings'; one wonders whether he hoped to convert Edward III or John of Gaunt or the young Richard II to his views. He was indeed writing just about the time of the negotiations for a concordat, but the English Crown, while ready to come to terms in practice, was always unwilling to concede a principle.

Easton is thoroughly familiar with the Continental literature on his subject, with Dante, Marsilius of Padua, John of Jandun,

12-2

Occam—more familiar probably than his contemporaries in England; it is doubtful for instance whether Wyclif knew of Marsilius. It was because of this familiarity with radical writers like Marsilius and John of Jandun that Wyclif's teaching aroused alarm at the Curia sooner than at home; Gregory XI, in condemning Wyclif in 1377, reproached the English bishops for their slowness to perceive the danger. Easton's polemic was primarily directed against Marsilius, Jandun and Occam; in the general plan of the work, they were to have two out of the six books devoted to them. But we can see that as Book I came to be written, Easton came to be more and more concerned with Wyclif and devoted a good deal of space to refuting him.

Easton was very polite to his opponents; he apparently referred to them as 'men of great learning and abundance of sanctity'. Evidently the controversy, at least when he began writing, was still at its gentlemanly stage. One is reminded of the Austin friar, Adam Stocton, who first described Wyclif in his notebook as *venerabilis doctor* and then later changed this to *execrabilis seductor*.[1]

Easton was among other things a devoted admirer and defender of St Brigit, the Swedish mystic who had vied with St Catherine of Siena in her denunciation of abuses and her appeals to the Papacy for reform. He may have known St Brigit at the Curia. He certainly wrote and laboured for her canonization, and he says that her intercession had comforted him under the tortures inflicted by Urban VI. About 1390–1 Easton sent Pope Boniface IX a treatise in which he refuted, in forty-one articles, certain criticisms made against the rule which St Brigit had made for the religious order (the Brigittines) which she founded.[2] The points to which the critics objected, and which Easton undertook to answer, were St Brigit's claim that the rule had been dictated to her by Our Lord, the clumsy and defective style of the rule, and certain allegedly heterodox passages; they also objected to a monastic rule being

---

[1] Gwynn, *English Austin Friars*, 239.
[2] Bodleian, MS. Hamilton 7, fo. 229, 248.

published by a woman. St Brigit was apparently the first woman to found a religious order, so that an important principle was at stake. The fact that Easton so ardently defended St Brigit shows that he was by no means a hide-bound conservative and that he had sympathy with the mystical movements of his day. It was a true instinct that made him support St Brigit and her order, for as the history of the fifteenth and sixteenth centuries was to show, the Brigittines, along with the Carthusians and the Friars Observant, represented the most fervent and heroic element in English monasticism.

Easton, as might be expected, was something of a bibliophile, and accumulated a large collection of books, which he bequeathed to his former monastery of Norwich;[1] they were sent from Rome to Norwich in six barrels, the king granting them a special clearance through the customs.[2] Some of his manuscripts survive; they include books on canon law, astronomy, a Hebrew dictionary, Origen, the Pseudo-Denys, and works on the mendicant controversy. One manuscript contains an illuminated copy of Fitz-Ralph's *De pauperie Salvatoris*,[3] with pictures of friars of the four orders accompanied by demons! An even more interesting manuscript is what seems to be Easton's copy of the *Policraticus* of John of Salisbury,[4] which may have been an important source of his political theory. Easton clearly valued it highly, for when he bought it, it was defective, and the missing parts (over sixty leaves) have been made good in what is apparently either Easton's own handwriting or that of his secretary—no small effort for a busy man.

[1] On Easton's books, see N. R. Ker in *Cambridge Bibliographical Society Transactions*, I (1949), 17; the books are nos. 50–2, and 80–4 in his list.
[2] Rymer (O), VIII, 501.
[3] Corpus Christi College, Cambridge, MS. 180.
[4] Balliol College, Oxford, MS. 300 B.

THOMAS BRUNTON, MONK OF NORWICH AND
BISHOP OF ROCHESTER

The career of Thomas Brunton (c. 1320–99)[1] is that of an outstanding monk-scholar, and so invites comparison with those of
Uthred of Boldon and Adam Easton. He led a more public life
than Uthred, while, unlike Easton, his public life, though begun at
the Roman Curia, was mainly led in an English bishopric. He is
the outstanding monk-bishop of the period, apart from Simon
Langham, and may perhaps be regarded as a Benedictine pendant
to the great friar-bishops of the late thirteenth century, Kilwardby
and Pecham. Here, as with Uthred and Easton, we can see the
thirteenth-century monastic experiment of establishing colleges at
the universities bearing fruit.

Brunton was probably born about 1320 and like Easton became
a monk of Norwich Cathedral Priory. The first phase of his adult
career was spent as a university student. According to a remark in
one of his sermons, he studied for a time at Cambridge, perhaps
c. 1352–3. He was at Gloucester College, Oxford, for a longer
period, perhaps c. 1355–63. He incepted as Doctor of Canon Law
c. 1363–4, apparently at the same time that Easton incepted as
Doctor of Divinity. The next phase of his career was at the Roman
Curia, where we find him acting as a papal penitentiary and proctor
for the English Benedictines, certainly by 1366; he may have been
a penitentiary as early as 1362. The last phase of his career was spent
as a bishop at home in England. In 1373 the monks of Rochester
elected their Prior as Bishop of Rochester. Their choice was set aside,
and the pope instead provided Brunton to the see of Rochester.
Brunton declared, in one of his sermons, that he owed his comparatively small and poor church, not to prayers or payment, not
to letters (on his behalf), not to his own pressure, but only to God

[1] For Brunton's career and sermons, see Sister M. A. Devlin, 'Bishop Brunton and his
sermons', in *Speculum*, XIV (1939), 324–44. Cf. also Pantin, *Chapters*, III, 61, 318
(*s.v.* Brinton); F. A. Gasquet, *The old English Bible and other essays* (London, 1897), 67;
Owst, *Preaching in medieval England* (Cambridge, 1926), 15, and *passim*.

and the pope. Brunton does in fact represent the type of man who would hardly have attained to a bishopric but for the help of a university career and papal provision; here at least we can see those two factors functioning at their best. It is to be noted, however, that he never rose higher than Rochester. It was not the last time that Rochester was given as a consolation prize to a distinguished scholar; St John Fisher is another example in a later age. Brunton died in 1389, but during his last years, from about 1382, he was an invalid and therefore out of action most of the time. His active period as bishop and preacher was thus between 1373 and 1382.

It is above all as a preacher that Brunton is well known to us, thanks especially to the collection of 103 sermons, preached between 1373 and 1383, that has survived.[1] These sermons were preached on various occasions: at Rochester, at St Paul's Cross, in Convocation and during Parliament, and at funerals. He was prominent in Parliament between 1376 and 1380, and preached a famous sermon on the day after the coronation of Richard II. Thus he was most active as a preacher just in a very critical period, the last years of Edward III and the first years of Richard II, the period of the Good Parliament and of the second recension of Piers Plowman, when the nation was seething with discontent. Brunton's career, like that of his predecessors Sheppey and Trillek, shows that a good preaching bishop was a very useful man to have at Rochester, within easy call of the capital; poor as it was, the see was not so insignificant a post as might at first sight appear.

Brunton's chief characteristic as a preacher is that he is an outspoken critic, in a great age of pulpit criticism. In the first place he attacks the abuses and especially the social abuses of the age. He attacks particularly the vices of the rich and their oppression of the poor, excessive taxation, anti-social sins like usury, unjust maintenance and false witness. He is equally prepared to denounce the excesses of the peasantry in the 1381 rising, or the ignorance of the

---

[1] British Museum, MS. Harl. 3760; these sermons have been edited by Sister Devlin in the Camden Third Series, vols. LXXXV and LXXXVI (London, 1954).

clergy; men, he says, will commit the custody of a thousand souls to men whom they would not trust with a thousand pears or apples. He particularly denounces the merciless exploitation of the poor by the rich, in which Christians compare unfavourably with Jews and Saracens. Among the Jews, money is collected from the rich to feed the poor; among the Christians, money is collected from the poor to maintain the rich in their pride. When tenths are levied on the churches or taxes on the people, no one thinks of applying the money to feed the poor who are dying of hunger.[1]

In the second place Brunton attacks the rich, the lay magnates, as persecutors and would-be despoilers of the Church, and he comes forward as a champion of the rights and liberties of the Church. We can see here the theoretical arguments of men like Uthred or Easton about the superiority of the Church being applied to practical politics. Brunton was one of the four bishops who in 1377 remonstrated with John of Gaunt over the taxation of the clergy; the clergy, they claimed, 'are of such authority and so free that laymen have no right to judge them or meddle with them'.[2] It is not surprising that Brunton came into conflict with Wyclif, who must have stood for all that was most repugnant to him. In more than one sermon, without mentioning names, he is obviously attacking the alliance of Gaunt and Wyclif; temporal lords, he says, take to themselves extraordinary masters, and support them in their errors, having itching ears,[3] and their aim is to reduce the Church to such a state that it shall have no rights, no privileges, no lordship except what they shall allow. Brunton urges the clergy to unite in the face of the manifest danger to the Church; 'every day we see Christ being crucified in His members, and Barabbas set free'.[4] He seems to think that the lesser clergy are less compliant and more zealous for ecclesiastical liberty than the prelates. What is specially interesting about Brunton is this combination of a rather

[1] Sister Devlin, art. cit. 337.
[2] The anonimalle chronicle, ed. V. H. Galbraith (Manchester, 1927), 100.
[3] Cf. II Tim. iv. 3   [4] Sister Devlin, art. cit. 340–2.

radical tone, of highly critical attacks on the rich and on social abuses, on the one hand, with a strongly conservative defence of ecclesiastical rights and liberties on the other.[1] It is interesting to compare and contrast his attitude with that of Langland and Wyclif; he has of course far more in common with Langland than with Wyclif. Like them, he criticizes social and moral evils, but unlike Langland, and still more unlike Wyclif, he will not allow the right of the lay power to coerce the Church.

[1] Cf. the *Memoriale presbiterorum*, below, p. 210.

PART III

RELIGIOUS LITERATURE

CHAPTER IX

MANUALS OF INSTRUCTION FOR PARISH PRIESTS

IN some respects, as in ecclesiastical politics, for instance, the fourteenth century, when viewed as the outcome of the thirteenth century, may seem disappointing, something of a misfit or an anticlimax; thus we may ask whether the episcopal appointments of the fourteenth century were what men like Innocent III had intended. But in the realm of religious literature we can see, in the clearest and most satisfactory way, the achievement of the fourteenth century as the logical outcome of forces at work in the thirteenth century and earlier.

There were three factors at work, which were closely interconnected. In the first place there was the disciplinary legislation of the Church; this was the product of the great movement for ecclesiastical reform, which had been going on from the eleventh to the thirteenth century, culminating in the Lateran Council of 1215 and in the synodal constitutions of the English bishops in the thirteenth century, which followed the lead of the Lateran Council.[1] These constitutions provided, among other things, an elaborate programme of religious instruction for the laity; and this was all the more necessary because of the great social and economic phenomenon of the age, the revival of town life and the consequent rise of an educated laity. It is impossible to exaggerate the importance of the educated layman in late medieval ecclesiastical history.

Secondly, there was the development of a technical literature, especially through the compilation of various *Summae*, dealing with

---

[1] M. Gibbs and J. Lang, *Bishops and Reform* (Oxford, 1934), part III, *passim*; C. R. Cheney, *English synodalia in the thirteenth century* (Oxford, 1941), *passim*; E. J. Arnould, *Le manuel des péchés* (Paris, 1940), chapter I.

canon law and moral theology;[1] while at the same time there was the development of preaching (especially helped on by the friars) and of manuals for preachers.[2] All this was in one way or another the outcome of that increasing systematization of knowledge which was encouraged in the schools of the twelfth and thirteenth centuries. Religious knowledge no longer meant browsing and ruminating over the sacred page; it was a matter of *distinctiones* and *schemata*, of definitions and subdivisions, of almost mathematical precision.

Thirdly, there was a particular line or process of devotional and mystical development, which had been going on since the eleventh century; it had begun with men like John of Fécamp, St Anselm and St Peter Damiani, and had been carried on, for instance, by St Bernard and the Victorines in the twelfth century and by the Franciscans, especially St Bonaventure, in the thirteenth century. In this line of development, devotion is concentrated, with an intensity of personal feeling and tenderness, more and more on the Person of Christ, and particularly on His Passion and on the Holy Name. Characteristic and familiar expressions of this can be seen, for instance, in the hymn *Jesu dulcis memoria* or, at a later date, in the Stations of the Cross. It is difficult to find a satisfactory name for this development: one might call it Christo-centric piety, or affective piety, or simply the devotional movement. Needless to say, this devotional movement continued to flourish and spread in the fourteenth century, and in one way or another has profoundly affected Christian spirituality ever since.[3]

The various types of fourteenth-century religious literature roughly correspond to the factors just enumerated. In the first

[1] Arnould, *op. cit.* 38–46; Cheney, *op. cit.* 53–4; J. Dietterle, 'Die summae confessorum von ihren Anfängen an bis zu Silverius Prierius', in *Zeitschrift für Kirchengeschichte*, XXIV–XXVIII (1903–7); A. Teetaert, *La confession aux laïques dans l'église latine* (Paris, 1926). 233–5, 347–59, 440–59. For a list of *Summae* produced in England during the thirteenth century, see Appendix below, p. 219.

[2] See below, p. 235; A. G. Little, *Studies in English Franciscan History*, chapter IV.

[3] P. Pourrat, *La spiritualité chrétienne* (Paris, 1946), II, especially chapter I; A. Wilmart, *Auteurs spirituels et textes dévots du moyen âge latin* (Paris, 1932), 62–3, 127–37, 476–82; *Poems of John of Hoveden*, ed. F. J. E. Raby (SS, CLIV, 1939), xviii; R. W. Southern, *The making of the middle ages* (London, 1953), 231 ff.

place there are the manuals of instruction for parish priests, mainly though not exclusively in Latin; these are the direct outcome of the first factor, the disciplinary legislation of the thirteenth-century bishops, but also owe something to the second factor, the canonical and moral literature.

Secondly, there are the vernacular religious and moral treatises, some in prose, some in verse, dealing with the vices and virtues, the ten commandments, and so forth, and intended for the laity as well as for the less educated clergy. This type of literature derives mainly from the second factor mentioned above, the literature of moral theology, of which it is essentially a popularization, but it is also connected with the first factor, the programmes of religious instruction laid down by the bishops, while in another direction it is influenced by the devotional and mystical movement. The vernacular treatises, it may be noticed, carry the purpose of the manuals for parish priests a stage further, by diffusing religious knowledge among the laity.

Thirdly, there are the writings of the mystics and the religious lyrics of the fourteenth century. These, of course, are mainly the result of the third factor, the Christo-centric devotional development, but are also connected, more closely than might be expected at first sight, with the moral treatises and even with the instructions for priests. Indeed, the marked taste for mystical literature among the more devout laity of the fourteenth and fifteenth centuries presupposes a thorough grounding in dogmatic and moral instruction, through the pulpit and the confessional as well as through reading. Such a state of affairs would have been impossible with a completely disorganized and ignorant clergy and laity, and it represents the final outcome, on however limited a scale, of what Innocent III and the bishops had been working for.

The starting point of the manuals of instruction is the legislation of the Lateran Council of 1215 and particularly the decree *Omnis utriusque sexus*, making annual confession to the parish priest and annual communion at Easter obligatory on all Christians. If this legislation was going to be carried out seriously, it meant that both priests and laity must be educated up to it, priests must be instructed in the elements of moral theology, particularly in the technique of hearing confessions, and the laity too must receive a minimum of necessary instruction. Subsequent documents show that confessors were expected to cross-examine penitents on their religious knowledge as well as on their sins, and in this way the confessional was as important as the pulpit as a potential means of religious instruction.[1] The correct use of the sacrament of penance is a theme which dominates or underlies most of the religious literature of the thirteenth and fourteenth centuries, from the constitutions of the bishops down to such unexpected places as certain passages in Langland, Chaucer and Gower.

Several of the thirteenth-century bishops had dealt in their synodal constitutions with religious instruction and the technique of confession. Alexander of Stavensby, Bishop of Lichfield, in his constitutions (c. 1224–37) provided a set of general regulations for parish priests; a model sermon to be preached by the priest on the seven deadly sins; and a treatise on confession, instructing the priest how to hear confessions and how to examine penitents, and dealing with satisfaction, excommunication and reserved sins. The bishop ordered that these constitutions should be copied and kept by every priest.[2] Walter Cantilupe, Bishop of Hereford, in his constitutions (c. 1240), dealt with the administration of the sacraments, and under the heading of confession, gave a programme of what the priest was to teach the people: the ten commandments, the seven sins, the seven sacraments, and the creed; he also mentioned a treatise on confession, which all priests were to possess and use.[3]

---

[1] On preaching and instruction in the confessional as alternatives, the author of the *Oculus sacerdotis* writes: 'But if the priest, on account of the shortness of time and the multitude of penitents, cannot explain such matters to each one individually, then he ought to preach them publicly at the beginning of Lent'; quoted in H. E. Allen, *Writings*, 103. Cf. also A. G. Little, *Studies in English Franciscan History*, 105, 120.

[2] Wilkins, I, 640; Cheney, *op. cit.* 42.   [3] Wilkins, I, 665; Cheney, *op. cit.* 42–3.

The great bishop Grosseteste of Lincoln probably took his pastoral duties more seriously than any bishop of his age. He wrote several treatises on confession, and also a short but elaborate manual of instruction for parish priests, named *Templum Domini*, which must have acquired some popularity, as some sixty-five manuscripts survive in English and foreign libraries.[1] The central part of the work is in effect a treatise on confession, but other topics, such as the ten commandments, the virtues and vices, and the sacraments, are worked in, and a great deal of instruction is ingeniously packed into a small space. Much of the matter is set out more or less in diagram form. Thus he shows how every virtue is a mean between two extremes, as for example with Hope:

Presumptio: hac sperantur speranda et non speranda: superfluum.
Spes: hac sperantur speranda et non speranda non sperantur: virtus.
Desperatio: hac nec speranda sperantur nec non speranda: diminutio.

Later in the thirteenth century there are two outstanding and elaborate examples of episcopal legislation on this subject. Archbishop Pecham, in the Provincial Council of Lambeth in 1281, issued an elaborate code, which among other things dealt with the administration of the sacraments and especially confession, and with the duty of publishing excommunications. It was this last matter that brought Pecham into conflict with the king, and this shows how easily a matter of practical instruction to parish priests could become a burning topic of controversy between Church and State. The most important part of Pecham's legislation for our purpose is the section *De informatione simplicium*, beginning *Ignorantia sacerdotum*; this gives a programme of religious instruction: the fourteen articles of faith, the ten commandments of the Law and the two commandments of the Gospel, the seven works of mercy, the seven virtues, the seven vices, and the seven sacraments.[2] These are to be expounded to the people in the vernacular four

[1] S. Harrison Thomson, *The writings of Robert Grosseteste* (Cambridge, 1940), 138.
[2] Wilkins, II, 54–7; for the influence of Pecham's legislation, see D. L. Douie, *Archbishop Pecham* (Oxford, 1952), 134, 138–42.

times a year. This, as a provincial constitution, became henceforth the standard legislation on the subject. Its influence was not confined to the southern province, for Archbishop Thoresby of York used it as the basis of his 'catechism' in 1357.

In 1287, Bishop Quivil of Exeter, besides making constitutions, also issued a *Summula* or treatise, of which all priests were to possess a copy; this deals with the ten commandments, the seven sins, and so forth, and instructs the priest both in the hearing of confessions and in giving religious instruction to the people.[1] This was evidently regarded as a standard work for the diocese, for in 1319 we find Bishop Stapeldon of Exeter telling an ill-instructed priest that he must learn Bishop Quivil's *Summula* by heart during the next six months, if he wants to keep his benefice.[2]

It should be noted that these bishops not only sketched out regulations and programmes of instruction for parish priests in their constitutions, but they also sent round tracts (for instance on confession) for priests to copy out and keep and learn by heart; and it is these episcopal tracts that are the ancestors of the fourteenth-century 'manual' literature that we are about to consider. There is an interesting contrast in method between the thirteenth and fourteenth centuries. In the thirteenth century, bishops were fond of legislating in synods; there are some twenty-three such synodal constitutions between 1219 and 1268, many of which are derived from each other, and altogether these represent a remarkable concerted effort. In the fourteenth century, the bishops' synodal legislation became much less frequent and less important, apart from the provincial constitutions made from time to time by the Archbishops of Canterbury. When a fourteenth-century bishop wanted to issue instructions on any subject, he preferred to do it by issuing a 'mandate' or circular letter, not unlike the pastoral letters of modern times; thus an energetic bishop like Grandisson of Exeter issued a very large number of these. And when it came to

[1] Wilkins, II, 162–8.
[2] *Register of Walter de Stapeldon*, ed. F. C. Hingeston-Randolph (Exeter, 1902), 242.

compiling tracts or manuals of instruction for parish priests, the work was almost entirely left to those who were not bishops; thus the fourteenth century is an age of non-episcopal compilations. We must now turn to examine these fourteenth-century manuals for parish priests, taking them as far as possible in chronological order.

THE 'OCULUS SACERDOTIS'

According to Boston of Bury (in the fifteenth century) and John Bale (in the sixteenth century),[1] this treatise was written by William of Pagula,[2] and there seems no reason for rejecting this. William of Pagula probably came from the village of Paull near Kingston-on-Hull, in Holderness, an area which produced a number of successful clerks in this period. He became Vicar of Winkfield, near Windsor, in the diocese of Salisbury, in 1314,[3] in the last year of Bishop Henry of Ghent's episcopate; the living was in the gift of the Dean and Chapter of Salisbury. In view of Henry of Ghent's interest in reviving theological teaching at Salisbury, and his packing the Salisbury chapter with learned men,[4] it is perhaps not an accident that the writer of this most important pastoral work should be connected with the Salisbury diocese and the Salisbury chapter; possibly he was a protégé of Ghent's. The writer of the *Oculus* tells us that he held the office of penitentiary, and we know that William of Pagula was a penitentiary in 1322 for the deanery of Reading and later for the whole archdeaconry of Berkshire.[5] The writer also cites the synodal constitutions of Salisbury, and this would be natural for William of Pagula.

In addition to the *Oculus sacerdotis*, which will be discussed presently, William of Pagula seems to be the author of several other

[1] Tanner, *Bibliotheca*, xl; J. Bale, *Index Britanniae scriptorum*, ed. R. L. Poole and M. Bateson (Oxford, 1902), 143.
[2] For what follows, I owe much to the help of Father Leonard Boyle, O.P., who is making a study of William of Pagula and his writings. Cf. also H. W. C. Davis, in *Zeitschrift der Savigny-Stiftung, Kanonistische Abteilung*, III (1913), 349.
[3] *Registrum Simonis de Gandavo*, II, 822.   [4] See above, p. 113.
[5] Salisbury Diocesan Registry, Reg. Mortival II, fo. 132.

works: the *Summa summarum*, a large compendium of canon law and theology in five books and 257 chapters, dealing with all the possible problems that could confront ecclesiastics, from prelates to parish priests, written *c.* 1325–7; the *Speculum prelatorum*, written *c.* 1320–6, an even larger work, which only survives in one manuscript; the *Speculum religiosorum*, written *c.* 1320–6, explaining the canon law affecting monks; and a very outspoken letter to Edward III,[1] written in 1331, denouncing the abuses of purveyance and forced labour by the king's servants, abuses which were specially felt in the neighbourhood of Windsor.

We know very little about William of Pagula's life. In one passage of the *Summa summarum* he seems to describe himself as Doctor of Canon Law at Oxford; he died probably about 1332, and there is no evidence that he ever rose higher than Vicar of Winkfield and penitentiary.[2] Perhaps this comparative obscurity was self-chosen; it is certainly remarkable, for he was one of the few outstanding canonist writers that later medieval England produced, comparable in his own way to John Acton or Lyndwood. He seems to be the first writer of a manual for English parish clergy to make use of the local English legislation, such as the constitutions of the thirteenth-century papal legates and Archbishops of Canterbury, as well as the general law of the Church, the Decretum, the Decretals, and so on. He is also remarkable for combining a mastery of canon law with a genuine interest in pastoral theology and a desire to improve the cure of souls; he reminds us that we cannot always put 'theologians' and 'canonists' into separate, watertight compartments, and that we must not dismiss the canonists as a race of soulless administrators. It is interesting to

---

[1] Printed in J. Moisant, *De speculo regis Edwardi III* (Paris, 1891), 83–123. The author does not hesitate to remind the young king of the fates of Gaveston, Despenser and Mortimer, *ibid.* 116, 119–120. For references to Windsor Forest, see *ibid.* 100, 102, 106. The identification of this letter as the work of William of Pagula is due to Father Leonard Boyle.

[2] That he resided on his benefice seems likely from his appointment as a local penitentiary and from his employment to carry out a sequestration, *Registrum Adae de Orleton*, ed. A. T. Bannister (C and YS, 1908), 318, 348, 353.

notice that some passages of William of Pagula's *Oculus sacerdotis* are incorporated into one of the treatises (the *Judica me*) of the contemporary mystic Richard Rolle;[1] there was evidently something in the canonist's work that appealed to the mystic.

The *Oculus sacerdotis* is divided into three parts: Part I is sometimes known as the *Pars oculi*, Part II as the *Dextra pars*, Part III as the *Sinistra pars*. Part I seems to have been written last, *c.* 1326–8, Parts II and III having been written apparently *c.* 1320–3.

Part I is a manual for confessors. It begins by instructing the priest how to hear confessions, how to interrogate the penitent concerning his religious knowledge and concerning the seven deadly sins and so forth. Special injunctions and interrogations are given as suitable for particular sorts and conditions of men and women, such as drunkards or wrathful men; a good deal of this is taken from the early thirteenth-century *Summa de penitentia* of Thomas of Chabham, subdean of Salisbury.

And the priest ought to inquire of the penitent, if he was drunk, how he got drunk, whether perchance because he did not know the power of the wine, or because of guests, or because of an exceeding thirst coming upon him. . . .

The priest ought to inquire of the penitent if he was accustomed to curse men or other creatures; for to be vehemently angry with God's creatures or with cattle, and to curse them, even with the ill will to harm them, which countrymen often do, cursing men and innocent animals, is a great sin; and also many men sin by this kind of sin, who do not believe that they are sinning, and few coming to confession confess concerning wrath; and the priest ought to enjoin on the wrathful man silence for a certain time, or for some hour of the day.[2]

There is even advice to be given to expectant mothers, who are to be told to avoid heavy work, and mothers are enjoined to suckle their own children, as this is shown to be best, both by Scripture and medical science.

[1] H. E. Allen, *Writings*, 101.
[2] Bodleian, MS. Rawlinson A 361, fo. 13; MS. Rawlinson A 370, fo. 14v; and see below, p. 268; cf. Thomas of Chabham, Oriel College MS. 17, fo. 84v, 86v.

The next section deals with canonical information; it gives long lists of penances prescribed by canon law (57 cases); sins whose absolution is reserved to the bishop or the pope; 35 ways of incurring irregularity and 73 ways of incurring greater excommunication; also a list of all the excommunications involved in breaking the Provincial Statutes, Magna Carta, and the Charter of the Forest. It is interesting to see how every parishioner was kept, or supposed to be kept, conscious of Magna Carta; it is clearly a mistake to imagine that the latter was something discovered by seventeenth-century politicians and lawyers. This part of the work ends with large extracts from the treatise of Pope Innocent III on the misery of mankind, a gloomy but extremely popular work.

Part II is a programme of instruction, laying down what the parish priest should expound to his parishioners. It opens with a striking quotation from the Decretum:

Multi sunt sacerdotes et pauci sunt sacerdotes. There are many priests and there are few priests. For there are many in name, but few in deed; XL. D. c. *Multi sunt.* For there are many priests in name, because in this life and especially at this time, nothing is easier and lighter and more attractive to men than the office of bishop and priest, but in God's sight, nothing is more miserable, sad, and damnable, if that office is carried out with negligence and flattery, XL. D. c. *Ante omnia.* But there are few priests in deed, because in this life and especially at this time, nothing is more difficult as to effect, laborious as to the person, and dangerous as to the soul than the office of bishop or priest, but in God's sight, nothing is more blessed, if the office is carried out in the way that Christ commands, XL. D. c. *Nichil est,* et in glosa....[1] But in order that many may become priests in deed, they ought to labour with great diligence in Holy Scripture....For priests ought to know the Holy Scriptures and the canons, at least penitential ones, and all their work should be in

---

[1] The whole of the preceding passage is taken from the *Decretum*, pars I, Dist. XL, c. 12 and c. 7; c. 12 is an extract from St John Chrysostom, c. 7 from St Augustine—which goes to show how careful one must be in using a treatise like the *Oculus sacerdotis* as evidence of contemporary conditions, though of course the author may well have been using time-honoured phrases to describe actual conditions.

preaching and teaching, and they ought to edify all both with the knowledge of the faith and the discipline of works.[1]

In the first place the priest is to expound to his parishioners the various practical duties of a layman. Thus the layman should know how to baptize in case of necessity; parents are warned against letting young children get smothered or overlaid in bed, against rashly tying them in their cradles, and against leaving them unattended by day or night; a child is easily killed if its mouth is covered by a cloth for even a little space of time (*per modicam horam*). These hints on what would now be called mothercraft are no doubt inspired by the fear of homicide with its moral and canonical penalties. Parents are to have their children confirmed within five years of birth, if the bishop is available. The problems of marriage and sexual morality are dealt with. Foresters and bedels are warned not to hold 'scotales' or other forced collections, under pain of excommunication, because this is against the Charter of the Forest. Instructions are given about annual confession and Easter communion, about devotions at Mass, about tithe-paying, about usury and magic arts—incantations cannot cure sick men or animals. There is to be reverent behaviour in church and churchyard: no sedition, clamour, *parliamenta*, vain or still less profane conversation; fairs and markets are not to be held there, nor those 'dissolute dances' and 'inhonest songs' which are wont to take place on the vigils of certain feasts; games or stone-throwing are not to take place there. (The medieval public, by some curious trick of tradition or psychology, seems to have been irresistibly drawn to use churches and churchyards for the most unsuitable purposes.) Finally, the lists of excommunicates are to be published on Sundays.

The second half of this programme of instruction is devoted to doctrine, and follows the same lines as Pecham's constitution. Every priest must expound to the people in the vulgar tongue four times a year the fourteen articles of faith (the account here given

[1] Bodleian, MS. Rawlinson A 361, fo. 50v; MS. Rawlinson A 370, fo. 47v; and see below, p. 268.

ends with a sermon on the Last Judgment), the seven sacraments (in so far as they affect laymen), the seven works of mercy, the seven virtues, the ten commandments of the law and the two of the gospel, and the seven sins. These last are dealt with at some length, with the divisions and subdivisions, the 'species' and 'members', and the remedies, of each sin. The section of avarice includes a denunciation of the frauds and extortions practised by all classes of society; the simony of prelates, the usury of burgesses, robbery, the false weights and measures of merchants and brewers, false oaths in assizes and inquisitions, the violence and intimidation practised by bedels and foresters, the unjust citations and extortions of the bailiffs and stewards of lords, the frauds of executors, false attorneys and pleaders, lords withholding their servants' wages, rural deans and archdeacons exacting palfreys and oxen for institutions to livings. These denunciations of extortionate officials represent a theme which was to be developed at much greater length in the *Memoriale presbiterorum* a generation later.

This second part of the *Oculus* ends with the remedies against sin, patience in tribulation, resistance to temptation, and the usefulness of temptation; and here, in the midst of this very practical manual, with its long lists of irregularities and excommunications, the articles of Magna Carta, the misdeeds of alewives and bedels, and so forth, we suddenly come upon a passage of great devotional feeling, which is worth quoting. This passage is not original, for it is taken bodily from the *Stimulus amoris* of the thirteenth-century Franciscan, James of Milan; but the very selection and reproduction of it in the *Oculus* does credit to the author, and reminds us that the age of William of Pagula was also the age of the English mystics. The passage runs thus:[1]

O happy temptation, which compels us to fly to God's embrace. O sweet Lord, who dost permit us to fly hither and thither, and dost

---

[1] Bodleian, MS. Rawlinson A 361, fo. 95; MS. Rawlinson A 370, fo. 84; and see below, p. 269; cf. *Stimulus Amoris fratris Iacobi Mediolanensis* (*Bibliotheca Franciscana ascetica medii aevi*, tom. IV, Quaracchi, 1905), c. VI, 28-9.

always give Thyself as a safe refuge, that we may dwell with Thee for ever. And always have this for a general rule: whenever you wish to bend God deeply towards you, bear in your heart the Wounds of Christ, and, sprinkled with His Blood, present yourself to the Father as His Only-begotten Son; and he will most sweetly and most fully provide for you. Turn to Christ, and humbly pray Him, that since it is not meet that He be wounded anew, let Him rubrish you wholly with His Blood, and so clad in the purple, you can enter into the palace. Think deeply on these Wounds every day; they will be to you a refreshment and solace; and doubt not that if you imprint them well upon your heart, no temptation will weigh you down.

Part III of the *Oculus* deals with the seven sacraments in turn, this time for the guidance of the priest, partly from a theological, partly from a canonical and practical point of view, discussing, for instance, such a question as whether a dumb man can baptize. The two longest sections are those on the Eucharist and on matrimony. The former includes a long exposition of the Mass. The latter includes such matters as clandestine marriages, consanguinity, impediments, dowries. The book ends with a consideration of the pros and cons of matrimony, discussed with a curious mixture of idealism and disparagement which characterizes so much medieval literature on this subject. On the one hand, the writer expounds eight reasons why husbands should love their wives, and eight reasons why matrimony should be commended, of which the first is the authority of Him Who instituted it: whereas other (religious) orders were instituted by various saints, the order of matrimony was instituted by God Himself, Who cannot err; if a transgressor of the order of St Benedict or St Augustine or St Francis is culpable, how much more so a transgressor of the order of God? On the other hand the traditional arguments are brought out to prove that the wise man does not marry, arguments that go back to St Jerome, Theophrastus, and the Stoic tradition. All the drawbacks of matrimony are set out: a wife will impede the study of philosophy, and a man cannot equally serve both his books and his wife. Anything else, a horse, an ass, an ox, a dog, or any other animal can be tried out before it is bought: only a wife has to be taken on trust. Is it better to marry a beautiful or an ugly wife? It is hard to keep one that everyone else is running after; it is irksome to have one that no one else wants: but on the whole, an ugly wife will bring less misery. To keep a poor wife is difficult, to put up with a rich one is torment. It was arguments such as these that roused the Wife of Bath to such fury against her fifth husband:

> The children of Mercurie and of Venus
> Been in hir wirking ful contrarious...
> Therfore no womman of no clerk is preysed.

The *Oculus sacerdotis* seems to have some of the marks of a pioneer work. While its general plan is clear and well-constructed, it has a certain garrulousness which is not unattractive, as though the writer is trying to bring in everything he can think of, in contrast for instance to the diagrammatic precision and terseness of Grosseteste's *Templum Domini*, where there is hardly a superfluous word.

THE 'CILIUM OCULI'[1]

This is a treatise of unknown date and authorship. As its name suggests, it is intended as a supplement, *quoddam additamentum*, to the *Oculus sacerdotis*, with the purpose of dealing with miscellaneous subjects left out or not sufficiently treated in the previous treatise. It has in particular a good deal more to say about the celebration of Mass, burials, tithe-paying, excommunication and interdict, and it ends with a section on preaching, discussing who should preach, and to whom, what should be preached, at what time and place, and for what reason. The whole work draws heavily upon the Decretals, and seems to be the work of a canonist rather than a parish priest.

[1] Balliol College, Oxford, MS. 86, fo. 231.

THE 'SPECULUM CURATORUM'[1]

This treatise is ascribed to Ranulph Higden, monk of Chester, the author of the *Polychronicon*, who died in 1364; it is said to have been compiled in 1340. It deals with the articles of faith, the ten commandments, vows, tithes, the Lord's prayer, the gifts of the Holy Ghost, the beatitudes, the virtues, the vices and their remedies, the sacraments.

THE 'REGIMEN ANIMARUM'

According to some manuscripts this treatise was compiled in 1343; the author is not named. The introduction mentions the sources from which it was compiled: the *Summa summarum*, the *Summa de paenitentia* of St Raymund of Pennaforte, the *Summa confessorum* of John de Friburgo, the *Compendium veritatis theologicae*, some works of St Anselm, and above all, the *Oculus sacerdotis*, most of which is incorporated *in extenso*. It thus represents another attempt to improve upon the work of William of Pagula. The work is divided into three parts.

The first part, containing thirty-six chapters, deals with the duties of parish priests (*de moribus et sciencia presbiterorum et aliorum clericorum*); it is based on canon law and on the *Summae* mentioned above, and chapters XXIV–XXXV, dealing with penances, excommunication, etc., are taken more or less bodily from Part I of the *Oculus sacerdotis*. This part includes, among other things, a good deal of interesting advice, apparently original and not borrowed, given to parish priests about the causes of discord between priest and parishioners, and particularly as to how discord over such matters as tithe-paying can be smoothed over:

And what if it is not the practice to pay tithes on certain things, when by law they ought to pay tithe? Say that then one should proceed according to law, but on account of the discord which can arise between

---

[1] Balliol College, Oxford, MS. 77, fo. 3; Cambridge University Library, MS. Mm. i. 20, fo. 216. I owe the reference to this work to Father Leonard Boyle.

a curate and his parishioners, this ought to be done cautiously and discreetly, and this can be done in two ways:

In the first way, thus: the curate ought to speak in a friendly way to his parishioners: 'My very dear sons, because this or that ought to pay tithes, and because this is not the practice among you, I counsel you that you choose two or three good and faithful men from among you, to come in my company before the ecclesiastical ordinaries, to have a discussion at my own expense, and I will be a faithful helper in your business and mine, because by no means do I desire your loss in temporal things, but I desire the salvation of your souls.' This first method works well in many dissensions which occur between very good curates and their parishioners who are also very good, or even middling good [*mediocriter bonos*]. But where there are middling good curates and middling bad parishioners, nay even very bad ones, then this first method is no good, but this following:

The second method is thus: Let the curate go cautiously and silently [*tacite*] to the official, or to the archdeacon if it is a great matter, none of his parishioners knowing for what cause, and let him say to him privately: 'My lord, such a thing in my parish ought to pay tithe, as it seems to me, but this is not the practice among my parishioners and so will you see whether they ought by law to pay tithe on the aforesaid things, and I pray you, that in your visitation at my church, you will inquire of the men cited before you from my parish, among other inquiries to be made, whether they pay tithe on such things, as they are bound to by law, or whether they do not pay tithe; and so it will be detected before you, in my absence, whether they say that they pay tithe, or that they do not pay; and let it be put into writing; and by your leave I will have a true copy by me, and will notify it to them.'[1]

In this passage one is forcibly reminded what difficulties the system of tithe-paying was liable to raise in the relations between the priest and the people, and that it must have required the tact of a saint to make the system run smoothly.

The second part, containing thirty-eight chapters, deals with religious instruction, the 'exhortations and teaching' which the parish priest ought to give to his people. This takes over Part II of

[1] Bodleian, MS. Hatton 11, fo. 6v; and see below, pp. 269–70.

the *Oculus sacerdotis* (virtues and vices, sacraments, command-ments, etc.) more or less bodily, but with some insertions. Thus in the chapter on the virtue of faith, we rather unexpectedly find inserted the whole of St Anselm's treatise on God's foreknowledge and freewill. Can this be an echo of the controversies that were being raised about this time by Bradwardine and Buckingham, and does it represent the intellectual preoccupations of the schools rather than the practical needs of the average parish? But possibly the fourteenth-century layman was worried by such questions; after all, Chaucer introduces a reference to the teaching of 'Boece and of bishop Bradwardyn' on predestination and freewill, in the Nonne Preestes Tale. In another passage there is a discussion of the four degrees of love, to which analogies are probably to be found in contemporary mystical writers. In another passage, Grosse-teste's scheme, showing how each virtue is a mean between two extremes, is taken bodily from the *Templum Domini*.

The third part, containing sixty-six chapters, deals with the seven sacraments and their administration: it has some resemblance to Part III of the *Oculus sacerdotis*, but is much remodelled.

THE 'MEMORIALE PRESBITERORUM'
(OR 'MEMORIALE SACERDOTUM')

This treatise is preserved in two manuscripts, one of which describes it as having been written by a Doctor of Canon Law at Avignon in 1344, and there is nothing in the work that is incon-sistent with this attribution and dating. It has not been possible so far to identify the author more exactly,[1] but he seems to have been an Englishman or at least writing for an English audience, to judge from references to Magna Carta, to the constitutions of the Arch-bishops of Canterbury, and so forth. The treatise was in the first place written for a friend who was a parish priest, as appears from

---

[1] He may possibly have been Thomas Fastolf, who was a prominent English canonist at Avignon about this time; see above, p. 21.

a letter appended at the end, concerning a problem of the law of burial. The author was possibly resident at the Roman Curia as a judge, or as a penitentiary or proctor, rather like Thomas de Brunton a generation later. He was evidently a secular or possibly a monk, as appears from his marked anti-mendicant bias; he takes much the same attitude as FitzRalph, with whom he may have had contact at the Curia *c.* 1337–44, and indeed he may have helped to inspire FitzRalph, whose attacks on the friars he anticipates by a few years.

The purpose of the treatise is to instruct parish priests how to hear confessions, and in particular how to impose appropriate penances; thus it is a manual for confessors similar to Part I of the *Oculus sacerdotis*, while from another point of view it is a belated specimen of the early medieval 'penitential' literature. The work falls roughly into three parts. First, the priest is told how he should instruct the penitent in the articles of faith, the commandments, etc., and how he should interrogate him; suitable interrogations are supplied, according to the sins committed and according to the occupations of the penitents, who range from ecclesiastics to peasants and sailors. Secondly, a long list is given of penances prescribed by canon law for various sins. Thirdly, the author deals with the problem of restitution, and gives particular advice as to the various classes most likely to be bound to make restitution, from prelates, archdeacons and lay lords to bailiffs, plundering soldiers, false witnesses and harlots.

One of the most interesting features of this treatise is the writer's preoccupation with social abuses, as seen in every class of society. This can best be illustrated by the following extracts:[1]

Concerning knights and their excesses and sins. You ought to inquire of a knight if he is proud or an adulterer or otherwise lecherous, as they almost all are nowadays, or if he has put away his wife....Item, if

[1] Corpus Christi College, Cambridge, MS. 148, fo. 21v, 65, 67v, 62, 62v, 23v, 63v, 70v; British Museum, MS. Harl. 3120, fo. 28v, 83, 85v, 79, 80, 31, 81v, 89v. (These references follow the order in which I have quoted the extracts given above.) See also below, pp. 270–6.

he has drawn clerks into his court against their will....Item, if he has made or caused to be made in his court any constitutions or statutes against the liberty of the Church....Item, if he has oppressed his tenants and especially his poor villeins [*rusticos*] with undue tallages and exactions....Item, if he has a chapel in his manor and has caused Mass to be celebrated there without the licence and authority of the pope or of his own bishop. Item, if he has caused justice to be done in his court equally to poor and rich....Item, if he has at any time encouraged his lord, the king perhaps, or an earl or baron, in carnal sins or other unlawful things or has spurred them on to unjust war....Item, if he has frequented tournaments.

The author is particularly severe on the various kinds of officials, ecclesiastical and lay:

Of archdeacons and their servants. If one may say so, the archdeacons of our time and also their servants, and also the others who are in charge of ecclesiastical jurisdiction as far as concerns making correction of sins, are like the hounds of hell [*canes infernales*], not only barking but also biting, and often unduly oppressing their subjects from exquisite and feigned causes and extorting money from them in various ways.... Moreover the servants of archdeacons are not content unless they receive gifts from the persons they visit, and if they do not receive gifts, they oppress such persons, sometimes superfluously spending (but God forbid that I should say stealing!) their goods, and sometimes falsely spreading sinister reports about them, and often procuring oppressions and molestations to be maliciously inflicted by their lords and other adherents of theirs upon those whom they thus visit, and in this they sin mortally.

Of apparitors and bedels and other servants of judges. The apparitors and catchpoles [*cacherelli*] of officials and secular judges, beyond what they receive as wages from their lords, sometimes in addition extort goods from their subjects by violence and oppression, as for instance thus: a bailiff or catchpole sees some rich men in his bailiwick, who contribute little or nothing to him by way of gratuity [*curialitatis*]. Hence in order to extort gifts, he puts them on assises or distrains by taking their goods, to the end that they be so compelled to buy off their annoyance, or causes them to be brought to law on their own behalf and without cause, and thus extorts various gifts from them....

Concerning temporal lords who oppress their subjects with tallages and exactions. It happens sometimes that temporal lords violently exact and extort both from their villeins [*rusticis*] and from their free tenants many goods beyond what the tenants ought and have been wont to pay, and they tallage them against their will and without cause, at their own will, sometimes once a year, sometimes more often, or whenever they like, now more, now less, extorting many goods by violence, whence it sometimes happens that such tenants being reduced to poverty have scarcely enough to provide themselves and their families with victuals; nor do such lords think they sin in this, because by civil law...it is laid down that whatever the serf acquires, he acquires for his lord [*quicquid servus acquirit, domino acquirit*], and so temporal lords, relying on this law, seize at their will all the goods of their villeins as their own. But they are badly mistaken, for no temporal lord ought by natural or canon law to exact anything from his tenant beyond what is owed him by the same, by custom or by contract made between him and the tenant, or by imposition made from of old, and if he has exacted more, he ought to confess this.... This ought to be enjoined upon him in confession and he should be effectively induced to it, namely that all that has been exacted beyond what is his due, should be restored to those from whom he extorted it or to their heirs, if he wishes to be saved.... You ought therefore to say to such lords, if they confess this to you, that all who do such things are robbers and men of bad faith. And that no custom can excuse them in this case from sin. The reason for this is that this custom of tallaging and extorting is uncertain, because lords tallage now more, now less, and as often as they please. Whence custom has no place in regard to this....

Concerning rustics and other tenants who withhold due and accustomed services from their lords.... You should know that everyone, whether free or serf, who holds temporalities from any kind of lord, at the creation of a new lord does him homage and fealty, promising him on his faith or on oath on the holy Gospels of God that he will be faithful to him and do faithfully to him the services which are due and accustomed by reason of the lands and tenements which he holds from him. If therefore anyone so swearing, withholds, withdraws, diminishes or knowingly conceals any of the services or rights due from him to his lord, he commits theft and also perjury.

Concerning villeins [*rusticos*]....In the first place they come together and make conventicles and illicit pacts, swearing and conspiring against their neighbours and especially against the poor, who have nothing to offer them, and disinherit them, and in many other ways cause them to be oppressed in the courts of their lords, against God and justice, and yet they get no profit out of this....Moreover a rich villein strives to sin in greater matters, and is less afraid to sin than a noble, who is led by a regulated sense [*sensu regulato*]. Of such a rich man it is said: the rich criminal fears no penalty because he thinks he can buy himself off with money....Item, villeins often deceitfully accuse their neighbours to their lords and their bailiffs of fictitious crimes and shortcomings, and so they are unjustly harassed and lose their goods....Item, villeins trust in auguries and the chattering [*garritu*] of birds and follow them. Item, they trust in certain evil casting of lots [*sortibus*] and superstitions which many old women hold and practise, and so go astray from the right and true faith and are ill believing.[1]

Concerning sailors and their sins....You must be very cautious and careful in inquiring, because you should know that the pen can scarcely suffice to write the sins in which they are involved, for such is their wickedness that it exceeds that of all other men. [The writer mentions piracy, robbing and killing of merchants, etc.]....In all the lands and regions that they touch upon, they contract matrimony *de facto* with different women, believing that it is lawful for them....

The writer discusses the problem of what constitutes a just war, and the unjust taking of plunder in war, and the position of those who buy plundered goods or, like the wives and families of robbers, live on the proceeds of plunder. He goes on to remark:

But whatever is written here or elsewhere about this matter [plunder in war] there is scarce found anyone who confesses to this sin, and if at any time anyone does do so, then many modern confessors, and especially those of the mendicant orders, blind leaders of the blind, having altogether no power to absolve such a sinner in this case, if some part of the plunder or something else is given to them, absolve *de facto* the plunderer and his adherents, taking altogether no care about seeing that restitution is made, as the law demands; but woe unto all such confessors!

[1] Although superstitious practices are denounced, the fear of witchcraft seems to play a much smaller part in the mentality of fourteenth-century Englishmen than in later times.

Of those who make unjust statutes. Temporal lords and sometimes their stewards and bailiffs make their statutes which are often contrary to written law, whereby their subjects are frequently aggrieved both in their goods and their persons.... And for this reason you ought to know that statutes or laws of this kind are sometimes made against the natural law which is contained in the Gospel and in canon law. Whence such statutes have no validity or binding power *ipso iure.* And often laymen make such statutes to the prejudice and grave damage of churches and their liberties and their clerks and their servants. Wherefore all legislators [*statuarii*] of this kind and their counsellors and the writers of the statutes and those who judge according to them and those who keep them and execute them are excommunicate *ipso iure....* And here is an example: certain country parishioners, being moved against their rector or vicar, decide among themselves that henceforward no one shall make an offering when any woman is churched, or for anyone that is dead, except one penny, or that no one shall offer on the anniversaries of their parents, and this they decide on and bind themselves to it, in order to annoy their rector or vicar, thereby prejudicing their mother church. Truly all such men are excommunicate *ipso facto* as has been said.

No doubt many of the vices which the author points to are to be found in every age, but it is tempting to see in his castigation of plundering in war some echo of the early years of the Hundred Years War and the ravages of the 'routiers', which were sufficiently felt or feared at Avignon to cause the rebuilding of its walls a few years after this treatise was written there. Perhaps also the writer's concern with the corruption of justice and the evils of officialdom may reflect the beginnings of 'bastard feudalism' and of that breakdown of law and order which reached its height in the fifteenth century. It is interesting to see that the writer regards the seigneurial courts as still sufficiently vigorous to be a source of real oppression. As a critic of the social evils of the times, he invites comparison with Langland and Chaucer a generation later. What is particularly striking is the way in which he combines a strong sympathy for the underdog, for the poor and the weak who are the victims of officials or powerful neighbours, and an outspoken criticism of clerical abuses, with a strong sense of clerical *esprit de corps* and a championship of clerical rights against any lay attacks, whether from lords or rustics. In this attitude he resembles Bishop Brunton.[1] Writings of this kind make it more clear than ever how untenable is the old view which regarded all critics of abuses as in some way forerunners or fellow-travellers of Lollardy. Fourteenth-century men cannot be neatly divided into radicals and reactionaries, and this particular brand of orthodox clerical criticism was probably widespread, as can be seen also in the sermon literature of the period.

Another interesting feature is that, as has been mentioned, the writer upholds the secular clergy against the mendicants, and criticizes the latter both for holding a lax moral theology and for exceeding their privileges and faculties, for instance by saying Mass in the chambers or private chapels of lords without the bishop's licence, or absolving sins reserved for bishops, or imposing too light a penance; 'and in this matter sin and err almost all those who hear confessions nowadays and especially religious confessors who serve and live in the courts of princes and magnates.... Such confessors, infected with the poison of adulation, mislead many magnates....'[2]

ARCHBISHOP THORESBY'S 'INSTRUCTIONS'
(THE SO-CALLED 'LAY-FOLK'S CATECHISM')

The author of this treatise, John Thoresby, Archbishop of York (1352–73), had the career of a successful civil servant, as chancery clerk, Keeper of the Privy Seal and Chancellor, and belonged to a group of interrelated administrative families, the Thoresbys, Walthams and Ravensers, who served the Crown for three generations.[3] He is a very interesting example of a great civil

[1] See above, p. 184.
[2] Corpus Christi College, Cambridge, MS. 148, fo. 55; British Museum, MS. Harl. 3120, fo. 70v; cf. above, p. 159.
[3] Tout, *Chapters*, III, 85, 158, 166, 206, 215.

servant bishop who took his episcopal duties seriously.[1] In 1357 he issued a Latin 'catechism' or summary of religious instruction, which was to be expounded in English by parish priests throughout the province of York. This was based on the instructions issued by Archbishop Pecham in 1281. At Archbishop Thoresby's command, John Gaytrick, a Benedictine monk of St Mary's, York, made an expanded English version of this 'catechism' in verse.[2] Thoresby's 'catechism' deals with the fourteen articles of belief, the ten commandments, the seven sacraments, the seven works of mercy, seven virtues and the seven sins; to encourage its popularization, an indulgence of forty days was offered to those who learnt it by heart. No doubt the putting of the English version into verse form was meant to make it easier to learn. This treatise has come to be known as a 'catechism', though it is not written in the form of question and answer like the catechisms of later times. As a scheme of religious instruction put forward officially by a bishop it may be regarded as a belated survival of thirteenth-century methods; while the official publication of a version in English links it with the vernacular literature of the period. At a later date a version of Gaytrick's translation was made which contained large interpolations of Lollard doctrine: the fact that the Lollard interpolators chose this particular treatise is indirectly a tribute to its popularity and respectability. A few years after Thoresby's publication of this for the province of York, Archbishop Islip published something similar for the diocese of Canterbury. On 21 February 1361 he sent round to all the parish priests of his diocese a *brevis libellus* containing the seven sins and their species and the ten commandments, ordering them to copy it, learn it and teach it to their parishioners before his next visitation after Easter.[3] The text of this *libellus* has not survived.

---

[1] Thoresby resigned the chancellorship in 1356.

[2] Both Latin and English versions, together with the Lollard version, are edited by T. F. Simmons and H. E. Nolloth as the 'Lay-folks catechism' in *EETS*, vol. 118; cf. Wells, *Manual*, 355 (VI, 17).

[3] Lambeth, Reg. Islip., fo. 182. I owe this reference to Mr J. R. L. Highfield.

THE 'PUPILLA OCULI'

This treatise is said to have been written by John de Burgo,[1] Chancellor of the University of Cambridge, in 1385. In the preface he gives his reasons for making this compilation. As the world grows old, human nature deteriorates, life is shorter, opportunity for acquiring knowledge is lessened. To provide a remedy, earlier writers had produced treatises, of which the *Oculus sacerdotis* is the most common. This is a useful work, but not well arranged, on account of the inordinate repetition [*replicatio*] of its contents. Other books are neglected by modern parish priests, because they are too prolix and modern men like brevity [*gaudent brevitate moderni*], or because they are too costly. Since the author has to a large extent based his work, he tells us, on the *Oculus sacerdotis*, he calls it the *Pupilla oculi*. As a matter of fact, however much he may be making use of the same materials as the *Oculus sacerdotis*, the *Pupilla* is not a mere summary of that work. Its structure is quite different; it is far more logical and clear-cut than any of the previous treatises of the fourteenth century, as perhaps one might expect from a distinguished academic compiler. The structure is based on the seven sacraments. There are ten books; Book I is introductory, on the sacraments in general; Books II–VIII cover each of the seven sacraments. Under each sacrament the author considers the minister, matter and form, intention, and so forth. The book on the Eucharist includes an exposition of the Mass, that on penance includes instructions on the hearing of confessions, interrogations, penances, doubtful cases, and so forth, as in Part I of the *Oculus sacerdotis*. Book IX is a miscellany, dealing with such matters as tithes, residence, burials and wills; Book X gives a programme of religious instruction, the fourteen articles, the ten commandments, the seven sins, etc., corresponding to Part II of the *Oculus sacerdotis*. Thus the *Pupilla oculi* represents a more scientific and successful recasting of the *Oculus sacerdotis*, which had been already attempted

[1] *DNB, s.v.* Borough.

in the *Regimen animarum*, but with greater prolixity. The *Pupilla oculi* became popular; there are many manuscript copies, and it was printed at Rouen in 1510, the only one of these fourteenth-century treatises to be printed at that period. It is uncertain how far it superseded the earlier treatises like the *Oculus sacerdotis* or the *Regimen animarum*.

Finally, at the end of the century, there are several works composed by John Mirk, the Prior of the Augustinian Priory of Lilleshall, Salop, *c.* 1400.

MIRK'S 'INSTRUCTIONS FOR PARISH PRIESTS'[1]

This consists of 1934 lines of English verse, suitable, like Gaytrick's catechism, for learning by heart. On some manuscripts it is described as a translation of the *Pars Oculi*, i.e. of Part I of the *Oculus sacerdotis*, but it is in fact not a complete or literal translation of that work. Its structure is as follows. There is a short prologue dealing with the behaviour of the parish priest, his clothing, and so forth. The next section deals with what the parish priest should teach his parishioners (corresponding to Part II of the *Oculus sacerdotis*); this includes lay-baptism in case of necessity, the duties of midwives, the care of children, regulations concerning marriage, reverent behaviour in church and churchyard, tithe-paying, witchcraft and usury; there are English versions of the Lord's prayer, the Hail Mary and the Creed; the fourteen articles of faith and the seven sacraments are also included. The last section explains what the priest ought to do in the administration of the sacraments (cf. Part III of the *Oculus sacerdotis*). The section on confession (over 1000 lines, more than half the whole poem) includes instruction on how to hear confessions with interrogation of the penitent as to his religious knowledge and as to his sins under the headings of the ten commandments, the seven sins and the five senses (cf. Part I of the *Oculus sacerdotis*).

[1] Ed. E. Peacock, in *EETS*, 31; Wells, *Manual*, 361 (VI, 38).

MIRK'S 'MANUALE SACERDOTIS'[1]

This treatise is written in Latin and is much more elaborate and learned than Mirk's *Instructions*; indeed, it is very interesting to see one man writing in two completely different styles, though both intended for parish priests. The *Manuale* is addressed to a certain 'I. de S., vicar of A.', a kinsman of Mirk. Mirk apologizes for his 'rustic speech', rather self-consciously, I think, or conventionally, because the work is obviously written in the 'elegant' style of the period. The *Manuale* is primarily a treatise on the responsibilities and duties of the priestly state. In some ways it may be regarded as the medieval equivalent of a book like George Herbert's *Priest to the Temple*, while from another point of view it perhaps has some affinities with medieval books of courtesy and instructions for household servants, with a great deal of moral advice and religious reflection thrown in.

The *Manuale* consists of five books. Book I is on the priestly state. The priest is reminded that 'the Gospel is the rule of priests'; there is much about the evils of frivolity and ignorance among priests, but Mirk points out that an unlearned but humble priest is better than a learned but presumptuous one. There are two interesting sketches, not unlike the 'characters' of the seventeenth century, of the 'life [*conversacio*] of the good priest' and the 'life of the bad priest'. It should be noted that both of these sketches, among other things, imply that the acting parish priest or 'curate' is normally not beneficed, but a salaried employee, working as an assistant or a substitute for an incumbent, or as chaplain to a lord. This can be illustrated by the following passages:

c. xi (*The good priest*). The priest of God, whose soul is in his hands always, knows that he is hired to celebrate every day...therefore he disposes himself to live soberly as to himself, justly as to the master he serves and piously towards God....The priest also lives justly, when he renders to each man what is his due. To his master indeed he

[1] Bodleian, MS. Bodley 549, fo. 121; MS. Bodley 632.

renders what is his due, when in return for the salary which he receives from him, he pays back spiritual commodities; not only by celebrating everyday for him one single Mass, but also in other spiritual services, as for instance the seven penitential psalms, the fifteen gradual psalms, devout litanies, offices of the dead, and other like spiritual things.

c. xii (*The worldly priest*). Him we call the worldly priest, who loves the world... [his aims are worldly, to be well fed, well clothed, to lead an easy life]... .Therefore to gain these things, they give themselves over to the world, that is they offer themselves to a certain worldly magnate, the patron of churches, to serve him, hoping to receive a church from him. Thus the world's priest works, through right and wrong, to the end that he may be wedded to the world and be bound to its service. On taking office, he goes to the altar, not when devotion invites him, but when his lord insinuates; not out of devotion, but from habit; thinking nothing of Christ's Passion, but only thinking how to prolong or shorten the Mass according to the will of his lord... . This man with sighs and groans tries to please his auditors, that without deserving it, he may get a name for himself for holiness. Wherefore he often bends the knee, raises his hands to heaven, beats his breast, utters groans; clearly he is acting like a madman, for this devotion does not proceed from the heart but from the mouth... .Nor does this priest only strive to please his lord whom he serves, but also the whole household, so that at the opportune time, that is, when any church falls vacant, of which his lord is patron, then they also may put in a good word for him to the lord... .Then on receiving the presentation to the church, he hastens to the bishop, taking with him Master Symon, because he is potent in work and word with the bishop and all his servants. And this Master Symon so speeds and expedites his business, that all impediments put on one side, he is at once admitted, and the business being done, he returns in haste rejoicing and cheerful. When he enters upon his church he carefully inquires, not about the burden of souls, but about the value of the church, for he thinks more about the number of marks than about the salvation of souls.[1]

Books II and III deal with the priest's daily life, the kind of clothes he should wear, the saying of office in church, the right keeping of his conscience and so forth. Book IV deals mostly with the Mass. Book V deals with the rest of the priest's day, his

[1] Bodleian, MS. Bodley 549, fo. 131v–132v; and see below, p. 275.

reading, his hearing of confessions, his meals. Here again we have two little pictures of the table-manners of the good priest and the bad priest; the latter is undisciplined and *minus facete educatus*, and his avidity and inordinate gestures are such that one wonders that he does not gouge out his eye with his knife! After dinner, 'honest manual work' is recommended, reading or writing, or gardening. I do not think the work contains any directions about house-to-house visiting in the parish, which would be an important part of the priest's duties by modern standards. Then the author deals with the priest in sickness and old age, and again we have sketches of the good old priest and the bad old priest. According to St Bernard, we are told,[1] the bad old priest is garrulous, wrathful, full of proverbs and given to fables; sitting among his boon companions, he recites the wars of princes [*bella principum*], and instils into the ears of his juniors anecdotes of his early life, which he ought to weep for rather than repeat. A deplorable character no doubt, but the modern student of medieval literature and folk-lore would give much to spend an hour or two with him. The *Manuale* ends with the priest's supper and bedtime; an allegorical discussion of the nightingale; and a meditation on Heaven and Hell. Mirk takes a gloomy view of his contemporaries, including the kinsman whom he is addressing. He is doing his best to improve them, but he doubts if it will be of much use.

MIRK'S 'FESTIALL'

This is the well-known collection of English sermons, arranged for the ecclesiastical year. It hardly comes into the category of literature that we are considering, except that it contains among other things a piece of advice to parish priests on how to deal with tiresome laymen who ask the priest difficult questions about the liturgy of Holy Week, in the hope of putting him to shame.[2] It throws a curious sidelight on medieval parish life and the relations of clergy and laity.

[1] I have not been able to identify this passage in St Bernard.
[2] *Speculum*, XI (1936), 224; *Mirk's Festiall*, ed. T. Erbe (*EETS, ES, 96*), 124.

It is interesting to examine the authors of these manuals, so far as we can identify them. They are a miscellaneous lot, ranging from an archbishop, a university chancellor and a canonist at the Roman Curia to a parish priest, an Augustinian canon and two Benedictine monks. It is curious how many of these writers, such as Archbishop Thoresby, the canonist, the two monks, and perhaps the university chancellor, were men who had probably little or no practical experience of work as a parish priest. The difficulty was no doubt that the clerical world was divided rather sharply into 'sublime and lettered persons' in high places, and a clerical proletariate which would be more or less inarticulate and unlikely to produce literary works. The important exception is William of Pagula, the author of the *Oculus sacerdotis*, who seems to have been a working parish priest all his life; and there may well be others yet to be identified.

The accumulated mass of the manuals that were turned out during the thirteenth and fourteenth centuries for the instruction of parish priests is very impressive. We can see many serious-minded men at work, trying hard to educate and improve the parish clergy. They knew well the need for such work, the ignorance and slackness and worse that had to be fought against; whatever other failings the men of that age had, complacency was not one of them, as we can tell from the contemporary sermon literature. If books could create an exemplary clergy, *omnia bene* might have been written against every parish. But unfortunately books in themselves were not enough; what was needed was a systematic training and formation of the clergy, of the kind given in earlier days in the bishop's *familia* or in the later seminaries, and that solution was not to be reached until the Council of Trent in the sixteenth century.

APPENDIX TO CHAPTER IX

The following *Summae* or manuals of pastoral theology were produced in England in the thirteenth century, and were the forerunners of the manuals which I have been discussing:

(1) The *Summa* 'Res grandis' of Robert of Flamborough, written at the request of Richard Poore, *c.* 1208–10; it is a penitential.

(2) The *Summa* 'Cum miseraciones Domini' or 'Summa de penitentia' of Thomas of Chabham, Sub-dean of Salisbury, written *c.* 1215–22; pastoral as well as penitential.

(3) The *Summa* 'Qui bene presunt', by Richard Wethershed (or Wethcringset), Chancellor of Cambridge, written *c.* 1220–9.

(4) The *Summa* 'Signaculum apostolatus mei', a manual for prelates, written perhaps *c.* 1245–50.

(5) The *Summa* 'Templum Domini' of Robert Grosseteste, written *c.* 1238–45.

(6) The *Summa* 'Speculum Iuniorum' (inc. 'Racionalem creaturam'), written *c.* 1250–60.

(7) The *Summa* 'Ad instructionem iuniorum' (sometimes called *Speculum iuniorum* or *minorum*) of Simon of Hinton, O.P., written *c.* 1250–60.

(8) The *Summa* 'Animarum regimen', a short treatise on confessional practice, written *c.* 1250–70.

I owe this list to Father Leonard Boyle, O.P.

CHAPTER X

RELIGIOUS AND MORAL TREATISES IN THE VERNACULAR

IN considering this type of literature, we are faced, as we all know, with a most alarming mass of material; contemporaries admitted that it would take a lifetime to read it all. Our task is all the more difficult, because in the past scholars have tended to consider these works from the linguistic and literary point of view, rather than as a body of theological or historical material; one is more likely to find such a work as *Handling Sin* or the *Azenbite of Inwit* as a prescribed text in an English literature course than in a theological or historical course. Yet these works are of vital interest to the ecclesiastical historian and the historian of theology, and one cannot get a complete picture of the fourteenth-century English Church without trying to understand them, so that it is at least worth making an attempt to analyse and classify them.

What were the sources of these works?[1] As regards their doctrine, the sources were of course manifold. They were specially influenced by the great thirteenth-century treatises on Vices and Virtues, the work of French theologians like the Dominican William Perrault or Peraldus (d. 1260) and William of Auvergne, Bishop of Paris (d. 1249), and the *Somme le roi* of the Dominican Friar Lorens (c. 1279). Considerable use was also made of works rightly or wrongly attributed to the Fathers, either directly from the original texts, or at second hand from the 'tables' and anthologies so popular in the later Middle Ages. There was also a good deal of moral theology to be got out of the *Corpus iuris canonici*. One finds the *Corpus* cited in the most unexpected fashion; thus one treatise, the *Summa summarum*,[2] opens 'To the honour and

---

[1] Cf. E. J. Arnould, *Le manuel des péchés*, chapters I and IV.
[2] The work of William of Pagula, see above, p. 196.

praise of the Name of Jesus, which whenever I recollect, I ought to bow the head and bend the knee, at least in my heart—see the Sext, *de immunitate ecclesiarum*, c. *Decet*, and the Decretum, *de consecratione*, dist. i, c. *Apostolica....*' Another important ingredient in these works was the use of *exempla* or illustrative stories.

As regards their structure, these works were probably influenced by the programmes of religious instruction put out in the constitutions of the thirteenth-century bishops; we find the same points dealt with; the ten commandments, the seven sins, the seven sacraments, the articles of the creed. In particular, an ingenious attempt was made to link together the various 'sevens'; vices and virtues, gifts of the Holy Ghost, petitions of the Lord's Prayer. Such a practice of dealing with groups of numbered items must always have figured in moral and ascetical teaching; Cassian, for instance, works through the seven petitions of the Lord's Prayer and the vices (of which however he makes eight, not seven).

The works we are considering were written in the vernacular, in English or in a few cases French; they were therefore intended both for the laity and for unlearned priests. They were sometimes in prose, but more often in verse. It seems possible that the verse form was adopted, as in the contemporary courtesy books, household regulations and instructions for servants,[1] to make it easier for the illiterate to learn at least the shorter works by heart. In much the same way, the rhyming headings or schemes which we find in contemporary sermons made it easier for the audience to carry something away of what they heard; they were the religious equivalent of such jingles as the gender rhymes in the Latin grammars.

Again, the verse treatises, especially the longer ones, were evidently intended as a substitute for and a pious counterfeit of the profane literature of the period—the romances—in order to beat the worldlings, like Mirk's 'bad old priest' with his *bella*

---

[1] Cf. *Early English Meals and Manners*, ed. F. J. Furnivall, *EETS*, 32.

principum, at their own game. The author of the *Speculum Vitae* addresses his audience thus:[1]

> Good men and women...
> I will make no vain speaking
> Of deeds of arms nor of amours,
> As do other minstrels and other gestours...
> Of Octavian and Isambrace
> Nor of Bevis of Hampton.

The same desire to make instruction attractive helps to explain the use of *exempla*.

The works which we have to consider may be roughly divided into five groups.

GROUP I

1. The starting point of this group of works is the *Mirror of Holy Church (Speculum ecclesiae)* written by St Edmund, Archbishop of Canterbury (d. 1240). This, of course, belongs to the previous century, but I include it here because it had so much subsequent influence. It exists in three versions: Latin (of which twenty-eight manuscripts survive), French (eighteen manuscripts) and English (twelve manuscripts); of these the French version was probably the original.[2] The rhythmical prose in which the French version was written may have influenced the style of Richard Rolle. Of the English versions, one, a Northern one, was made *c*. 1350.

The main theme of the *Mirror* is the three degrees of the knowledge of God by contemplation. First there is the contemplation of God in His creatures. Secondly, there is the contemplation of God in Holy Scripture, which gives us a knowledge of the seven sins, the seven beatitudes, the seven gifts of the Holy Ghost, the ten commandments, the seven virtues, the twelve articles of the

---

[1] *Englische Studien*, VII, 469.

[2] H. W. Robbins, *Le Merure de Seinte Eglise* (Lewisburg, 1925); C. Horstmann, *Yorkshire writers, Richard Rolle* (London, 1895), I, 218–61; *EETS*, 26; Wells, *Manual*, 346 (VI, 5); the Latin version in De la Bigne, *Maxima Bibliotheca veterum patrum* (Cologne, 1618), XIII, 355.

creed, the seven sacraments, the seven works of mercy, the seven petitions of the Lord's Prayer, the seven joys of the body and seven joys of the soul in Heaven, and the seven pains of Hell. The resemblance to the episcopal programmes of instruction is obvious. Thirdly, there is the contemplation of God in Himself, both in His Manhood and in His Godhead. When speaking of the contemplation of God in His Manhood, St Edmund outlines a double series of meditations on different scenes in the life of Christ and especially in the Passion. These are arranged so that there are two meditations for each of the seven canonical hours of the day, and for each meditation he gives an elaborate and vivid word-picture. These meditations of St Edmund are extremely important in the history of medieval spirituality. One example may be quoted, the meditation on the birth of Christ:

Now dear friend, before matins shalt thou think of the sweet birth of Jesu Christ first, and afterwards of His Passion. Of His birth, shall thou think busily the time and the place and the hour that Our Lord Jesu Christ was born of His Mother Mary. The time was in mid-winter, when it was most cold; the hour was at midnight, the hardest hour that is; the place was in mid-ward the street, in a house withouten walls; in clouts was He wounden, and as a child was He bounden, and in a crib before an ox and an ass that lovely Lord was laid, for there was no other place void. And there shalt thou think of the keeping of Mary about her Child, and of her spouse Joseph, what joy Jesu sent them. Thou shalt also think of the shepherds that saw the token of His birth, and thou shalt think of the sweet fellowship of angels, and raise up thy heart and sing with them: *Gloria in excelsis Deo.*

The *Mirror* was apparently intended primarily for religious, though probably first written in vernacular French. It is the earliest of the treatises which we shall be considering, and the most remarkable. In particular St Edmund, like some other thirteenth-century writers, St Bonaventure for instance, manages to combine a love of highly elaborate schematization, of divisions and subdivisions, with the most vivid imagination, affection and devotion. This kind of writing must have had a profound effect on the development of English mystical writing.

2. Besides the complete English translations of the *Mirror*, there are two derivative works in English: the *Prick of Love*, a free version of the *Mirror*, in verse, belonging to the middle or end of the fourteenth century (it mentions Henry Duke of Lancaster's foundation at Leicester); and *How a man shall live perfectly*, an English version of the first part of the *Mirror*.

GROUP II

1. The starting point of this group is the *Manuel des péchés*.[1] The author is uncertain; William de Waddington was perhaps the author or compiler, perhaps only a copyist, but the author was certainly an Englishman writing in French or 'Anglo-Norman' verse. The date is probably *c.* 1260. It is a poem of over 12,000 lines. Twenty-four manuscripts of it are known. As regards its structure, although the name suggests that it is simply a treatise on the Vices, it is in fact more comprehensive. Books I–V go over the familiar programme: the twelve articles of the creed; the ten commandments; the seven sins, to which is added sacrilege; the seven sacraments. Books VI–IX apparently represent additions of a revision; they include a sermon, a treatise on how to make a good confession, and a treatise on prayer. The work includes a number of *exempla*. The *Summae* of Peraldus on the vices and virtues provide much of the doctrine but not the structure.

2. *Handling Sin*[2] is an English verse translation of the *Manuel des péchés* by Robert Mannyng, of Brun (or Bourne), a Gilbertine canon of Sempringham in Lincolnshire; he was writing in 1303. It is a poem of 12,628 lines. Mannyng takes some liberties with his original, for instance by omitting the articles of the creed; what

---

[1] See E. J. Arnould, *Le manuel des péchés*, *passim*.

[2] Ed. F. J. Furnivall, *EETS*, 119, 123; Wells, *Manual*, 342 (VI, 2). D. W. Robertson, 'The cultural tradition of Handlyng Synne', in *Speculum*, XXII (1947), 162–85, points out that *Handlyng Synne* and the *Manuel des péchés* may be regarded as belonging to the class of confessional manuals, or aids to confession.

remains is thus mainly moral: the ten commandments, the seven sins, the seven sacraments, and the requisites and graces of confession. Mannyng above all excels in his use of *exempla*, adding some to his original and generally improving them. It is his skill as a story-teller that makes his work so attractive. His aim was to avoid pedantry and dullness, and deliberately to compete with profane tales and rhymes. To modern eyes, Mannyng has a very important place in the history of English literature, but among medieval readers, he seems to have been less popular than might have been expected, for his work only survives in four manuscripts.

3. An English prose version of the *Manuel* was made with the title *Of shrift and penance*. This has been attributed on linguistic grounds to a date *c.* 1350 and to the neighbourhood of London.[1]

GROUP III

1. This group has as its starting point the *Somme le Roi*, written in 1279, in French prose, by Friar Lorens, the Dominican confessor of Philip III of France.[2] It deals with the ten commandments; the twelve articles of the creed; the seven sins, very elaborately divided and subdivided; an *Ars moriendi*; and treatises on the Lord's Prayer and on the seven gifts of the Holy Ghost. The *Somme le Roi* has a complicated pre-history, and only the latter part of it is Lorens's own original work. While dealing with similar subject matter, it is more clearly and elaborately articulated than the works of the *Manuel des péchés* group, and not so much interrupted by stories; it is in fact more scholastic.

2. The well-known *Azenbite of Inwit* (or 'Remorse of conscience', as we should say) is a translation of the *Somme le Roi* into English prose in the Kentish dialect by Dan Michael of Northgate, monk of St Augustine's, Canterbury, in 1340.[3] Dan Michael

---

[1] Arnould, *op. cit.* 319–34.

[2] Cf. the *Book of Vices and Virtues*, ed. W. N. Francis, *EETS*, 217 (1942), xiiiff.; *Romania*, XIV, 532, XXIII, 449, XXVII, 109.

[3] Ed. R. Morris, *EETS*, 23 (1866); Wells, *Manual*, 345 (VI, 4).

seems to have been a man of remarkable and varied intellectual interests, to judge from the collection of books that he left to the library of St Augustine's.[1] As one might expect, these books include a number of moral and devotional treatises, such as the *Mirror* of St Edmund, the *Stimulus amoris*, the *Somme le Roi*, and his own translation (which still survives); also two copies of a remarkable twelfth-century treatise on natural ethics, known as the *Moralium dogma philosophorum*; besides these, nearly half the collection are books on natural science (including Roger Bacon's 'Experimental science'), on surgery, astronomy and alchemy. One of these volumes, a miscellany of treatises, begins with penance and the seven deadly sins and ends with veterinary surgery. It is very interesting that such a man should have taken the trouble to make the work of a French king's confessor available to Kentish clerks and laymen.

3. The *Book of Vices and Virtues* is another English prose translation of the *Somme le Roi*, made perhaps c. 1375; there is no evidence as to authorship. It survives in three manuscripts.[2]

The *Somme le Roi* seems to have been one of the most popular books of its kind. There are six other translations, and a version was printed by Caxton in 1486, entitled *The Royal Book*.

Comparable to Groups II and III, though not dependent upon either, are several well-known passages in contemporary literature which deal with virtues and vices and with confession. First there is the passage in Langland's *Piers Plowman* (C-text, passus VII and VIII), where the seven deadly sins, personified, make their confession; this is a fanciful and imaginative treatment of the type of literature that we have been considering. Secondly, there is Chaucer's Parson's Tale; this is a good, straightforward, rather conventional example of a treatise on confession and on the seven

---

[1] M. R. James, *Ancient libraries of Canterbury and Dover* (Cambridge, 1903), lxxvii, and Index of Donors, *s.v.* Northgate.
[2] Ed. W. N. Francis, *EETS*, 217 (1942).

sins and their remedies. It ultimately derives from the episcopal constitutions and tracts of the thirteenth century, and from the work of Raymund of Pennaforte and Peraldus; and it has analogies with similar matter in priest's manuals like the *Oculus sacerdotis*. Thirdly, John Gower's *Miroir de l'homme* (*Speculum meditantis*) includes among other things a manual of vices and virtues. His *Confessio amantis* is even more interesting for our purpose. In this, the lover is told by Venus to confess to her priest, Genius; the lover makes his confession, working through the seven sins, with interrogations and instructions by the priest. Here we have in fact an elegant, moral parody of the contemporary treatises on confession. At first sight it sounds like a piece of profanity, but it is simply an example of the medieval love of allegory; men were as ready to make a moral allegory out of the technique of confession as they were to make a moral allegory out of Noah's Ark or Ovid's *Metamorphoses*.

GROUP IV

The chief characteristic of this group is an ingenious attempt to equate the various groups of 'sevens'. An early example of this is in St Anselm's Homily on the Beatitudes, where he equates the seven beatitudes with the seven gifts of the Holy Ghost and with the seven petitions of the Lord's Prayer; thus *Spiritus timoris* = *Beati pauperes* = *Libera nos a malo*.[1] Other equations of the 'sevens' were made with increasing elaborateness throughout the twelfth and thirteenth centuries. Simon of Hinton, O.P., c. 1250–60, equates as many as seven different categories of 'sevens'.[2] Grosseteste in his manual of pastoral care, *Templum Domini*, compares the sinner to a patient and the priest to a doctor. The seven vices are the patient's infirmities; corresponding to these, the seven petitions of the Lord's prayer are the patient's complaints to the doctor; the seven beatitudes and seven moral habits are the medicinal preparations;

---

[1] Migne, *Pat. Lat.* CLVIII, 595–7; cf. Hugh of St Victor, *De quinque septenis*, in Migne, *Pat. Lat.* CLXXV, 405; St Augustine, in Migne, *Pat. Lat.* XXXIV, 1286; *RTAM*, IX (1937), 9n.
[2] *RTAM*, IX (1937), 11.

the seven virtues represent health restored. Grosseteste sets these out in diagram form, and concludes by saying: *In hac tabula est tota cura pastoralis officii.*[1] If these diagrams and equations seem quaint and even childish to a modern reader, one can only say that they did not seem so to one of the most acute minds and most practical and devoted pastors of the Middle Ages.

These curious experiments in theological mathematics are chiefly important for our present purpose from the fact that they seem to be the basis or background of one of the most popular of all Middle English religious poems, namely the *Speculum vitae.*[2] This is a late fourteenth-century English poem of great length. In some manuscripts it is attributed to William Nassington,[3] apparently an advocate in the court of the Archbishop of York, one of a class of men not usually given to writing religious poetry. The work exists in two forms: as a poem (of which thirty-five manuscripts survive) and in a prose version (of which three manuscripts survive). The *Speculum vitae* as regards its structure is based on the seven petitions of the Lord's Prayer and other 'sevens'. The first quarter of the work consists of what might be called a preliminary run through the Lord's Prayer, taking in its stride some other familiar features of the instruction programmes—the twelve articles of the creed, the ten commandments, and so forth. Then, after pointing out the correspondence of the seven petitions, the seven gifts of the Holy Ghost, the seven sins, the seven virtues, the seven beatitudes and the seven rewards, the author proceeds, in the remaining three-quarters of the work, to go steadily through the seven vices and corresponding virtues, taken together with the seven gifts of the Holy Ghost and the seven petitions of the Lord's Prayer. Thus in answer to the prayer *Sed libera nos a malo*, the gift of fear roots out the sin of pride and puts in the virtue of humility. The vices and virtues are elaborately divided and subdivided, and show much in

[1] Bodleian, MS. Bodley 631, fo. 186v–7.
[2] Wells, *Manual*, 348 (VI, 8); H. E. Allen in *PMLA*, XXXII, 133–62; the opening lines have been printed in *Englische Studien*, VII, 468. I have used MS. Bodley 446.
[3] Wells, *Manual*, 463; H. E. Allen, *Writings*, 371–2.

common with the *Somme le Roi*. Pride has seven roots: infidelity, contempt, presumptuousness, ambition, vainglory, hypocrisy, false shame; of these, hypocrisy, for instance, is subdivided into 'foul' hypocrisy, sinning in secret; 'foolish' hypocrisy, doing good for the sake of praise; 'subtle' hypocrisy, behaving well in order to obtain office and dignity. These minutely articulated analyses of virtues and vices are not to be despised, for they constitute a very important body of medieval ethical and psychological doctrine, which deserves careful study; they need to be compared, for instance, with the ethical teaching of the twelfth-century humanists and with the revived Aristotelian doctrine of the thirteenth century.

A note in some manuscripts of the *Speculum vitae* tells us that it was on one occasion subjected to a careful scrutiny by the University of Cambridge:[1]

In the year of Our Lord 1384, this compilation was examined at Cambridge in this manner. While it was left there by a certain priest, in order to be bound, it was carefully looked at by certain scholars, and read through and presented to the Chancellor of the University and his Council, in order to be examined for defects and heresies; lest the unlearned should carelessly deceive the people through its means, and fallaciously lead them into various errors. Then by command of the Chancellor, before him and the whole Council of the University, it was examined for four days with all care and diligence, and tested in every college on every side; and on the fifth day all the doctors of both laws and the masters of theology, together with the Chancellor, declared and affirmed that it was well and subtly drawn out of the sacred laws and divine books, and that it was alleged, affirmed and founded on the authority of all the Doctors of the Sacred Page. Therefore whoever you are, O reader, do not despise this work, because without a doubt, if any defects had been found in it, it would have been burnt before the University of Cambridge.

Here one has a vivid picture of some inquisitive don picking up the *quaterni* as they lay in the bookbinder's or stationer's shop, and the suspicion of Lollardy—it might have come from that

[1] MS. Bodley 446, fo. 1; the text is printed in *PMLA*, xxxii, 148. The note also appears in Cambridge University Library, MS. Ii. i. 36 and Caius College, Cambridge, MS. 160.

well-known fountain of heresy at Oxford. It is probable that the Chancellor concerned was John de Burgo, the author of the *Pupilla oculi*.

GROUP V

Finally we have a number of miscellaneous treatises, which it will be most convenient to take more or less in chronological order.

1. William of Shoreham, a Kentish parish priest, wrote poems, *c.* 1320, which include treatises on the seven sacraments, the ten commandments and the seven sins, as well as devotional pieces on the five joys of the Blessed Virgin and on the history of the Creation and Redemption.[1]

2. *The Prick of Conscience*[2] is a long English poem, of 4812 couplets, of the mid-fourteenth century; there is a Latin as well as an English version. It deals mainly with the wretchedness of man's state and of the world, and with the four last things: Death, Judgment, Hell and Heaven. Unlike most other didactic religious poems of this period it does not include the seven sins, the sacraments, or the commandments; it represents quite a specialized type of its own. It was perhaps the most popular of all these poems, for over a hundred manuscripts of it survive, in contrast, for instance, to the four manuscripts of *Handling Sin*. Moreover, its description of the Last Judgment is represented in a stained-glass window in All Saints' Church, North Street, York. It is a very rare, almost unique distinction to find a contemporary literary work directly represented in wall-painting or stained-glass. It is difficult to know why the poem was so popular. The author is unknown; he was apparently not Richard Rolle (as was at one time thought), nor was he William Nassington.

3. The *Speculum Christiani*[3] is by an unknown author, the date is after 1350. It is a large, comprehensive work in eight 'tables' or

---

[1] Ed. M. Konrath, EETS, ES, 86 (1902); Wells, *Manual*, 349 (VI, 10).
[2] Ed. R. Morris, *Phil. Soc.* (Berlin, 1863); Wells, *Manual*, 447 (XI, 4); H. E. Allen, *Writings*, 372.
[3] Ed. G. Holmstedt, EETS, 182 (1929).

books. The first four books include the usual programme: the creed, the commandments, the works of mercy, the virtues and vices. The fifth book deals with impediments and aids to spiritual progress, and resembles Book IV of Richard Rolle's *Amending of Life*, though it is not derived from it. Some versions of this work are partly in English and partly in Latin; others are entirely in English. A special feature is the use of numerous extracts from the Fathers. It was a very popular work; sixty-six manuscripts survive, and it was printed four times between *c.* 1480 and 1513.

4. The *Livre de Seyntz Medicines*[1] is one of the most remarkable religious works of the fourteenth century. It was written in 1354, in French, and is the work of a devout layman, Henry Duke of Lancaster, who was born *c.* 1300–1310 and died of the plague in 1361. He was celebrated as a diplomat and soldier, and was active in the Hundred Years' War; Froissart calls him a 'good knight' and a 'valiant lord, wise and imaginative'. He was alderman of the guild of Corpus Christi at Cambridge at the time of the founding of Corpus Christi College there, and he founded a great collegiate church at Leicester. He was one of the original knights of the Order of the Garter in 1348.

The book is an allegory. As a wounded man needs a physician, so mankind, wounded with the various wounds of sin, wounds of the ears, eyes, nose, and mouth, needs Christ as a physician, to apply remedies. There is an allegorical treatment of the various remedies required: beverages, ointments, lotions, bandages, and so forth. Summarized like that, the work sounds rather banal, but it is certainly not so; on the contrary it is a work of great freshness and simplicity, and Froissart was right in calling the author 'imaginative'. It gives the impression of being not, like so many medieval works, a mass of literary borrowings, except perhaps for the influence of bestiaries or romances; it seems rather to be based on

---

[1] Ed. J. Arnould, *Anglo-Norman Text Society*, 1940; cf. J. Arnould, in *Bulletin of the John Rylands Library*, Manchester, XXI (1937), 352–86. One of the two surviving MSS. (the Stonyhurst MS.) belonged to Humphrey Duke of Gloucester.

personal feelings and on the experience of courtly life. The writer speaks with a disarming frankness about himself, for instance, about his pride in his shapely arms, in his garters and rings, in his skill in dancing, about his love of scarlet cloth—he liked the smell of it; and he lets us know that his sensuality did not stop short at smelling scarlet cloth. He has something of that consciousness of social abuses which we have seen in the *Memoriale presbiterorum*. He accuses himself of extorting money mercilessly from the poor who need it most, and of acquiring property that he covets, a piece of land, a castle or a manor, by prayers or threats, or by pleadings or light judgments in his court; and in the madness of his wrath he has ordered or incited the killing, beating or maiming of his fellow-men, 'my neighbour, my brother'. He is ashamed of shrinking from the stench of the sick and the poor, or of feeling resentment when it is proposed that the remains of a feast should be given to the poor. At the same time, he is not a leveller or a prude, and he accepts the standards of contemporary aristocratic life. While condemning his own gluttony and self-indulgence, he admits that feasting on fine food and drink is legitimate for lords and others, in moderation, 'according as their estate demands', and the same is true of dancing and jousting. There is a most elaborate and realistic description of the digging out and smoking out of foxes, with terriers and rods and spades; this is an allegory of a good confession, with the shrift-father digging out the penitent's sins. He anticipates Langland in comparing the Passion to Christ fighting for us in a tournament: 'le turnoy estoit pur nous quant il par turment tourna nostre dolour en joie et vanquy mort par mort.' The whole work is written in the second person, addressed in a very personal and affectionate way to Christ—'Tresdouz Sire Jesu Christ', 'Beau Sire Deux', 'Douz Sire Meistre', or to the Blessed Virgin—'Douce Dame'.

In its general purpose and scheme the *Livre de Seyntz Medicines* resembles the familiar literature about the seven sins and their remedies which we have already considered, but it is remarkable as having been written from the point of view of the layman, the self-examining penitent, the amateur, so to speak, rather than that of the professional, the moral theologian and confessor. Duke Henry is not haunted, like the author of the *Oculus sacerdotis* or the *Memoriale presbiterorum*, by canonical complications and responsibilities, by the seventy-two cases of excommunication and the twenty-nine irregularities and the lists of reserved sins, and one may doubt whether he had ever heard of the Lateran Council of 1215 or even of Pecham's constitutions. And yet, at the same time, in all fairness, one must remember that this attractive phenomenon of the devout knight expressing himself so finely and spontaneously would not have been possible without an army of ecclesiastical technicians, bishops and canonists, confessors and preachers, at work for the previous century and a half. This treatise is also interesting as being halfway between the didactic literature which we have already been considering, and the more devotional or mystical literature and lyrics of the century; it is worth remembering that Duke Henry is an almost exact contemporary of Richard Rolle.

Finally, Duke Henry's work shows how unsafe it is to judge by superficial appearances and to condemn a whole class, however unprepossessing. *Spiritus ubi vult spirat*—great spiritual literature can come from any milieu, from an ecclesiastical lawyer like Nassington, from the clerical proletariate as with Langland, and, as here, from the world of bastard feudalism, court life and patronage. Henry of Lancaster is one of those lords whom one meets not only in Froissart but also in records like the papal registers, over and over again, loyally pushing their clerks for provision to benefices.

5. John Gaytrick's translation of Archbishop Thoresby's catechism, already discussed,[1] should be mentioned here, as it was apparently not merely intended for the use of parish priests, but also for the laity to read or learn and to teach their children; to encourage its use, as has been said, an indulgence of forty days was

[1] See above, p. 212.

granted to those who taught it or learned it, and parish priests were ordered to examine their penitents in their knowledge of its subject matter. Perhaps, as M. Arnould has suggested,[1] Gaytrick's comparatively short piece represents a reaction against or at least an alternative to the excessively long and elaborate poems like the *Speculum vitae*, the *Prick of Conscience* and the *Speculum Christiani*— works so formidable that they rather tended to defeat the aim of easy popular instruction; the laity could hardly be expected to learn them by heart, however many indulgences might be attached. Perhaps the truth is that there were two kinds of public for these vernacular treatises: the ordinary run of laymen, many of them illiterate, for whom the simpler pieces like Gaytrick's were intended; and the more devout, educated and sophisticated laymen, who would collect and read the more elaborate treatises.

6. At the end of the century, *c.* 1400, comes the most elaborate treatise of all, the *Desert of Religion*,[2] which is probably known to most students from the picture of Richard Rolle contained in some of the manuscripts, which has been reproduced more than once.[3] A northern English poem, surviving in three manuscripts, it is a comprehensive allegory, made to include all the allegories that the author could find. The Desert is the religious life, with its penances and its temptations. The author's idea of the Desert is not at all like the Thebaid; with a characteristically north-European point of view, he conceives the Desert as a forest full of trees and wild beasts. We are introduced to no less than twenty allegorical trees, each with its various branches. Moralists had long been fond of dividing the virtues and vices into so many 'roots' or 'branches'; our author is carrying this to its logical conclusion, and giving us a whole forest of such trees. Thus there is a tree of the seven virtues (that is, of seven branches) and another tree of the seven vices; a tree of the seven degrees of meekness and another of the seven

---

[1] J. Arnould, *Manuel des péchés*, 36–7.
[2] Printed in *Herrig's Archiv*, cxxvi, 58 ff., 360 ff.; Wells, *Manual*, 371 (vi, 50); H. E. Allen, *Writings*, 309.
[3] E.g. as the frontispiece to R. M. Clay, *Hermits and anchorites of England* (London, 1914).

degrees of pride; a tree of the twelve abuses in religion and another of the twelve abuses in the world, and so forth, ending with the fourteen pains of Hell and the fourteen blessednesses of Heaven. It should be observed that this is a very symmetrical forest, more like an avenue or a pleached alley! The poem is accompanied by a series of illustrations of Abraham, Moses, St John the Baptist, St Mary Magdalen, St Mary of Egypt, St Paul the first hermit, St Antony, St Hilarion, St Benedict, St Giles, St Hilda, St Godric and Richard Rolle. With all its quaintness, this poem is an impressive reminder of the hold that the idea of the Desert, the Desert Fathers and the solitary life had upon the later Middle Ages. It is not surprising that the solitaries and the Carthusians were the most active and influential spiritual writers and spiritual guides of the time.

We have been concerned in the two preceding chapters with the literature of religious and moral instruction. But we cannot leave this subject without mentioning, however briefly, two other important media of such instruction, the one oral, the other visual, namely sermons and wall-paintings. For every one person who took the trouble or had the education to read one of the treatises or poems, there must have been hundreds or thousands who listened to sermons or looked at the painted walls of their churches; they could hardly avoid doing so.

The importance of preaching in England in the later Middle Ages has only recently been fully realized, after centuries of neglect. Professor G. R. Owst has done valiant work in excavating this field and making it known,[1] and it is to be hoped that other scholars will follow his lead by working on medieval English sermons. What we badly need is a systematic catalogue or repertory of medieval English preachers and their sermons.

---

[1] G. R. Owst, *Preaching in medieval England* (Cambridge, 1926); and *Literature and pulpit in medieval England* (Cambridge, 1933). Cardinal Gasquet had earlier drawn attention to the importance of medieval sermons in an essay reprinted in *The Old English Bible and other essays* (London, 1897), 63–101. For the art of preaching, and the medieval English writers on the subject, see T. M. Charland, *Artes praedicandi* (Paris, 1936).

In preaching, as in so much else, we can see the efforts of the thirteenth century bearing fruit in the fourteenth. The pulpit and the confessional had been the two sides of pastoral work which the thirteenth-century reformers had developed most vigorously. We have seen how thoroughly the manuals for parish priests dealt with both confession and religious instruction. The revival of preaching was one of the things that helped to transform the everyday life of the Church in the thirteenth century and to give the laity a more active and informed participation in that life; it is impossible to overestimate its importance.[1] The revival was due to various causes, but especially to the activity of reforming bishops and the work and example of the friars.[2] The growth of the towns also, by providing ready-made audiences in concentrated populations of more educated people, provided both the need and the opportunity for preaching. We can see the effect of this upon Church architecture, among other things; the friars developed a particular type of church plan, where the nave was a spacious preaching-house, and this type came to be adopted in the larger parish churches as well.[3]

The fourteenth century was perhaps the classic age of preaching in medieval England, when sermons were abundant, vigorous and influential, hardly less so than they were, say, in the seventeenth century. Every walk of ecclesiastical life produced great preachers: bishops like FitzRalph and Brunton,[4] friars like Bromyard and Waldeby[5], monks like Robert Rypon, the Sub-prior of Durham,[6] secular chaplains like Thomas Wimbledon.[7] Men were prepared to take a great deal of trouble to make themselves efficient preachers.

[1] D. W. Robertson, 'The frequency of preaching in thirteenth century England', in *Speculum*, XXIV (1949), 376–88; J. Sweet, in *Journal of Eccles. History*, IV (1953), 27–36.
[2] Little, *Studies in English Franciscan history*, chapter IV.
[3] A. W. Clapham, 'The friars as builders', in A. W. Clapham and W. H. Godfrey, *Some famous buildings and their story* (London, n.d.), 241–67; A. R. Martin, *Franciscan architecture in England* (British Society for Franciscan studies, 1937), 13–29; W. A. Hinnebusch, *The early English Friars Preachers* (Rome, 1951), 135–48.
[4] See above, pp. 151 ff., 182 ff.   [5] See above, pp. 147, 150.
[6] Owst, *Preaching in medieval England*, 54 ff., and see Index, *s.v.* Rypon.
[7] *Ibid.* 360.

Some of the monk-students were sent to university solely or mainly for this purpose.[1] A man of affairs like the great Thomas de la Mare (later Abbot of St Albans) spent three years of his time as Prior of Tynemouth in training himself as a preacher both in Latin and English; he surrounded himself with a circle of clerks and masters, both seculars and mendicants, to coach him in this art.[2] Sermons were of different types suited to different audiences and occasions. There were university sermons, often preached as part of the exercises required for a degree;[3] these might be earnest discourses like Simon of Ghent's Ash Wednesday sermon,[4] or they might include a certain amount of mild, donnish ribaldry, like Robert Holcot's *Sermo finalis*.[5] There were sermons to the clergy and to religious, at synods and visitations; sermons preached before civic audiences at St Paul's Cross; funeral sermons; the sermons of friars and the sermons of parish priests. We have seen how Pecham's constitutions and the manuals laid down the programme of instruction that every parish priest was supposed to cover four times a year. In a sufficiently explosive atmosphere a sermon might start a controversy, like Thomas Waleys's sermon at Avignon[6] or FitzRalph's sermon against the friars at St Paul's Cross.[7] The popularity of sermons, especially by noted preachers, among the laity is well illustrated in Margery Kempe's autobiography.[8] While the sermons *ad clerum* would be in Latin, the sermons to the people would of course be in the vernacular, either in English, or possibly in French, in so far as that language was still used for polite audiences. One wonders when the last French sermon was preached in England. Henry Duke of Lancaster wrote his *Livre de Seyntz Medicines* in 1354 in French; did he have sermons preached to him in that language?

The sermons of the fourteenth century form a vast body of material for religious, literary and social history, still insufficiently

[1] Pantin, *Chapters*, II, 75.
[2] T. Walsingham, *Gesta abbatum mon. S. Albani*, II, 380.
[3] Little and Pelster, *Oxford theology and theologians*, 149–215.
[4] See above, p. 112. [5] See above, p. 145. [6] See above, p. 145.
[7] See above, p. 162. [8] See below, p. 259.

exploited. Almost all the points dealt with in the manuals and poems that we have been considering, the analyses of virtues and vices, of the commandments and the Lord's Prayer, the denunciations of social abuses, and all the material of satire and complaint that we find in Chaucer or Langland or the political poems, can be paralleled in the sermons of the day.[1]

The candour and the capacity for criticism among the preachers and writers of this period is remarkable. The one failing that cannot be charged against the fourteenth-century English Church is that of complacency. There were indeed plenty of abuses, but at least men did not fall into the fatal mistake of ignoring them or keeping silence about them. Everyone, high and low alike, was aware of abuses and anxious to remedy them. *Clama, ne cesses*—there was a spate of denunciation and criticism, whether from the preachers, or the bishops, or the writers of manuals, or the chroniclers, or the satirists. It is very much to the credit of the men of the fourteenth century that it is they themselves who have supplied so liberally and openly the very materials with which modern historians have criticized them. And their self-criticisms were for a large part not private and confidential, like the *comperta* of visitations, but open and public. If the newly-revealed denunciations of the preachers, after centuries of neglect, have been something of a revelation to historians in our own day, they must have been only too familiar to the fourteenth-century public. Above all, until towards the end of the century, no one had any suspicion that there might be anything disloyal or heterodox in criticism. The more orthodox men were, the more violently they criticized and demanded reform, as St Jerome and St Peter Damiani, St Bernard and Grosseteste had done before them. One of the most disastrous and blighting effects of Wycliffism was that, for the first time in the history of this country, it associated criticism with heterodoxy, and it must have tended to make orthodox reformers think twice about what they said. Readers of Chaucer's *Canterbury Tales* will remember that the

[1] See Owst, *Literature and pulpit*, especially chapters v–vii.

perfectly orthodox Parson could not rebuke a man for swearing without being accused of Lollardy. Fortunately the spirit of loyal and outspoken criticism did not die, as we can see from Gascoigne in the next century, but if anything might have killed it, it was the intemperance of the Wycliffite attack.

Medieval English wall-paintings also represent something of a re-discovery. A great deal has been done during the last hundred years by way of uncovering, preserving and scientifically studying them,[1] and it is now realized that there was a vigorous native art that can bear comparison with continental work. The destruction, both deliberate and accidental, has been immense, and what survives can be only a fragment of what once covered the walls of churches.

What concerns us here is not the artistic character of these paintings, but their subject matter. In both religious and secular art, medieval people liked every picture to tell a story. What stories did these paintings tell? In some cases, particularly where individual saints were depicted, the choice might be dictated by the particular devotion of the donor, or even by the spaces to be filled; a row of angels, prophets, apostles, evangelists or doctors of the Church would be very suitable for filling the panels of a rood-screen or a pulpit, or the lights of a window. Such figures might be part of a didactic scheme, however; the apostles would each carry a sentence of the creed, the prophets some sentence relating to the Incarnation or the Passion. From the point of view of religious instruction, the most impressive feature in most churches would be the great painting of the Last Judgment over the chancel arch; this would be a sermon in itself, and indeed corresponds precisely with one of the sermons outlined in the *Oculus sacerdotis*. The little

[1] C. E. Keyser, *A list of buildings in Great Britain and Ireland having mural and other painted decorations* (London, 1883) is of fundamental importance and deserves a new edition. Professor E. W. Tristram's volumes on *English medieval wall paintings* have not reached the fourteenth century. Cf. also O. E. Saunders, *English art in the middle ages* (Oxford, 1931), chapter XIV; C. H. Collins and M. R. James, *British painting* (London, 1933), 10–15; T. Borenius and E. W. Tristram, *English medieval painting* (Paris, 1927), chapter IV.

naked figures rising from their tombs and coming to judgment would include one or two wearing crowns or mitres, or a usurer clutching his money bag, in keeping with the prevalent denunciation of social abuses.

Other subjects of paintings reflect the teaching which we find in the manuals and poems, such as the virtues and vices, the seven sacraments, the seven works of mercy; these sometimes take the form of trees, with so many branches, like the allegorical trees in the *Desert of Religion*. Other moral subjects are the wheel of fortune (at Rochester placed rather pointedly opposite the bishop's throne) and the legend of the 'three living and the three dead'. The latter, a popular subject, represents three pleasure-loving young princes meeting three grisly corpses, who exclaim: 'As ye are now, so once were we; as we are now, so you shall be.' It used to be fashionable among historians to connect such gruesome themes with the Black Death, but that is quite unnecessary, for they must always have been among the stock-in-trade of the moralists.

One type of painting shows Christ covered with wounds and surrounded by the implements of various trades. This has sometimes been called the 'Christ of the trades' or 'Christ as Piers Plowman', and has been interpreted to represent Christ as sanctifying labour, or as suffering in the sufferings of His people. The correct meaning is probably more prosaic and more moralizing; it seems to be directed either against Sabbath-breaking, or against the use of oaths such as 'God's wounds', by showing how Christ's body is continually wounded and dismembered by men who blaspheme in the course of their daily work.[1]

Another particularly interesting type is the scenes or 'histories' from the life of Our Lord and of His Mother. These are sometimes arranged in two cycles of considerable length, one centred round the Annunciation and the Nativity, the other round the Passion,

---

[1] C. Woodforde, 'A medieval campaign against blasphemy', in *Downside Review*, LV (1937), 357. For the older view, see T. Borenius and E. W. Tristram, *English medieval painting*, 29–37.

the Resurrection and the Assumption. The two series together might nearly fill the walls of the chancel or nave of a village church. There are two very good examples of these cycles surviving from the fourteenth century, one at Croughton church in Northampton-shire,[1] the other at Chalgrove church in Oxfordshire. Each individual picture attempts to portray the scene in question, such as the Nativity or the Last Supper or the Crucifixion, with feeling and imagination; these scenes are the exact equivalent of those meditations recommended in St Edmund's *Mirror*.[2] and would also be echoed in certain types of sermon. These Nativity and Passion cycles were a very important way of bringing home to people that devotion to the Person and Passion of Christ which was characteristic of this period. We can see, from Margery Kempe's autobiography, how a sensitive person would react to them.[3]

On the whole the religious art of the fourteenth century seems to aim at making a fairly simple and direct moral and emotional appeal; we do not seem to find that very erudite and allusive kind of religious art, consisting of types and anti-types, drawing parallels between the Old and New Testaments, such as the twelfth century delighted in,[4] though such themes reappear at a later date, as in the windows of King's College Chapel, Cambridge.

Instructive wall-paintings were put up not only in churches, but in domestic buildings as well. A good example of this is at Long-thorpe Tower, near Peterborough, a house where the lay Stewards of the Liberties of Peterborough Abbey lived in the fourteenth century. Here the Great Chamber or Solar, the best room in the house, in about the year 1330 had its walls, window recesses and

---

[1] See *Archaeologia*, LXXVI (1927), 178–204. These cycles or 'histories' of the life of Christ and the Blessed Virgin go back to the thirteenth century; there are good examples at Brook (Kent), Ashampstead (Berks) and West Chiltington (Sussex); cf. E. W. Tristram, *English medieval wall painting* (Oxford, 1950), 46–9, 228, 275, 309, 470–3, 501, 510, 525.

[2] See above, p. 223.   [3] See below, p. 257.

[4] For instance in the 'theological windows' at Canterbury Cathedral, and the paintings (now destroyed) which formerly decorated the roof of Peterborough Cathedral and the chapter house at Worcester; cf. also M. R. James, 'Pictor in carmine', in *Archaeologia*, XCV (1951), 141–66.

vaulted ceiling entirely covered with a very remarkable series of paintings, which constitute an encyclopaedia of scriptural, moral and secular subjects. These subjects include the Nativity of Our Lord, the four evangelists, the twelve apostles (carrying scrolls), figures and scenes representing the active and the contemplative life, the seven ages of man, the occupations of the twelve months of the year, the 'wheel of the five senses' (controlled by a crowned figure probably representing Reason), and the story of 'the three living and the three dead'; there are also two enthroned figures which may represent King Edward II or III and Edmund of Woodstock.[1] In an earlier period, the directions for the decoration of the royal residences given in the *Liberate* Rolls of Henry III show how the walls of halls and chambers, as well as chapels, were covered with religious and moral 'histories', like Dives and Lazarus or the Wheel of Fortune.

One other form of art should be mentioned, which has much in common with the visual instruction of the wall-paintings and the oral instruction of the sermons, namely the religious drama of the period, the miracle plays or mystery plays. The period from the middle of the thirteenth to the middle of the fourteenth century was a turning point in the development of religious drama, for it was then apparently that the strictly liturgical drama of the early Middle Ages, performed in churches in Latin, gave place to more elaborate vernacular plays, performed outside the churches, in churchyards, in market-places or in the streets.[2] This popularization of religious drama is closely parallel to the popularization of religious instruction that led from the penitential literature of the thirteenth century to works like the *Lay-folk's Catechism* or Mirk's *Instructions*.

In their fully developed form these plays consisted of cycles of anything up to fifty scenes or more, representing episodes from the Old and New Testaments, from the fall of Lucifer and the Creation

---

[1] The Longthorpe paintings are illustrated and described by Mr E. Clive Rouse in the *Illustrated London News*, 5 Nov. 1949, p. 705.

[2] See E. K. Chambers, *The Medieval Stage* (Oxford, 1903), II, chapters XX–XXII; Wells, *Manual*, chapter XIV; E. K. Chambers, *English Literature at the close of the Middle Ages* (Oxford, 1945), 1–49.

to the Last Judgment, the story of the Nativity and of the Passion being given in special detail.[1] As performed in the larger towns like York and Chester, these plays were organized by the municipal authorities, and each of the various trade-guilds made itself responsible for a particular scene. The scenes were sometimes allocated with a quaint appropriateness, as when the shipwrights were made responsible for Noah's ark, or the goldsmiths for the Adoration of the Magi. It became usual to act the scenes on a series of stages which were moved from place to place through the streets.

There is an obvious analogy between these plays and the cycles of scenes or 'histories' of the Nativity and Passion found among the wall-paintings; and Professor Owst has pointed out how much common ground is covered by the plays and the sermons, so that 'the expanded vernacular play itself often seems to be little more than a dramatized sermon or set of sermons'.[2] The plays had their crude and comic side, and were calculated to amuse as well as to instruct (as with the episode of the sheep-stealing shepherds in the Townely plays), and perhaps for this reason they had their critics both among the orthodox like Bromyard and among the Lollards. But undoubtedly they must have been important as a vehicle of religious instruction, reaching a wider public than the religious poems or treatises or even the sermons. They presented in a very vivid and forceful way the story of the Incarnation; they were capable of dignity and pathos, as well as quaintness, and they brought home to the most stolid and unimaginative onlookers just those scenes of the Nativity and the Passion which St Edmund's *Mirror* had recommended to the imagination of the devout. They thus formed an important element in that devotion to the Person and Passion of Christ which was so characteristic of this age.[3]

---

[1] See the lists in Chambers, *The Medieval Stage*, II, Appendix T.

[2] Owst, *Pulpit and literature*, chapter VIII.

[3] The morality plays (which developed rather later than the miracle plays) have also a strong resemblance to the treatises and poems of religious instruction, especially when they deal with topics like the *Paternoster* or the conflict of virtues and vices; cf. Chambers, *English literature*, 49 ff.

CHAPTER XI

ENGLISH MYSTICAL LITERATURE OF THE FOURTEENTH CENTURY

THE purpose of what follows is not to attempt to give a full account of the English mystics, but simply to offer some observations, and especially to attempt to relate this subject with what has gone before, namely the manuals of instruction for parish priests and the religious and moral didactic literature.

The materials of fourteenth-century English mysticism are very diverse.[1] In the first place there are the four great and outstanding writers: Richard Rolle, who died in 1349; the anonymous author of the *Cloud of Unknowing*, who probably lived in the late fourteenth century; Walter Hilton, the author of the *Scale of Perfection*, who died in 1396; and Dame Julian of Norwich, the author of the *Revelations of Divine Love*, who was writing *c.* 1373. These represent widely different types, living under different conditions. Richard Rolle was a hermit, living in the country and acting at the end of his life as the spiritual director of some Cistercian nuns; a self-made mystic and highly individualistic. The author of the *Cloud* has so far proved quite elusive, but it has been conjectured that he may have been a secular priest. Hilton was an Augustinian canon of Thurgarton in Nottinghamshire. Dame Julian was an enclosed solitary, living in a cell adjoining a town church, in Norwich. They also differ in the basis of their literary fame. Dame Julian is only known for one work. The author of the *Cloud* and Hilton, while they wrote several treatises, are each mainly remembered for one outstanding work. Rolle, on the other hand, was a prolific and versatile writer. Some of his works are Latin prose treatises, including his commentaries on Scripture; some are Latin verse, such as his *Canticum amoris*; some are English prose,

---

[1] For the English mystics in general, see M. D. Knowles, *The English Mystics* (London, 1927).

such as his English commentary on the Psalter and his letters addressed to nuns or solitaries; and some are English lyrics.

I suppose the things that interest and attract most modern readers are Rolle's English works, and especially his shorter treatises and lyrics; but here, as always, it is interesting to compare modern taste with medieval preferences, as reflected in the number of surviving manuscripts.[1] One has to allow for the element of accident in the survival of manuscripts, but we probably have here a very rough indication of the relative popularity of the various works. On this basis, the most popular seems to have been the *Emendatio vitae* (*Amendment of Life*), of which there survive ninety-four manuscripts of the Latin version and fifteen of English translations. Next in popularity comes his commentary on the Psalter, with fifty-eight manuscripts of the English and Latin versions altogether. Then come the Latin *Incendium amoris*, with forty-two manuscripts, and the Latin *Job*, with the same number. The latter was a commentary on the lessons in the Office of the Dead, dwelling on sin and 'the four last things' and calculated to inspire penitence; it had something of the same appeal as the *Prick of Conscience*. The English treatise, the *Form of living*, survives in thirty-eight manuscripts. It seems clear that it was the more systematic and practical of Rolle's works that had the greatest popularity, those that served as a general directory of spiritual life or as commentaries on those parts of Scriptures that were in everyday liturgical use, like the Psalter and the Job lessons. Rolle's lyrics and his more individualistic and autobiographical treatise, the *Melum contemplativorum*, survive in far fewer manuscripts.

In addition to the four great writers, there are one or two minor figures who deserve attention. First, there is an anonymous fourteenth-century monk of Durham who became a solitary on Farne Island[2]—here we have another northern equivalent of the Desert. He wrote (*c.* 1349) some remarkable meditations, in Latin,

[1] H. E. Allen, *Writings, passim.*
[2] W. A. Pantin, 'The Monk-Solitary of Farne', in *EHR*, LIX (1944), 162–86.

addressed to Christ Crucified, to the Blessed Virgin, to the Angels, to Abraham and David, to St John the Evangelist and to St Cuthbert. These form a very interesting link between the old and the new; in style they are Latin meditative prayers, rather in the twelfth-century manner of St Anselm and St Bernard, and the doctrine that the author propounded of the 'degrees of love' seems to be derived from St Bernard; while in his fervent personal devotion to Christ and the way in which he expresses it, he shows himself very much a contemporary of Rolle. In one passage he describes a mystical experience that he had, a revelation or 'showing' comparable to those described by Dame Julian. He had evidently been through a period of spiritual crisis, dominated by the fear of judgment and the wrath to come and by anxiety as to how to obtain salvation; and he tells us that Christ spoke to him in person, saying 'Love, and you will be saved' (*Dilige et salvus eris*), and that He spoke these words with a smile (*quasi enim ridendo ista dicebas*). Throughout the meditation addressed to the Crucified Christ there runs a remarkable combination of fear of judgment with the love of Christ, which is well summed up in his apostrophe: 'O Domine Sabaoth, amabilis Jhesu.'

Secondly there is William Flete,[1] an Austin friar and a Bachelor of Divinity of Cambridge, who left England in 1359 to go to Italy and settled as a hermit at Lecceto near Siena, where he was known as '*il Baccalliere della Selva del Lago*'. He became the friend and disciple of St Catherine of Siena, and wrote an interesting series of letters to his English brethren, mainly concerned with spiritual direction, but also urging reform in Church and State and loyalty to Pope Urban VI during the Schism. He criticized royal intervention in episcopal elections and the use of writs of prohibition to impede religious discipline, and he feared that God's punishment would fall on England and that the English people might fail in war on account of their sins. 'Pray, pray for England,'

---

[1] Gwynn, *English Austin Friars*, 107, 139–210. Flete came forward as a defender of St Catherine, rather as Easton came forward as a defender of St Brigit (see above, p. 180).

he wrote, 'England is much in my mind, England and the English King.'[1] He was writing in 1380, when the state of England was probably more critical than he can have fully realized in his retirement. It has been suggested that he was perhaps not so much the disciple as the director of St Catherine. He is certainly a very interesting illustration of the contact between English and Italian mysticism in this period, and he is also a striking example of a man turning his back on an academic career to embrace the solitary, mystical life, like St Benedict, *scienter nescius, sapienter indoctus.*

I have mentioned these two men particularly, because they are comparatively obscure and little known; we owe our entire knowledge of the Durham monk-solitary to the survival of a single manuscript. It seems to me that further research among the manuscript materials of fourteenth-century spiritual literature may well reveal more figures of this type. We badly need a scholar of the type of Dom Wilmart or Henri Bremond to explore and record the later Middle Ages from this point of view.

Finally, there is the great mass of anonymous mystical and devotional writings, in prose and verse: *turba magna, quam dinumerare nemo potest.* Some of these have been incorrectly attributed to Richard Rolle or even more arbitrarily to the school of Wyclif. Many pieces were printed over fifty years ago by the indefatigable Horstman;[2] a selection of the religious lyrics has been printed by Carleton Brown,[3] and the same author has listed between two and three thousand poems, a considerable proportion of which, perhaps a thousand, must belong to the fourteenth century.[4] Of the numerous anonymous treatises one of the most interesting and striking is that known as *A talking of the Love of*

[1] Gwynn, *English Austin Friars,* 201–3.

[2] C. Horstman, *Yorkshire writers, Richard Rolle of Hampole...and his followers* (London, 1895–6).

[3] *Religious lyrics of the fourteenth century* (Oxford, 1924).

[4] Carleton Brown, *A Register of Middle English religious and didactic verse,* 2 vols., Oxford, 1916; Carleton Brown and R. H. Robbins, *The Index of Middle English verse,* New York, 1943.

God,[1] a composition in rhythmical prose, which is a fourteenth-century recasting of two earlier thirteenth-century pieces; it consists almost entirely of a series of lyrical outbursts, of apostrophes addressed to Christ and His Mother, and is intended as a preparation and preliminary to affective prayer. It is impossible to exaggerate the importance of this vast sea of minor religious literature in the religious history of fourteenth-century England, for it means that the great spiritual writers like Rolle and Hilton did not stand alone in a vacuum, but had numberless followers and imitators. Nothing could illustrate better the thoroughness with which the piety of the age had seeped throughout society. From the historian's point of view a mass of even second-rate material is often as revealing and impressive as the work of a single writer of genius.

What relation had this mystical and devotional literature to the manuals for parish priests and the didactic English treatises, the rather more humdrum literature which we have already been considering? I think there is more relation than might at first sight appear. Thus, for instance, St Edmund's *Mirror*, which we have already considered as one of the treatises of religious instruction,[2] besides containing the usual material about the virtues and vices and commandments, does also contain those remarkably elaborate meditations on the life and Passion of Christ, which have been quoted above, and in fact the main theme of the *Mirror* is contemplation, the contemplation of God in His creatures, in Holy Scripture and in Himself.

A still more striking link is Richard Rolle's *Iudica me*. This is a Latin prose treatise written *c.* 1322, for the instruction of a friend who was a parish priest; it deals with the priest's duties and particularly with the method of hearing confessions. It incorporates considerable sections of William of Pagula's *Oculus sacerdotis*, but with certain characteristic additions by Rolle. Here we have one of the leading mystics taking a hand in giving practical instructions for a parish priest, and for that purpose borrowing from one of the

---

[1] *A Talkyng of þe love of God*, ed. Sister M. Salvina Westra, O.P. (The Hague, 1950).
[2] Cf. above, p. 222.

most popular manuals of the period. Rolle is not only concerned with instructing contemplatives; he has like so many others an interest in improving the parish clergy of his day.[1]

The anonymous treatise known as *Poor Caitiff*,[2] which survives in many manuscripts, probably dates from the late fourteenth century. It has sometimes been attributed to the school of Wyclif, but apparently without foundation. It is particularly instructive for our purpose in showing the link between didactic and mystical literature, for it begins with simple elementary instructions on the creed, the commandments and the Lord's Prayer, and these lead on to a number of short tracts of a more mystical character, 'exciting men to heavenly desire'.

This treatise [the prologue runs] compiled of a poor caitiff and needy of ghostly help of all Christian people, by the great mercy and help of God, shall teach simple men and women of good will the right way to heaven, if they will busy themselves to have it in mind and work thereafter, without multiplication in many books. And as a child, willing to be a clerk, beginneth at the ground, that is his A B C, so he who thus desires to speed the better beginneth at the ground of health, that is the *Christian men's belief* [the creed];... but for as much as the belief by it self is not sufficient to man's salvation, without good works of charity, as Christ saith by His Apostle St James, therefore he purposeth with God's help ensuingly to tell the *Commandments of God*, in which the charitable works be contained that belong to the belief. And for as much as it is hard to purchase aught of God in prayer, until a man verily believe and live after His Commandments, as He Himself says in the Gospel,... therefore, following after these Commandments, he thinketh with the help of God to show shortly the *prayer* that Jesu Christ taught to His disciples, that is to say the *Pater noster*; and after these, some short *sentences exciting men to heavenly desire*; for thus it behoveth to climb up as by a ladder of diverse rungs, from the *ground of belief* unto the keeping of *God's Commandments*, and so up from *virtue to virtue*, till he see the God of Sion reigning in everlasting bliss.[3]

[1] H. E. Allen, *Writings*, 101, 108, 124, 142, 147, 151.
[2] Wells, *Manual*, 482 (XII, 74); H. E. Allen, *Writings*, 406; *Modern Language Review*, XVIII, 3; M. Deanesly, *The Lollard Bible* (Cambridge, 1920), 346–8.
[3] Bodleian, MS. Ashmole 1286, fo. 32v; cf. Deanesly, *op. cit.* 346.

The short mystical tracts with which the work concludes deal with the counsels of perfection; with patience in tribulation; 'the charter of heaven'; 'Horse and Rider' (or the 'rule of man's body'); 'learn to love Jesu'; 'Desire of Jesu'; 'Of meekness'; 'the affect of will'; 'Active and contemplative life'; 'the Mirror of chastity'. These tracts incorporate some borrowings from Rolle and Hilton.

In general it may be said that the more advanced and, so to speak, lyrical writings of the mystics presuppose a solid, severe, astringent preparation of dogmatic teaching and ascetical training. Both Rolle and Hilton, for instance, have much to say about sin and conversion from sin; this is the main theme of Rolle's *Amendment of Life*, and the destruction of the 'image of sin' in man's soul and the formation of the 'image of Christ' plays an important part in Hilton's *Scale of Perfection*. Thus all the treatises on confession and on penance, and on the virtues and vices, with their relentless analysis and their divisions and subdivisions of every sin—literature which may seem dreary reading to modern students—and all the mass of moralizing and critical sermons, cannot be ignored or passed over, because they were the necessary preparation or groundwork, without which one could not have had the exquisite flowering of the mystical literature. The mystics in fact presuppose an audience thoroughly and severely drilled in the rudiments of faith and morals, and the widespread appeal of vernacular mystical literature in the later Middle Ages seems to argue that the programme of religious instruction planned by the reforming bishops of the thirteenth century did succeed in reaching and indoctrinating certain sections of the laity. If the devout and literate layman was something of a problem to the Church, he was also in some respects a product of the Church's own work. We should have a misleading and superficial picture of fourteenth-century English spirituality if we looked only at the great mystics without also looking at the more pedestrian literature of religious instruction which lies behind them; the two go together.

It will be useful for our purpose to consider some of the characteristics of the fourteenth-century English mystics. In the first place we find a very strong, intimate and affectionate concentration on and devotion to the Person of Christ.[1] This type of devotion, as has been mentioned already, goes back to the eleventh century, to writers like John of Fécamp, St Peter Damiani and St Anselm; it was continued in the twelfth century, notably by St Bernard and other Cistercian writers, and in the thirteenth century by Franciscans, such as St Bonaventure. It reached its height in the fourteenth century when it takes a very vivid and even emotional form, as for instance in Richard Rolle, and it was particularly concentrated on the Passion of Christ and on the Holy Name of Jesus. This type of devotion is most marked in Rolle, least in the author of the *Cloud*. Rolle was the great propagandist of the cult of the Holy Name in England, rather as St Bernardino of Siena was later to be in Italy.

Another characteristic is anti-intellectualism. The fourteenth-century English mystics naturally shared in that reaction against the excessive intellectualism of the schools, which we have already noticed, for instance, in FitzRalph's 'conversion' from philosophy to theology.[2] This is very marked in Richard Rolle and in the monk-solitary of Farne. Richard Rolle complains of the contempt which the intellectuals, trained in the schools, show for those whose learning is derived from mystical experience:

But those who are taught by means of wisdom which is acquired, not infused, and are puffed up with complicated argumentations, are disdainful towards him [the mystic], saying: 'Where did he learn? What doctor did he attend?' They do not believe that the lovers of eternity can be taught by the doctor within, to speak more eloquently than those who are taught by men, who all the time study for the sake of vain honours.[3]

The monk-solitary of Farne makes the same point:

'I have had understanding above the ancients; because I have sought Thy commandments.' Behold the reason why he [the psalmist] confesses

[1] See above, p. 190. [2] See above, p. 132.
[3] *Incendium Amoris*, ed. M. Deanesly (Manchester, 1915), 240.

that he understands the things of God. He does not say 'because
I have gone to the schools, because I have learnt from learned men',
but 'because I have sought Thy commandments'. And truly it is so.
For there is a certain instruction and understanding of holy scripture
which the Lord promises to give to those who walk in the way of His
commandments; as Bernard learnt among the beech trees and the
oaks....Let the sons of Agar the bond-woman listen to this, who seek
the wisdom of earth, the sons of Belial, puffed up with knowledge, who
are wont to despise simple and ignorant men because they are not
powerful in letters as they are.

Let the meek hear and rejoice, that there is a certain knowledge of
holy scripture which is learnt from the Holy Ghost and manifested in
good works, which often the layman knows and the clerk does not,
the fisherman knows and not the rhetorician, the old woman has learnt
and not the doctor of theology.[1]

Another characteristic of the mystics is their individualism.
Rolle is the most markedly individualistic of all. But in general it
is noticeable how mysticism especially flourished, in England in
the later Middle Ages, not so much in religious communities as
among solitaries, like Rolle and Dame Julian, or in that religious
order, the Carthusians, which most cultivated the solitary life; and
where we do find a Benedictine mystic, like the monk of Farne,
he is a monk who has turned solitary.

From a geographical point of view it is interesting to note that
the English mystical writers of the fourteenth century were mainly
drawn from the northern and eastern parts of England, from what
had been the Danelaw in fact—roughly the same area where in the
twelfth century the Cistercian foundations had been concentrated.

Perhaps the most remarkable characteristic of all is the vernacular
element in fourteenth-century English mystical literature. While
some of the writers, such as Rolle, put some of their work into Latin,
yet on the whole the English mystics wrote their most important
works in the vernacular, in English. We find the same practice
of writing mystical works in the vernacular on the Continent at

[1] *EHR*, LIX (1944), 177.

this period, in Germany, the Netherlands and Italy, among such writers as Eckhart, Tauler, Suso, Ruysbroeck, and St Catherine of Siena. The importance of this vernacular English mystical writing in helping to maintain the 'continuity of English prose' from Anglo-Saxon times to the later Middle Ages has, of course, been well pointed out by R. W. Chambers[1] and others. It was important for the English language as well as for literature, for it meant that English was being used for describing the most abstract and intricate spiritual and psychological matters, for which hitherto Latin had been used.

The vernacular mystical writings, while partly intended for the use of unlearned clerics and religious, including nuns and anchoresses, were also read by devout lay people. And this brings us to one of the most important phenomena of the religious history of the later Middle Ages, namely the rise of the devout layman. Of course there had been devout laymen in every age, but in the fourteenth and fifteenth centuries it was possible for a devout and literate layman, with the help of all the apparatus of religious instruction, sermons, and devotional literature, to take a more intelligent, educated, active, and, so to speak, professional part in the life of the Church. Thus laymen were enabled and encouraged to attempt the practice of contemplative prayer. Walter Hilton's treatise on the 'Mixed Life'[2] is expressly intended to teach how laymen immersed in affairs, 'the which have sovereignty', as he puts it—in fact men like Henry Duke of Lancaster—can at the same time try to live a contemplative life. Again, a very popular treatise of this period, the *Abbey of the Holy Ghost*,[3] has as its purpose to show how a devout laywoman can, so to speak, live in a 'spiritual' convent, live the religious life in spirit while still remaining in the world. And of course the institution of the third orders of the mendicants had for a long time past offered lay men and women active membership

---

[1] *On the Continuity of English Prose* (extract from *EETS*, 186).

[2] Printed in Horstmann, *Yorkshire writers*, I, 264–92; D. Jones, *Minor works of Walter Hilton* (London, 1929); cf. Wells, *Manual*, 461 (XI, 55); Deanesly, *op. cit.* 218.

[3] Wells, *Manual*, 368 (VI, 46); printed in Horstman, *op. cit.* I, 321–37; *EETS*, 26.

of and participation in a religious order. To this type of the devout layman, at a later period, belonged such different personalities as King Henry VI and St Thomas More; and a good example of the devout laywoman is Cicely Duchess of York, the mother of Edward IV and Richard III, whose daily life has been described for us in detail:[1]

Me seemeth it is requisite to understand the order of her own person concerning God and the world. She useth to arise at seven of the clock, and hath ready her chaplain to say with her matins of the day and matins of Our Lady; and when she is full ready, she hath a low Mass in her chamber, and after Mass she taketh somewhat to recreate nature; and so goeth to the chapel, hearing the divine service and two low Masses; from thence to dinner, during the time whereof she hath a reading of holy matter, either Hilton of Active and Contemplative Life, Bonaventure *De infancia Salvatoris*, the Golden Legend, St Maud [Mechtild], St Katherine of Siena, or the Revelations of St Brigit.

After dinner she giveth audience to all such as have any matter to show unto her, by the space of one hour; and then she sleepeth one quarter of an hour; and after she hath slept, she continueth in prayer unto the first peal of evensong; then she drinketh wine or ale at her pleasure. Forthwith her chaplain is ready to say with her both evensongs; and after the last peal she goeth to the chapel, and heareth evensong by note [sung]; from thence to supper, and in the time of supper, she reciteth the reading that was had at dinner to those that be in her presence.

After supper she disposeth herself to be familiar with her gentle women, to the following of honest mirth; and one hour before her going to bed, she taketh a cup of wine, and after that goeth to her private closet and taketh her leave of God for all night, making an end of her prayers for that day; and by eight of the clock is in bed. I trust to Our Lord's mercy that this noble princess thus divideth the hours to His High pleasure.

It was for a lower level of society, for the devout layman who was head of a family, that Richard Whitford, a monk of Syon, published his *Work for householders* (1530). Besides giving a form

[1] *A Collection of Ordinances and Regulations for the Government of the Royal Household* (published by the Society of Antiquaries, London, 1790), 37.

of morning and night prayers for personal use, he gives an English paraphrase of the Lord's Prayer, the Hail Mary and the Creed, for family use; he directs that this shall be recited in a loud voice, so that all can hear, at every meal or at least once a day, and that all persons in the house shall be required to learn this by heart. He also tells the householder that 'it should be a good pastime and much meritorious, for you that can read, to gather your neighbours about you on the holy day, specially the young sort, and read to them this poor lesson' (i.e. the treatise). It would be a mistake to think that family piety, 'pure religion breathing household laws', was solely a post-medieval development. The difficulty is that the medieval layman was largely inarticulate and this side of his domestic habits unrecorded. It is only occasionally that we are given glimpses. To take an example from fourteenth-century France, the great theologian, John Gerson, gives us a vivid description of a certain father (it is clearly his own father) telling his child the story of Christ's Passion, standing with outstretched arms against the wall and saying: 'See, my son, this was how your God, who made you and saved you, was crucified and died.'[1] Gerson wrote letters and treatises of spiritual direction to his six sisters, who all lived at home and devoted themselves to religion; the Gerson home must have resembled a miniature Béguinage, a fourteenth-century Little Gidding.

For fourteenth-century England, Bishop John Sheppey of Rochester gives us an interesting picture of a devout laywoman, in a sermon which he prepared for the funeral of Lady Cobham in 1344; I say 'prepared', because, as he tells us, the Archbishop of Canterbury turned up and preached instead. He takes (rather boldly, according to our modern taste) as his text *Ecce ancilla Domini*: 'Lo here God's servant, that worshipped Him wonderfully in lusts and likings forsaking, pleased Him lovelily in her good workings doing, followed Him goodly in holy bedes and speakings saying.' He holds up Lady Cobham as an example in such matters

[1] J. L. Connolly, *John Gerson, reformer and mystic* (Louvain, 1928), 21.

as Sunday observance and reverence in church, and describes her devout practices and her deathbed:

But lo, in such things this lady was well instructed; for as regards prayers, every day was a feast day with her. For unless there was some greater necessity, on no day would she willingly come down from her chamber or speak with any stranger, until she had said matins and the hours of Our Lady, the seven psalms and the litany, almost every day; and then at Mass, when the priest was silent, she said some private prayers in French and some Paternosters and Hail Marys. And in her last days, when mortal illness took hold of her, she still showed the devotion which she had had in her prayers; for when I came to her in the fifth day of her illness, she complained to me more about not being able to say her matins, than about her illness; and for the space of a league, a little before her death, she made the priest that was present say with her the litanies and Hail Marys.[1]

Another extremely interesting and well-documented example of a devout laywoman is Margery Kempe of King's Lynn, whose autobiography is one of the most remarkable discoveries in medieval English literature.[2] Although Margery's spiritual adventures lay in the early fifteenth century, she may be regarded as a product of fourteenth-century conditions. Margery was of course abnormal in several ways, but she was an abnormal specimen of what was a large and familiar class of devout lay people—the sort of people whom she so disturbed at Mass or sermon by her hysterical outbursts. Her whole life presupposes a background of devout laymen. And just because Margery was abnormally sensitive and hysterical, she serves very conveniently as a kind of spiritual seismograph; she records the devout layman's reactions to the devotional stimuli of the time, and shows how men used the contemporary apparatus of piety.

In the first place, Margery provides a very good example of what has already been referred to, namely intense devotion to the Person of Christ and especially to the Passion. That devotion was clearly

[1] New College, Oxford, MS. 92, fo. 152, 155; and see below, p. 276.
[2] *The Book of Margery Kempe*, ed. S. B. Meech and H. E. Allen, *EETS*, 212 (1939); modernized version by W. Butler-Bowdon, World's Classics ed., 543 (Oxford, 1954).

the centre of her spiritual life and of her thought. In this she is typical and normal, and that this was so was very much to her credit, however tiresome she may have been in other respects— by her hysterical outbursts, for instance. An important element in this devotion was detailed meditation on the scenes of Christ's life and Passion, as had long been recommended, for instance, by such books as St Edmund's *Mirror* and the *Meditations of the Life of Christ* attributed to St Bonaventure. Margery of course makes these meditations; sometimes she does this more or less spontaneously and deliberately, with an ease that other devout people envied:

When she was there [in the Priory cloister at St Margaret's, Lynn], she had so great mind of the Passion of Our Lord Jesu Christ and of His precious wounds and how dearly He bought her, that she cried and roared wonderfully, so that she might be heard a great way off, and might not restrain herself therefrom. Then had she great wonder how Our Lady might suffer or endure to see His precious body be scourged and hanged on the cross. Also it came to her mind how men had said to her before, that Our Lady, Christ's own Mother, cried not as she did, and that caused her to say in her crying, 'Lord, I am not Thy Mother. Take away this pain from me, for I may not bear it. Thy passion will slay me.' Then there came by her a worshipful clerk, a doctor of divinity, and said, 'I had sooner than twenty pounds that I might have such a sorrow for Our Lord's Passion.'[1]

Sometimes, however, meditations, vivid pictures in her mind of the Passion or the Nativity, are suggested to her by sermons that she hears, or by the sight of an image, a crucifix or a *pietà*:

And there [at Leicester] she came into a fair church, where she beheld a crucifix that was piteously devised and lamentable to behold, through beholding which the Passion of Our Lord entered her mind, whereby she began to melt and dissolve utterly in tears of pity and compassion. Then the fire of love kindled so quickly in her heart that she might not keep it privy, for, whether she would or no, it caused her to break out with a loud voice and cry marvellously and weep and sob full hideously, so that many a man and woman wondered at her therefore.[2]

---

[1] Meech and Allen, *op. cit.* 164; Butler-Bowdon, *op. cit.* 215.
[2] Meech and Allen, 111; Butler-Bowdon, 144.

On another occasion, when she went into a church at Norwich, this creature saw a fair image of Our Lady called a 'pity'. And through the beholding of that pity her mind was all wholly occupied in the Passion of Our Lord Jesu Christ and in the compassion of Our Lady Saint Mary, by which she was compelled to cry full loud and weep full sore, as though she should have died. Then came to her a priest saying, 'Damsel, Jesu is dead long since.' When her crying was ceased, she said to the priest, 'Sir, His death is as fresh to me, as if He has died this same day, and so me thinketh it ought to be to you and to all Christian people. We ought ever to have mind of His kindness, and ever to think of the doleful death that He died for us.'[1]

When she was on pilgrimage to the Holy Land, visits to the holy places of Jerusalem inevitably had the same effect:

Then the friars lifted up a cross and led the pilgrims about from one place to another where Our Lord had suffered His pains and His passions, every man and woman bearing a wax candle in her hand, and the friars always, as they went about, told them what Our Lord suffered in every place. And the foresaid creature wept and sobbed so plenteously as though she had seen Our Lord with her bodily eye suffering His Passion at that time. Before her in her soul she saw Him verily by contemplation and that caused her to have compassion.[2]

Particularly curious is the account of Margery's meeting with a fellow-pilgrim, a woman, who carried about a chest with an image (probably of the Christ-Child), and the effect of this upon Margery:

And the woman that had the image in the chest, when they came into good cities, she took the image out of her chest, and set it in the laps of worshipful wives; and they would put clothes upon it, and kiss it as though it had been God Himself. And when the creature [i.e. Margery] saw the worship and the reverence that they did to the image, she was taken with such sweet devotion and sweet meditations that she wept with great sobbing and loud crying. And she was moved so much the more, because while she was in England, she had high meditations on the birth and childhood of Christ, and she thanked God

[1] Meech and Allen, 148; Butler-Bowdon, 193.
[2] Meech and Allen, 68; Butler-Bowdon, 87.

forasmuch as she saw these creatures have so great faith in what she saw with her bodily eye, like as she had before with her ghostly eye.[1]

The interesting thing to notice is that these manifestations of popular piety, like image-worship and pilgrimages—the very things that the Lollards attacked, and that may seem to a modern observer to take a childish or superstitious form—were to a devout person like Margery not a hindrance but a direct help and stimulus to a more spiritual devotion. There seems in fact to be a direct connexion between the use of images and the practice of meditation in the later Middle Ages, which needs studying. As has already been mentioned, it is in this period that we find those cycles of scenes of the Nativity and Passion of Christ painted on the walls of village churches, as at Chalgrove and Croughton, which must have served as a kind of text-book or programme of meditations for the devout.

Margery Kempe also illustrates the love of sermons among the devout laity of her period. 'Alas, Lord,' she exclaims, 'so many clerks Thou hast in this world, and yet Thou wouldest not send me one of them that might fill my soul with Thy word and with reading of Holy Scripture; for all the clerks that preach may not fill it; for me thinketh that my soul is ever alike hungry. If I had gold enough, I would give every day a noble for to have every day a sermon, for Thy word is more worthy to me than all the goods in this world.'[2] When a famous preacher came to Lynn, her friends came to her and said, 'Margery, now shall you have preaching enough, for there is come one of the most famous friars in England to this town.' When she was forbidden to attend this preacher's sermons, on account of the disturbance she caused by her outbursts, 'she had so much sorrow that she knew not what she might do, for she was put from the sermon which was to her the highest comfort in earth when she might hear it, and right so the contrary was to her the greatest pain in earth when she might not hear it'.[3]

---

[1] Meech and Allen, 77–8; Butler-Bowdon, 99.
[2] Meech and Allen, 142; Butler-Bowdon, 186.
[3] Meech and Allen, 148, 151; Butler-Bowdon, 194, 198.

17-2

She tells us that some enthusiasts would follow a favourite preacher from town to town.[1] She throws light on the popularity and influence of certain spiritual books, which she had read to her—for she seems to have been illiterate herself—such as Hilton, St Brigit's *Revelations*, St Bonaventure, the *Stimulus amoris*, and Rolle's *Incendium amoris*,[2] and illustrates the contemporary practice of spiritual direction and the relations of penitent and director.

Margery is also interesting as exercising a kind of lay apostolate. She was very fond of giving what she calls 'good words'—moral stories, *exempla*, texts from the Gospel, spiritual advice, and she was particularly concerned to rebuke people for swearing oaths; she reproved the Archbishop of Canterbury for allowing his servants to do this. On one occasion, her 'good words' got her into serious trouble, for she was accused of persuading Lady Westmorland's daughter to leave her husband. The Archbishop of York, who was examining Margery, asked her what it was that she had said to Lady Westmorland. Margery answered, 'I told her a good tale of a lady that was damned, for she would not love her enemies, and of a bailiff that was saved, for he loved his enemies and forgave that they had trespassed against him, and yet he was held an evil man.' The archbishop said it was a good tale.[3] This use of 'good words' not unnaturally made her unpopular with some people, for instance with her neighbours and fellow-pilgrims, especially when she talked about religion at the dinner table; when she exclaimed 'It is full merry in Heaven,' they replied, 'Why speak ye so much of the mirth that is in Heaven? Ye know it not and ye have not been there, no more than we.'[4] Her 'good words' must have seemed dangerously like lay preaching, and so helped to bring on her the suspicion of Lollardy. But I suspect that the practice was not so uncommon as one might think; Cicely, Duchess of York, as we have seen, used to rehearse at supper, to her companions, the

[1] Meech and Allen, 152; Butler-Bowdon, 199.
[2] Meech and Allen, 143; Butler-Bowdon, 188.
[3] Meech and Allen, 133–4; Butler-Bowdon, 175.
[4] Meech and Allen, 11; Butler-Bowdon, 15.

spiritual reading that they had had at dinner, and some parts at least of the Canterbury Tales might come under the category of 'good words'.

In spite of much that was morbid and hysterical in her behaviour, on the whole Margery Kempe comes out well as a creditable specimen of the devout lay person of the later Middle Ages. If her troubles and sufferings were to some extent of her own making, she was never embittered by them; she impresses one as sincere, generous and affectionate, and completely lacking in that harshness which has sometimes marked the pious laity. It would be difficult to imagine anyone less like Mrs Proudie.

In the earlier part of this book we examined first the social structure of the fourteenth-century English Church, the relations of Church and State, and of Crown and Papacy; and secondly we examined the organization of learning, the scholars and the con-troversies of the period. Finally, we have now examined the religious literature of the period. As I have already suggested, it is probably in this last sphere of religious instruction that we can see the most constructive achievement of the fourteenth-century English Church, the direction in which men succeeded most clearly and directly in carrying out the aims of the thirteenth-century church reformers. The legislation of the Lateran Council and of the thirteenth-century English bishops led on logically to the production of manuals, written by a variety of authors, all eager to instruct the parish priest in every detail of his work. In particular we can see how much importance was attached to both the confessional and the pulpit as means of religious instruction and spiritual direction. We can see fourteenth-century religion in its most intensely personal aspect, in the minute care, integrity and sympathy with which each individual conscience was approached. We can also see the preoccupation of the age with social evils and with the misdeeds and problems of every class from judges to prostitutes. So much for the technical literature of the cure of souls, which, in the absence of a seminary system, was probably the most serious provision that the age made for the training of its priests. Next, the work of religious instruction was carried a stage further by the provision of less technical, but still often quite formidable works of moral and devotional teaching, written in the vernacular, and so available to a wider public of devout laymen as well as clergy. At least one of these vernacular treatises was written by a layman for laymen. The devout and literate layman was one of the most important phenomena of this period; he represented an opportunity as well as a problem for the Church, and the opportunity was at any rate not ignored. The process is carried a stage further still by the remarkable output of mystical literature in the vernacular, so that even the practice of contemplation is made possible for laymen; and this would not have been possible without the solid substructure of moral and doctrinal instruction that had been established. How many priests and laymen actually availed themselves of all this literature we can never know; the important thing is that it was offered to them.

APPENDIX I

Certain of the passages quoted in translation throughout this book are taken from unprinted manuscript sources. The following is the Latin text of these passages.

(i) PAGE 20. Extract from a letter of John Lutterel to a friend concerning the Beatific Vision (c. 1333-4):

Cambridge University Library, MS. Ii. III. 10

[fo. 91 v]
Epistola magistri Iohannis Lutterel Anglici, doctoris sacre theologie, ad quendam et[1] curie Romane disputantem.

[fo. 94 v]
...Sed michi opponitis quod nobis Anglicis frequenter hic opponunt; 'Ecce secundum logicam respondistis; tolle, tolle, secundum theologiam responde.' Ergo apud theologos superfluit logica? Revera non est periculosior bestia, si assit presumpcio, quam theologus sine logica. Vultis tractare questionem sine logica? Materiam queritis murum sine cemento. Audivi cum essem iuvenis quendam magnum[2] dicentem quod theologus sine bona logica asinus esset cornutus.

(ii) PAGE 114. Extracts from the *Questiones* of Thomas Buckingham (c. 1346-50):

New College, Oxford, MS. 134

[fo. 324]
Questiones tractate per Thomam de Bukyngham, nuper ecclesie Exoniensis cancellarium, ostendentes inter errores Pelagii, Cicheronis et Scoti catholicum medium invenire, predestinacionem, preordinacionem, prevolucionem eternam concursumque Dei stare cum libera voluntate et merito creature, et ideo ab effectu ostensivo meriti libere accionis sequens opusculum nominatur, et iuxta modum Oxonie actenus observatum in sua incepcione seu principio questionem materias quas tractare disposuit continentem proposuit sub hac forma....

---

[1] *sic* MS.   [2] *sic* MS., perhaps for *magistrum*?

[fo. 395 v]

Quia pretacte materie est annexum de statu primorum[1] sanctorum in limbo usque ad Christi adventum sub potestate diaboli detentorum, hic inserere questionem que Exonie[2] inter quosdam doctores diucius vertebatur [   ],[3] et fuit questio sub hac forma: *questio 67*;[4] Utrum omnes adulti et parvuli mortui ante Christum in culpa mortali et sine presentis iustificacionis et remissionis ac gratificacionis gracia decesserunt ad carenciam visionis divine perpetuam obligati?

Qui partem affirmativam tenere videtur, eam sanctorum dictis et racionibus variis persuasit, et ad auctoritates ac raciones sibi contrarias apparenter respondet; cuius dicta ad questionem et ad contrarias raciones summarie colligenti videtur quod doctor dicat multa sanctorum dictis opposita et in scolis communiter inaudita; de quibus multis colligere volo pauca et eo ut potero infirmare.[5]

1. Quod ante mortem Christi nec penitencia, nec circumcisio, nec aliquod sacramentum vel cerimonia veteris testamenti valebant ad originalis vel actualis peccati mortalis purgacionem et delecionem tunc actu et in re factam, sed tantum in spe, et primo in morte Christi in re et actualiter faciendam.

2. Quod Iohannes baptista, Moyses, Abraham et alii sancti patres actu et in re solummodo iusti erant iusticia legali morali et iuris nature.

3. Quod Maria mater Dei, si in originali peccato concepta fuit, continue in peccato mortali mansit, nec graciam remissionis peccati mortalis vel iustificacionis presentis et gratificacionis ad vitam eternam habuit ante mortem Christi.

4. Quod si ipsa Maria sine omni peccato concepta vel nata fuit, vel si graciam et caritatem habuit iustificacionis presentis, et qualem quilibet nunc de lege habet qui est extra peccatum mortale, et quali caret quilibet in mortali existens, sibi fuit ianua regni celestis aperta ante mortem Christi.

5. Quod nulli fuit ianua regni celestis clausa nisi in culpa mortali actualiter existenti.

6. Quod opera bona sanctorum patrum, quamvis fuerunt facta in reatu peccati mortalis et pro tanto mortua per carenciam gracie tem-

---

[1] *Parentum* expunged.   [2] The MS. clearly reads *Exonie*, not *Oxonie*.
[3] A blank occurs here in the MS.; some word like *curavi* or *curabo* seems needed.
[4] *Questio 67* in left margin.
[5] The thirteen articles that follow are omitted in the translated version on p. 114 above; I have given them here for the sake of completeness.

poralis, per mortem Christi sunt vivificata et iam in celis remunerata vita eterna per graciam subsequentem, et primo in morte[1] Christi eis infusam,'et tunc primo fuerunt vita eterna digni,[2] et sic dicit quod opera mortalia in culpa mortali facta, et sine presentis iustificacionis gracia de qua superius est loqutum, ad vitam eternam viviscunt per graciam subsequentem, quemadmodum illa opera que sine peccato et in gracia ac caritate fuerunt facta.

8. Quod de triplici caritate quam posuit doctor predestinacionis divine, iustificacionis presentis quam vocat remissionis graciam, et ut dicit est et gracia baptismalis, et Augustinus eam vocat graciam temporalem, que a gracia predestinacionis divine differt, eo quod aliqui habent primam et non secundam, sicut multi qui sunt modo in peccato mortali et tamen predestinati, aliqui e contra sunt extra omne peccatum mortale et sic habent illam graciam sed non predestinati, et de tercia caritate que dicitur redamacionis, de qua dicit Iohannes: Diligamus Deum quoniam ipse prior dilexit nos, et hanc nominat caritatem seu graciam adquisitam.

Caritas media se habet per modum vestis, et sicut honesta vestis in scutiffero et mundicia vasis pro ferculo faciunt ministerium acceptum domino, ita est de illa gracia temporali, et non se habet ad bona opera per modum principii activi, sed gracia et caritas predestinacionis et redamacionis sufficiunt cum libero arbitrio tanquam principia activa bonorum operum.

9. Quod nulla opera bona mortificata vel mortua possunt vivificari, nisi procedant de caritate divine predestinacionis et humane redamacionis.

10. Quod obligacio ad eternam penam sensus per penitenciam antiquorum et alia bona opera, que in vita fecerunt, fuit eis remissa et in toto deleta, non obstante quod in culpa mortali et sine illa gracia tali, de qua superius est loqutum, continuo permanserunt.

11. Quod Deus remittit unum peccatum mortale quantum ad penam sensus alias infligendam, ipso mortali et alio remanente, sed non remissione acceptoria ad vitam eternam.

12. Quod semper culpa et debitum pene pro culpa simul sunt, nec unquam est debitum pene pro culpa, nisi pro culpa actualiter tunc manente; sed sicut pena partibiliter remittitur, sic secundum eandem proporcionem remittitur ipsa culpa.

[1] *mortem* MS.   [2] Article 7 apparently begins about here.

13. Quod in penitentibus extra articulum necessitatis, per quem intelligo articulum mortis, peccatum mortale in eis manet, donec sint per applicacionem clavium actualiter absoluti; et de cathecuminis et baptismo aque dicit eodem modo quod culpa mortalis deletur primo, et gracia remissionis et iustificacionis presentis, de qua superius est loqutum, infunditur in ipsa applicacione actuali sacramenti, non ante in cordis contricione et firmo proposito confitendi et satisfaciendi quamcicius facultatem habebit.

Multa alia prenarratis similia vel peiora fuerunt dicta, que per sequencia denudantur ac multis racionibus denudantur.[1] Hii articuli, salva semper reverencia opinantis, videntur quasi in toto erronei ac sanctorum scriptis et scole principiis repugnantes, et ego partem contrariam catholicam reputo et[2] fidelem, quam spero probabiliter declarare, et primo et[3] omnia dicta mea correccioni ecclesie et prelati mei ex corde submitto, quorum doctrinam in omnibus sequi opto; nulli errorem vel falsum impono, quia si dicta non sint vel dicta et finaliter sint correcta, hoc est quod quero, et ne in posterum aliquis ista credat, scribo.

[fo. 399 v]

Nunc racionibus reverendi doctoris ut spero veraciter persolutis, restat partem meam, immo opinionem communem racionibus et sanctorum testimoniis declarare; et quia doctor, contra cuius dicta sermonem accepi, conclusiones suas apparencias nominat, ego magis desiderans veritatem antiquam quam novam apparenciam vacuam et fallacem, iuxta articulos pertractandos elicio veritates....

(iii) PAGE 146. Extract from Thomas Waleys on Judges i. 1:

New College, Oxford, MS. 30

[fo. 47 v]

...Et certe sicut dicit Solinus, apud elephantes maximus ducit agmen, id est gregem; de quibus dicit Ambrosius, *Exameron*, quod rex excellit magnitudine et mansuetudine; unde hoc videtur animalibus inditum a natura, ut preditus melioribus naturalibus regat. Si sic esset modo in ecclesia, optime fieret et esset tempus eximium. Sed iam promoventur in ecclesia non divino consilio, sed parentum et amicorum carnalium, illi qui omnino sunt indigni divino iudicio, et est de eis sicut de fetu

---

[1] *Sic* MS.; perhaps for *declarantur?*   [2] *spero* expunged.   [3] *sic* MS.

ursi, nota alibi. Ps. *Quis ascendet in montem Domini*, id est ad gradum prelacionis, et respondet: *Innocens manibus et mundo corde* et cetera.

(iv) PAGE 159. A bill of complaint against the Mendicant Friars, delivered to the Convocation of Canterbury (c. November 1355): Public Record Office, D.L., 42/8 (Selby Register)¹

[fo. 79 v]

Billa liberata in consilio Cantuariensi provinciali contra fratres mendicantes
    Reverendis in Christo patribus, domino Cantuariensi archiepiscopo, tocius Anglie primati et apostolice sedis legato, et ceteris episcopis Cantuariensis provincie in consilio provinciali congregatis, graviter conquerendo demonstrat clerus vester Cantuariensis provincie, quod religiosi, quibus deceret² tribuere victum questus mendicitatis incerte, suis laxatis habenis, deliciis affluentes, in palefridis nobilibus propriis cellisque et frenis nimis exquisite ornatis, ultra morem maiorum prelatorum in Anglia, ad curias magnatum et loca publica et populosa frequenter incedentes, et archiepiscoporum, episcoporum et aliorum prelatorum Cantuariensis provincie et ecclesie Anglicane et iurium et canonum censuras non verentes, efficiuntur mordacissimi detractores, adulatores magnatum, confessores ac negociorum secularium et spiritualium erga dominum nostrum regem et alios terre proceres ac magnates, in preiudicium cleri et ecclesie Anglicane, quibus ⟨ultra laicos⟩³ hiis diebus opido sunt infesti,⁴ astuti et inequales mediatores, corrupti et sub velamento religionis fucati, eciam contractuum⁵ matrimonialium frequenter illicite voluntarie fiunt mediatores protervi [?] ac fallaces negociorum gestores; tantamque dominorum et dominarum/[fo. 80] regni Anglie benevolenciam blandiciis adquirunt, quod ecclesie regni Anglie quamplures quibus adversantur in sua iusticia enormiter oprimuntur; et quod flebilius est, huiusmodi dominorum et dominarum nobilium confessores, quin pocius proditores et animarum deceptores notorii, emendaciones peccatorum soli et poli iure lesis restituendas convertunt eisdem⁶ in predam, ac posito

---

¹ Letter-book of Geoffrey de Gaddesby, Abbot of Selby, 1342–64. This document occurs between documents of December 1355 and January 1356; it presumably refers to the Convocation of Canterbury summoned at St Paul's, 16 November 1355 (Wilkins, III, 33). The document is in places very difficult to read.
² Perhaps for *deberet*?   ³ Added above the line.
⁴ Cf. the opening words of the Bull of Pope Boniface VIII: *Clericis laicos infestos opido tradit antiquitas.*
⁵ *contractum* MS.   ⁶ or *eis*?

pulvillo blandiendi sub capite peccatoris quiescentis [?] in peccato, de bonis gravati, rubentes buccas pascunt, ventres inflant, et ecclesie Anglicane, in huiusmodi fomento peccati merito obiurgati, intollerabiles indies parant incidias, et hiis revora[1] latenter committunt, de quibus ad presens eis sic dominantibus non expedit loqui. Unde rogat clerus vester pro salute ecclesie Anglicane, quatinus contra huiusmodi insolencias dictorum mendicancium in hoc presenti consilio vel provisione sedis apostolice remedium procuretis adhibere oportunum.

(v) PAGES 197, 198, 200. Extracts from the *Oculus sacerdotis* of William of Pagula (*c.* 1317-33):

Bodleian Library, MS. Rawlinson A 361 (cited as R 1); MS. Rawlinson A 370 (cited as R 2); New College, Oxford, MS. 292 (cited as N)

[R 1 fo. 13; R 2 fo. 14v; N fo. 10]

Et[2] debet sacerdos inquirere a penitente qui[3] fuit ebriosus, quomodo[4] se inebriavit, vel quia forte ignoravit potenciam vini, vel propter hospites, vel eciam propter nimiam sitim supervenientem, quia in talibus casibus ebrietas est veniale peccatum. . . .

Sacerdos confessor debet inquirere a peccatore confitente, si assuetus fuerit maledicere hominibus vel aliis creaturis; vehementer enim irasci creaturis Dei vel pecoribus,[5] et maledicere eis cum[6] malicia nocendi, quod sepe faciunt rustici et homines maliciosi, est peccatum magnum. Magna est enim malicia irasci contra homines et animalia innocencia, et multi[7] homines in hoc genere peccati peccant, qui sepe peccare non credunt, et pauci ad confessionem venientes confitentur de ira. Et debet sacerdos iniungere iracundo silencium per aliquod tempus vel per aliquam horam diei. . . .

[R 1 fo. 50v; R 2 fo. 47v; N fo. 34]

Multi sunt sacerdotes et pauci sunt sacerdotes. Multi sunt nomine, pauci in[8] opere, XL di. *Multi sunt.*[9] Multi enim sunt[10] sacerdotes nomine, quia nichil est in hac vita et maxime hoc tempore facilius et levius et hominibus acceptabilius episcopi aut presbiteri officio; sed

---

[1] *sic* MS., perhaps for *peiora*?
[2] *Et* R 1 R 2; *Item* N.   [3] *qui* R 1 N; *si* R 2.
[4] *ebriosus quomodo* N; *ebriosus et quomodo* R 1 R 2.
[5] *pecoribus* N; *peccatoribus* R 1 R 2.
[6] *et maledicere eis cum* N; *et maledicere eis et cum* R 1; *vel maledicere eciam eis cum* R 2.
[7] *et multi* R 1 N; *et eciam multi* R 2.   [8] *in* R 2 N; *et* R 1.
[9] *Decretum*, Pars I, Dist. XL, c. 12.   [10] *sunt* R 1 R 2; om. N.

apud Deum nichil[1] miserabilius, tristius et dampnabilius, si negligenter atque adulatorie officium illud[2] agatur, XL di. c. *Ante omnia.*[3] Sed pauci sunt sacerdotes in opere, quia nichil est in hac vita et maxime hoc[4] tempore difficilius quo ad effectum, laboriosius quo ad personam, periculosius quo ad animam, episcopi aut presbiteri officio; sed apud Deum nichil[5] beatius, si eo modo militetur et fiat officium, quo Christus iubet, XL di. c. *Nichil est,*[6] et in glosa.... Ut autem multi fiant sacerdotes in opere, debent in sacra scriptura cum magna diligencia laborare.... Scire enim debent sacerdotes sacras scripturas et canones saltem[7] pentitenciales, et omne opus eorum debet esse in predicacione et doctrina atque cunctos debent edificare tam fidei sciencia quam operum disciplina.

[R1 fo. 95; R2 fo. 84; N fo. 63; S (= *Stimulus Amoris,* cap. VI)]

O felix temptacio, que ad divinos amplexus fugere nos compellit. O dulcis Domine, qui nos permittis undique effugari, et te semper tribuis refugium salutare, ut tecum omni tempore commoremur.[8] Et hoc semper habeas pro regula generali, quod quandocumque Deum ad te profunde volueris inclinare, in corde tuo vulnera Christi porta, et eius consparsus sanguine te Patri tanquam unigenitum presentabis,[9] et ipse tanquam Pater dulcissimus tibi plenarie providebit. Accede ad Christum et eum suppliciter depreceris ut ex quo non decet ipsum denuo vulnerari, dignetur te totaliter suo sanguine rubricare, et sic[10] indutus purpura poteris introire regis palacium. Hec autem vulnera cotidie intime cogitare; erunt tibi refrigerium[11] et solamen. Nec dubites quod si bene ea in corde tuo expresseris,[12] nulla temptacio te gravabit.[13]

(vi) PAGE 203. Extract from the *Regimen animarum* about tithe-paying (1343):

Bodleian Library, MS. Hatton 11

[fo. 6v]

Et quid si non sit in usu decimare de rebus aliquibus, cum de iure debeat decimare? Dic quod tunc procedatur secundum iura, sed

---

[1] add *est* R2.
[2] *illud* R2 N; *idem* R1.
[3] *Decretum,* Pars I, Dist. XL, c. 7.
[4] *in hoc* R1.
[5] add *est* N.
[6] *Decretum,* Pars I, Dist. XL, c. 7.
[7] om. R1.
[8] *commemoremur* N.
[9] *presentandum* N.
[10] *sic* om. N.
[11] *refrigerium* N R1 R2; *refugium* S.
[12] *impresseris* S.
[13] *regnabit* R1; *nullus tentationi aditus apparebit* S.

propter discordiam qua de causa possit oriri inter curatorem et parochianos suos oporteat fieri caute et discrete, et hoc duobus modis
potest fieri: Primo modo sic: debet curator parochianis suis amica-
biliter loqui: 'Filii mei karissimi, quia hoc vel hoc debet decimari, sed
quia non est in usu apud vos, consulo vobis ut eligatis duos vel tres
probos et fideles homines ex vobis, ut veniant in consorcio meo coram
ordinariis ecclesiasticis ad discussionem faciendam sumptibus meis
propriis, et ero fidelis coadiutor in negociis vestris et meis, quia nullo
modo volo dampnum vestrum in rebus temporalibus, sed desidero
animarum vestrarum salutem.' Iste primus modus valet in multis
dissensionibus que contingunt inter valde bonos curatores et suos
parochianos eciam valde bonos, immo mediocriter bonos. Sed ubi
sunt mediocriter boni curatores et mediocriter mali parochiani, immo
valde mali, tunc non valet iste primus modus, sed iste sequens:

Secundo modo ita fiet: Accedat curator caute et tacite ad officialem
vel ad archidiaconum, si magnum sit negocium, nesciente aliquo ex
parochianis suis qua de causa, et dicat ei privatim: 'Domine mi, talis
res in parochia mea decimari deberet, ut michi videtur, sed non est
in usu apud parochianos meos, et ideo videatis si de iure decimare
deberent de rebus iam supradictis, et supplico te, ut in visitacione
tua apud ecclesiam meam volueris inquirere ex viris coram vobis
citatis de parochia mea inter alias inquisiciones faciendas, utrum deci-
marent de talibus rebus, sicut de iure tenentur, vel non decimant, et ita
detectum erit coram vobis me absente, sive dicant quod decimant, sive
quod non decimant, et redigetur in scriptis, et secundum licenciam
vestram habebo copiam penes me, et illis notificabo.'

(vii) PAGES 206–10. Extracts from the *Memoriale presbiterorum* (1344):
Corpus Christi College, Cambridge, MS. 148 (cited as C), collated with
British Museum, Harleian MS. 3120 (cited as H):[1]

[C fo. 21v; H fo. 28v]

Circa milites.[2] Inquirere debes a milite si fuerit superbus vel adulter
vel alias luxuriosus, secundum quod sunt quasi[3] omnes moderni, vel si
uxorem suam a se abiecerit. . . .Item si traxerit clericos ad curiam suam

Corpus MS. 148 is a fourteenth-century MS., probably from Norwich Cathedral Priory.
Harleian MS. 3120 is a fifteenth-century MS., of unidentified provenance; its text is very
corrupt. I have only reproduced a small selection of its variant readings, many of which
are evidently the accidental mistakes or omissions of a careless scribe.
² add *et de eorum excessibus et peccatis* H.   ³ *communiter* H.

270

contra eorum voluntatem....Item si ediderit, statuerit, edi vel statui fecerit in curia sua aliquas constituciones vel statuta contra ecclesiasticam libertatem....Item si talliis et[1] exactionibus indebitis suos tenentes et maxime pauperes rusticos gravaverit....Item si habuerit capellam in manerio suo et in ea celebrari fecerit sine licencia et auctoritate pape vel proprii episcopi....Item si in curia sua iustiticiam servari et fieri fecerit equaliter pauperi sicut et diviti. Item si domino suo, regi forsan, comiti vel baroni aliquando favebat vel[2] fovebat eum in peccatis carnalibus vel aliis illicitis, vel si eum ad bellum iniustum stimulabat....Item si frequentaverit torneamenta....

[C fo. 65; H fo. 83]

De archidiaconis et eorum ministris. Si phas esset dicere, archidiaconi nostri temporis[3] et eorum ministri et eciam ceteri qui ecclesiastice presunt iurisdiccioni, quo ad correccionem peccatorum faciendam, tanquam canes infernales non solum latrando sed eciam devorando[4] suos subditos multociens ex causis exquisitis et fictis gravant plus debito, et pecunias varie extorquent ab eisdem....Preterea familiares archidiaconorum non sunt contenti, nisi dona recipiant a personis visitatis, et si dona non receperunt, gravant personas tales, quandoque bona sua superflue expendendo, sed absit quod furando, et quandoque sinistra falso predicando de eisdem, et multociens procurando gravamina et molestias per suos dominos et alios sibi adherentes inferri maliciose taliter visitatis; et in hoc peccant mortaliter.

[C fo. 67v; H fo. 85v]

De apparitoribus et bedellis ac aliis ministris iudicum.[5] Apparitores et cacherelli officialium et iudicum secularium, ultra id quod a dominis suis pro stipendiis suis recipiunt, nonnumquam ultra bona extorquent a subditis suis, aliquando per violenciam et oppressionem, verbi gracia: bedellus vel cacherellus videt aliquos divites in baliva sua, qui parum aut nichil curialitatis sibi conferunt. Unde pro muneribus extorquendis ponit eos in assisis, vel distringit per capcionem bonorum suorum, ea occasione, ut sic compellantur redimere vexacionem suam; vel facit eos vocari in ius ex proprio capite et sine causa, et sic varia dona

---

[1] A blank follows between *et* and *exactionibus* in H.
[2] *favebat vel* om. H.   [3] *nostri temporis* om. H.
[4] *non latratando* [sic] *sed devorando* H.
[5] *De ballivis et servientibus magnatum* H: this title really belongs to the next chapter, as rightly given in C.

extorquet ab eisdem, et aliquando per immoderatam improbitatem, et sic subditos suos multipliciter iniuriose gravat. . . .

[C fo. 62; H fo. 79]

De dominis temporalibus qui gravant subditos suos talliis et exaccionibus.
Contingit interdum quod domini temporales violenter exigunt et extorquent tam a rusticis suis, quam libere[1] tenentibus multa bona, ultra id quod tenentes ipsi[2] solvere debent et consueverunt, et ipsos invitos et absque causa talliant pro voluntate sua quandoque semel in anno, quandoque pluries, vel quociens eis videtur, nunc plus, nunc minus, quamplura bona per violenciam extorquendo; unde quandoque evenit, quod tenentes huiusmodi depauperati vix habeant unde possunt sibi et suis in victualibus providere; nec credunt tales domini se peccare in hoc, quia de iure civili,[3] quod hodie in omnibus casibus, in quibus vertitur periculum anime et peccatum committitur, si observetur ad litteram, tollitur omnino, cavetur quod quicquid servus adquirit, domino adquirit,[4] et sic huic legi innitentes domini temporales omnia bona rusticorum suorum pro sua voluntate occupant tanquam sua. Sed male decipiuntur, quia nullus dominus temporalis debet de iure naturali seu canonico aliquid exigere a tenente suo, preter id quod sibi debetur ab eodem de consuetudine, vel ex convencione inter ipsum et tenentem suum inita, vel ex imposicione facta ab antiquo; et si plus exegerit, debet hoc confiteri. . . . Et in confessione sibi debet iniungi et efficaciter induci, quod totum id quod ultra sibi debitum exegit, restituat illis a quibus illud extorsit, vel eorum heredibus, si salvari voluerit. . . . Debes igitur talibus dominis dicere, si tibi de hoc confiteantur, quod omnes qui talia faciunt, predones sunt et male fidei. Et quod nulla consuetudo poterit eos excusare in hoc casu a peccato. Racio est quia consuetudo ista talliandi et extorquendi est incerta,[5] quia nunc plus, nunc minus, et quociens placuerit dominis talliare.

[C fo. 62v; H fo. 80]

De rusticis et aliis tenentibus subtrahentibus dominis suis servicia et iura[6] sibi debita et consueta.[7] . . . Scire debes quod quilibet, tam liber, quam servus, a dominis quibuscumque temporalia tenens, in creacione novi domini sui facit[8] sibi homagium vel fidelitatem, spondendo in fide sua

[1] *liberis* H.	[2] *ipsis* H.	[3] *civili* om. H.
[4] *adquiritur* H.	[5] *iniusta* H.	[6] *iura* om. C.
[7] *et consueta* om. H.	[8] *faciat* H.	

vel iurando ad sancta Dei evangelia, quod sibi erit fidelis et quod faciet fideliter servicia sibi debita et consueta racione terrarum seu tenementorum, que vel quas tenet ab eodem. Si igitur aliquis taliter iurans aliquid de serviciis vel iuribus ab eodem debitis domino suo retinuerit,[1] subtraxerit, diminuerit vel ex certa sciencia concelaverit, furtum committit et eciam periurium.

[C fo. 24v; H fo. 31v]

Circa rusticos.... In primis ineunt inter se et faciunt conventicula et pacciones illicitas, coniurando et conspirando contra proximos et maxime contra pauperes, qui non habent quid eis offerant, et ipsos exheredant, et multis aliis modis opprimi procurant in curiis dominorum suorum, contra Deum et iusticiam et tamen sibi ipsis ex hoc nichil accrescit.... Preterea rusticus dives in maioribus peccare nititur, et minus peccare formidat quam nobilis sensu regulato ductus. De tali enim divite dicitur: Reus dives nullam culpam pertimescit, quam nummis se redimere existimat.... Item rustici frequenter accusant vicinos suos fraudulenter erga dominos suos et eorum balivos super criminibus et defectibus fictis, et sic fatigantur iniuste et bona sua amittunt.... Item rustici confidunt in auguriis et garritu avium, et ea sequuntur. Item confidunt in quibusdam malis[2] sortibus et supersticionibus, quas vetule plurime tenent et faciunt, et sic deviant a recta[3] et vera fide, et male sunt credentes.

[C fo. 23v; H fo. 31]

Circa nautas.[4] Tu confessor, si contingat te audire aliquem nautam in confessione, necesse habebis caute et studiose te habere in inquirendo; quia scire debes quod vix sufficit calamus scribere peccata quibus involvuntur. Tanta est enim illorum malicia, quod omnium hominum aliorum peccata excedit.... Item non solum occidunt clericos et laicos dum sunt in terra, sed eciam quando sunt in mari, piraticam exercent pravitatem, rapiendo bona aliorum et potissime[5] mercatorum mare transeuncium, et eos crudeliter[6] interficiunt.... Item omnes sunt adulteri et fornicatores, quia in singulis terris et regionibus quas ingrediuntur, vel contrahunt matrimonia de facto cum diversis mulieribus, credendo hoc sibi licere, vel fornicantur passim et indistincte cum meretricibus....

---

[1] *detinuerit* H.   [2] *quibusdam malis* C; *aliis* H; ⟨*alias aliis*⟩ added in margin C.
[3] add *via* H.   [4] add *et peccata eorum* H.
[5] *precipue* H.   [6] add *tractant et* H.

[C fo. 63 v; H fo. 81 v]

...Sed quicquid hic vel alibi scribatur de materia ista [plunder in war], vix reperitur aliquis qui de hoc peccato confiteatur, et si aliquociens forsan hoc contingat, plerique tunc confessores moderni, et maxime de ordinibus mendicancium, ceci et duces cecorum, nullam penitus talem peccatorem in hoc casu absolvendi potestatem habentes, data sibi aliqua parte huiusmodi prede, vel re alia, predonem et alios sibi adherentes absolvunt de facto, de restitucione, prout ius exigit, facienda penitus non curantes; sed ve omnibus talibus confessoribus.

[C fo. 70 v; H fo. 89 v]

De his qui iniqua statuta condunt. Domini temporales et quandoque eorum senescalli et ballivi faciunt[1] statuta sua multociens iuri scripto contraria, per que subditi sui frequenter gravantur, tam in rebus, quam personis.... Et ob[2] hoc scire debes, quod huiusmodi statuta sive leges quandoque fiunt contra ius naturale, quod continetur in evangelio et in iure canonico. Unde talia statuta non valent neque tenent ipso iure. Et multociens laici talia statuta faciunt in preiudicium et grave dampnum ecclesiarum et libertatum ac[3] clericorum et ministrorum earundem.[4] Propter quod omnes huiusmodi statuarii et eorum consiliarii necnon statutorum scriptores ac secundum ea iudicantes et ea servantes et eciam exequentes sunt excommunicati ipso iure. Et nichilominus obligantur in solidum ad restitucionem omnium dampnorum faciendam illis, qui per huiusmodi statuta iniqua fuerant lesi et que ipsorum occasione incurrerunt, ut patet per exemplum: Ecce rustici parochiani contra suum rectorem vel vicarium moti, statuunt inter se quod de cetero nullus offeret cum aliqua muliere se purificante vel pro aliquo mortuo nisi unum denarium, vel non offeret die anniversariorum parentum suorum, et hoc statuunt et eciam tenent, ad gravandum suum rectorem vel vicarium, sue ecclesie matrici in hoc preiudicando. Certe omnes tales sunt excommunicati ipso facto, ut supra tangitur.

[The following colophon is found only in H, fo. 104 v]

Explicit memoriale sacerdotum compositum a quodam doctore decretorum apud Avenonem, anno Domini millesimo CCC° quadragesimo quarto, ad informacionem iura non intelligencium, ita quod ex frequente iteracione iura penitencialia, que in canonibus reperiuntur, secundum diversa capitula aliqualiter sciunt, et eciam modum penitencie penitentibus sciunt inponere, secundum quod ordo iuris exigit.

[1] *condunt* H.   [2] *ad* C.   [3] *ac* om. H.   [4] *eorundem* H.

(viii) PAGE 215. Extracts from the *Manuale sacerdotis* of John Mirk (*c.* 1400):

Bodleian Library, MS. Bodley 549 (cited as A) collated with Bodleian Library, MS. Bodley 632 (cited as B), and Bodleian Library MS. Digby 75 (cited as C)

[A fo. 130v; B fo. 73; C fo. 169]

De conversacione sacerdotis boni. Dei vero sacerdos, cuius anima in manibus eius est semper,[1] sciens se conductum esse ad celebrandum quotidie....Idcirco se sobrie, iuste et pie vivere disponit, ita ut sobrie sibi, iuste magistro cui servit, et pie Deo cui preces offerre debet....Iuste eciam sacerdos vivit, dum cuique quod suum est reddit. Magistro quidem[2] suo reddit quod suum est, dum pro salario quod ab illo recipit, spiritualia commercia rependit, non ut tantum quotidie pro eo unam singulam[3] missam celebret,[4] sed eciam in aliis[5] spiritualibus obsequiis, ut puta vij psalmis penitencialibus, xv graduum psalmis,[6] devotis letaniis, mortuorum obsequiis, et huiusmodi aliis spiritualibus suffragiis.

[A fo. 131v; B fo. 73v; C fo. 171v]

De conversacione sacerdotis mundani. Illum namque sacerdotem mundi appellamus, qui mundum diligit....Igitur ut hec[7] predicta consequantur [good food and clothing], mundo se conferunt, hoc est cuidam mundano magnati, ecclesiarum patrono, se ad serviendum offerunt, sperantes ab eo ecclesiam fore[8] accepturos. Sic agit sacerdos mundi per fas et nephas, ut mundo copuletur et in illius servicium mancipetur. Accepto vero officio, ad altare accedit, non quando devocio illum invitat, sed quando dominus eius insinuat, non devocione, sed consuetudine,[9] de Christi passione nichil pensans, sed de prolongacione sive abbreviacione misse secundum velle domini sui cogitans....Hic cum suspiriis et gemitibus placere audientibus, ut absque merito nomen sibi extorqueat sanctitatis, satagit.[10] Quamobrem sepe genua flectit, manus ad celum tollit, tundit pectus, emittit gemitus, delirans plane, quia non de corde sed tantum de ore procedit devocio ista....Nec tantum studet sacerdos iste placere domino suo cui servit, sed eciam

---

[1] Cf. Ps. cxviii. 109. [2] *quidem* om. C.
[3] *singularem* B. [4] *celebraret* C. [5] *aliis* om. C.
[6] *penitencialibus, xv graduum psalmis* om. A. [7] *hec* om. C. [8] *fore* om. B.
[9] *devocionis consuetudine* (sic) C. [10] *nomen sibi sanctitatis extorquere satagit* B.

toti familie, quatinus et ipsi tempore opportuno, hoc est quando aliqua vacat ecclesia, cuius dominus eius patronus est, ut tunc loquantur pro eo bonum domino....Denique presentacione ad ecclesiam accepta, festinat ad episcopum, sumens secum magistrum Symonem, eo quod ipse potens sit in opere et sermone coram episcopo et omnibus sibi famulantibus. Hic vero magister Symon ita negocium suum maturat et expedit, quod omnibus impedimentis postpositis statim admittitur, et expleto negocio cum festinacione gaudens et hilaris revertitur. Ingressus vero ecclesiam, non de onere animarum, sed de ecclesie valore solicite inquirit, quia plus pensat de numero marcarum quam de salute animarum.

(ix) PAGE 256. Extract from Bishop Sheppey's funeral sermon on Lady Cobham (1344):

New College, Oxford, MS. 92

[fo. 152]

Iste sermo fuit ordinatus pro exequiis domine de Cobham anno Christi 1344, sed non dicebatur pro eo quod archiepiscopus Cantuariensis predicavit ibidem.

[fo. 155]

Sed ecce in talibus fuit ista domina bene instructa, quia quantum ad oraciones fuit cum ea quolibet die dies festivus; quia nisi esset maior necessitas, nullo die libenter descenderet de camera vel loqueretur cum aliquo extraneo, donec dixisset matutinas et horas de domina, 7 psalmos et letaniam, fere omni die; et tunc in missa, quando sacerdos siluit, alias privatas oraciones in gallico et alias oraciones dominicas et salutaciones angelicas; et in extremis diebus suis, quando infirmitas mortalis eam occupavit et tenuit, adhuc ostendit devocionem quam habuit alias[1] in oracionibus suis; quia quando accessi ad eam 5 die infirmitatis sue, plus conquesta est michi, quod non potuit dicere matutinas suas, quam de infirmitate sua; et per spacium unius leuce vix ante mortem suam fecit unum sacerdotem qui presens est dicere secum letaniam et salutaciones angelicas. Videtur michi quod esset magna ignorancia homini scienti ista, quando oraret, nisi haberet ratum et gratum quod ipsa, qui tantum delectabatur et amavit oraciones, esset particeps; et ideo amore Dei oretis pro anima eius, quod Deus pro sua misericordia perducat eam ad gaudium sempiternum....

[1] *al'* or *ad'* MS.

APPENDIX II

In addition to the manuals for priests and the vernacular treatises described in Chapters IX and X, attention should be drawn to a certain class of manuscripts, namely miscellaneous collections of short didactic treatises, which were very popular in the later Middle Ages. Two examples, out of many, will illustrate the type of compilation that I have in mind.

(i) British Museum, MS. Burney 356. This is a remarkable compilation known as the *Flos florum*, written at the beginning of the fifteenth century, and containing twenty-two 'books' or treatises of various dates and authorship (there was formerly a twenty-third which has now disappeared). Some of these are devotional treatises such as the Meditations ascribed to St Augustine, St Anselm, and St Bernard, Innocent III's *De miseria humanae conditionis*, Richard Rolle's *Emendatio vitae*; but nine of the treatises form part of the literature of religious instruction. They are as follows:

Book I, fo. 8. A treatise on the Lord's Prayer, which also deals with the seven Gifts of the Holy Ghost, the seven sins, the seven virtues, the seven beatitudes: 'Per istas vii peticiones impetrantur vii dona Spiritus Sancti, que extrahunt a corde hominis vii peccata mortalia, et plantant in corde hominis vii virtutes principales, que nos perducant ad vii beatitudes et eorum merita' (fo. 9v).

Book II, fo. 20v. The *Templum Domini* of Robert Grosseteste (see above, p. 193).

Book III, fo. 29v. 'Hic incipit capitulum qualiter sacerdotes, qui alios regere presumunt, seipsos primo regere debent ad exemplum subditorum. Cum sacerdotis dignitas....' This is a treatise in ten chapters on the priest's way of life, on the celebration of Mass, on the Lord's Prayer, on the seven articles of faith, the Ten Commandments, the seven sacraments, and the seven sins; the later chapters include interrogations for the use of the priest in confession. The seven articles of faith and the seven sacraments are said to correspond with the seven seals in the Apocalypse.

Book IV, fo. 36v. 'In nomine Domini Ihesu Christi, volentes simplicium sacerdotum ignoranciis subvenire, pauca collegimus ex patrum nostrorum doctrinis, que poterunt sacerdotes curati secure populis predicare, et in sacramentis securius ministrare. Hec autem subscripsimus sub rudibus verbis et quasi puerilibus, ne quis ob eorum ignoranciam se poterit excusare....' This is a popular treatise known as 'Quinque verba', probably of the late thirteenth century, giving an outline of instructions for parish priests, under five headings: [i] *Que sunt credenda*; [ii] *Que sunt diligenda* (the seven virtues); [iii] *Que sunt observanda* (the ten commandments); [iv] *Que sunt vitanda* (the seven sins); [v] *Que sunt exercenda* [the seven sacraments, including a section *De modo confitendi et absolvendi*]. The treatise is followed on fo. 39 v by some constitutions of the Archbishops of Canterbury, from Langton to Islip (1349–66).

Book v, fo. 43 v. 'Quilibet sacerdos parochialis sive curatus tenetur parochianos suos predicare (sic) et docere in lingua materna quater in anno videlicet....' This is a scheme of religious instruction, in Latin and English, for the use of parish priests, in accordance with Archbishop Pecham's constitution *Ignorancia sacerdotum;* it deals with the Lord's Prayer, the Hail Mary, the Creed, the Ten Commandments, the seven sins, the seven works of mercy, the seven virtues, the seven sacraments, the five senses, the sentence of greater excommunication *secundum usum Sarum*, and the bidding prayer.

Book vii, fo. 65. Richard Rolle's treatise *Iudica me*, arranged and divided into chapters to form a manual of instruction for priests, and dealing with the articles of faith, the Ten Commandments, the seven sins and their remedies, preaching and hearing confessions (cf. p. 248 above, and Allen, *Writings*, p. 96).

Book x, fo. 105 v. 'Hic incipit de officio sacerdotis et quomodo viverent et se haberent. De officio sacerdotis est breviter pertractandum. Licet ex sentencia evangelica....' This is an enlarged version, divided into three books, of the *Speculum sacerdotis* (or *sacerdotum*), or *Speculum regis Edwardi*, of which books two and three appear in many other manuscripts. It probably belongs to the mid-thirteenth century. It deals with the priest's way of life and duties, preaching, prayer, the administration of the sacraments; it includes denunciations of clerical abuses and numerous moral anecdotes. One of these concerns a prophecy of St Edward the Confessor. In some ways this work is a forerunner of Mirk's *Manuale Sacerdotis* (above p. 214).

Book xiv, fo. 156. 'Tractatus de vii sacramentis et aliis multis que sunt capellanis necessaria. Infirmitatem contractam per peccatum primorum parentum....' This is a treatise divided into two books, the first dealing with the seven sacraments, the second with the seven sins, the seven virtues, the fourteen articles of faith, the Ten Commandments, the seven gifts of the Holy Ghost, and the seven petitions of the Lord's Prayer, probably thirteenth or early fourteenth century; there are other copies in British Museum, MS. Royal 11 A.I, fo. 119, and Merton College, Oxford, MS. 144, fo. 129v.

Book XVII, fo. 176: 'De modo et ordine confessionis faciende breviter tractemus. Primo in confessione quid sit observandum. De opere, capitulum i. De me totum nichil dixi et totum dixi....' This is a very short treatise on confession. It is followed by Book XVIII, fo. 177v: 'Nunc dicendum est qualiter servandum sit cor in vigiliis nocturnis. c. i. Nunc quomodo preparandum sit cor tuum....' The latter is a series of meditations for the different hours and occupations of the monastic day; these two pieces apparently together form a single treatise, a remarkable piece of writing, the work of a certain Thomas of Woburn, probably a Cistercian monk of the early thirteenth century (cf. Bale, *Index Britanniae Scriptorum*, ed. R. L. Poole, 460; M. R. James, *Ancient Libraries of Canterbury and Dover*, St Augustine's catalogue, nos. 782, 798, 799, 1593, 1595; St John's College, Cambridge, MS. 168, fo. 119v; Corpus Christi College, Cambridge, MS. 63, fo. 31v; Bodleian, MS. Hatton 101, p. 404; MS. Laud Misc. 8, fo. 63).

(ii) Bodleian, MS. Bodley 110 (S.C. 1963). This is a compilation written in the early fifteenth century, containing eleven treatises. Some of these are devotional, such as the Meditations on the Passion ascribed to St Bonaventure, and Rolle's Form of living; there is a collection of short lives of Saints; and the following deal with religious instruction:

3, fo. 36. The *Speculum ecclesiae* of St Edmund Rich (see above p. 222).

5, fo. 99. The *Speculum sacerdotum* (cf. MS. Burney 356, fo. 105v, described above).

10, fo. 155. A scheme of instruction in Latin and English, which is substantially the same as in MS. Burney 356, fo. 43v, described above; the Bidding prayer refers to the King and the Queen, the Prince, the Duke, and all their children, and so is perhaps after the creation of John of Gaunt as Duke of Lancaster in 1362.

A note states that this manuscript was bought in 1463 by William Cleve, Rector of Clyve (Cliffe), Kent, from a London stationer, and given by him to a chantry priest and his successors. We know therefore that it was in the hands of more than one member of the parochial clergy.

There are several points to be noticed about these compilations. They mostly consist of quite short treatises, a good deal shorter than such works as the *Oculus sacerdotis* or the *Regimen animarum* or the *Pupilla oculi*; most of those in the *Flos florum*, for instance, are about ten or twelve folios long. They are concerned mainly with helping to carry out Pecham's constitutional *Ignorancia sacerdotum*, by giving instructions about preaching or the hearing of confessions; but they only provide a kind of syllabus or outline of points for preaching, and not the actual sermons, which would have to be filled out by the parish priest to the best of his ability. In purpose therefore they resemble the manuals for priests described in Chapter IX, while in their subject matter, the Lord's Prayer, the virtues, the Commandments, and so forth—they resemble the vernacular treatises described in Chapter x. The dates of these treatises range over the thirteenth and fourteenth centuries; they were evidently still popular in the fifteenth century, when they were copied into these manuscripts. The *Flos florum* strikes one as a curious product of the collector's habit, which accumulated these short treatises until in bulk they together exceeded one of the larger works like the *Oculus sacerdotis*. But no doubt these short treatises often, perhaps normally, circulated as isolated pamphlets; probably the stock-in-trade of many parish priests would consist of one or two such *quaterni*, or gatherings of a few leaves, unbound and well-thumbed, which like school-books would have little chance of survival. It is only when such tracts have been copied or bound together in a substantial volume that they have survived.

INDEX